ALLIES OF THE STATE

*China's Private Entrepreneurs
and Democratic Change*

JIE CHEN

BRUCE J. DICKSON

Harvard University Press
Cambridge, Massachusetts, and London, England   2010

Library of Congress Cataloging-in-Publication Data

Chen, Jie, 1955–
Allies of the state : China's private entrepreneurs and democratic change / Jie Chen,
Bruce J. Dickson.
p.   cm.
Includes bibliographical references and index.
ISBN 978-0-674-04896-6 (alk. paper)
1. China—Politics and government—2002–
2. China—Economic policy—2000–
3. Democratization—China.   4. Capitalists and financiers—China—Political
activity.   5. Businessmen—China—Political activity.   6. Entrepreneurship—
Political aspects—China.   7. Capitalism—China.   I. Dickson, Bruce J.   II. Title.
JQ1516.C433   2010
322'.30951—dc22   2009040026

To our families
Yanping and Jackie
&
Benita, Andrew, and Caitlin

Contents

Acknowledgments

When we began several years ago to design the research project presented in this book, we drew insights from previous studies about the political role of private entrepreneurs in China's political change. These insights helped us sharpen the focus of our research and clarify key theoretical and empirical issues dealt with in this project. Over the years, a variety of people and institutions provided us with invaluable assistance in conducting this research. Without their assistance, we would never have been able to complete this project. We would therefore like to acknowledge and thank these people and institutions.

We want to express our heartfelt gratitude to our colleagues and friends for their invaluable guidance and assistance. Particularly, our thanks go to Li Lulu, chair of the Department of Sociology of People's University *(Renda)* of China, and Dai Jianzhong, vice director of the Institute of Sociology of the Beijing Academy of Social Sciences, for helping us design and implement the five-province survey on which the study is based. Both are extremely knowledgeable about China's private entrepreneurs and have extensive experience in conducting national and regional surveys of private entrepreneurs. They offered detailed advice on all stages of the survey, from questionnaire design to sampling frame and interview strategy. Their advice helped us prevent potential pitfalls that could have disrupted the survey.

For their comments and suggestions at different stages of the writing process, we want to thank Scott Kennedy, Pierre Landry, Lianjiang Li, Melanie Manion, Wenfang Tang, Kellee Tsai, and one still anonymous reviewer. Their critical and constructive comments on earlier conference papers or the full book manuscript allowed us to discover new ways of analyzing and presenting our findings. For their invaluable research assistance, we would like to thank Jeffrey Becker, Chunlong Lu, Huhe Narisong, and Frank Tsai.

We would like to thank several institutions that played critical roles in facilitating our research. First and foremost, acknowledgments are due to the National Science Foundation for its provision of a generous grant (SES-0550444/0550518) supporting our research for this book. Any opinions, findings, and conclusions or recommendations expressed in this material are those of the author(s) and do not necessarily reflect the views of the National Science Foundation. We greatly appreciate each of our respective institutions, George Washington University and Old Dominion University, for granting us research leaves during this research project. We also want to thank the colleagues in our departments who offered support and assistance along the way. At George Washington, we thank Ikuko Turner and Suzanne Stephenson for the difficult task of managing the grant that made the research possible.

Parts of this book previously appeared in "Allies of the State: Democratic Support and Regime Support among China's Private Entrepreneurs," *China Quarterly*, no. 196 (December 2008), pp. 780–804, and are printed here with the permission of Cambridge University Press.

Our sincere gratitude also goes to Kathleen McDermott, our editor at Harvard University Press, for shepherding the book through the publication process. Throughout the entire process, she enthusiastically supported us and this project. Moreover, she offered substantive as well as editorial suggestions, all of which improved the final version of the book.

Finally, we both want to express many thanks to our respective families for willingly putting up with our obsession with this project that sometimes competed with our family obligations. Because we live in different corners of Virginia, we rarely had opportunities to work together. A series of vacations to Virginia Beach provided rare opportunities to meet face to face but resulted in a bit less beach time. Our families also got to accompany us on one or more trips to China during the course of our research. So even though we were often distracted by our research, it was not a complete loss for our families. As we both are deeply indebted to our families, therefore, we dedicate this book to them.

Allies of the State

CHAPTER ONE

Introduction

THE EMERGENCE and growth of the private sector in China has been one of the most profound socioeconomic changes in China since the onset of the post-Mao reforms. From the early 1990s, the number of private enterprises increased by 35 percent annually and now totals over 5 million. The private sector is the main source of economic growth in China: by 2007, it contributed 66 percent of gross domestic product (GDP) and 71 percent of tax revenues. It is also the main source of new jobs: between 2002 and 2006, the private sector created almost 44 million urban jobs, whereas employment in state-owned and collective enterprises shrank by nearly 11 million.[1] As private enterprises have gained increased prominence in the national economy, private entrepreneurs have begun to play an increasingly important role in China's political life. Their economic and political status has been further enhanced and institutionalized by the constitutional protection of private property promulgated in 2003 (later put into law in 2007) and the Chinese Communist Party's (CCP) lifting of its ban on recruiting private entrepreneurs into the party in 2001.

As the number of capitalists continues to grow, what impact are they having on China's political system? Particularly, does this new social class think and act democratically and hence serve as the harbinger of democratization in that country, as many scholars and policy makers in the West have expected? Due to the growing economic and political clout of China's private entrepreneurs, scholars have become more and more interested in these questions and have begun to speculate on the possibility that China's private entrepreneurs will promote political change and eventually a democratic system. Thus far, the findings from recent empirical studies suggest that China's entrepreneurs are generally status-quo oriented and not supportive of change for democracy.[2] However, these studies are not definitive. Some are based on a single city or industrial sector; others focus on relatively large-scale firms. Moreover, the indicators of support for democracy used in these studies are not theoretically robust enough to capture private entrepreneurs' orientations toward democracy and democratization.

To explore China's private entrepreneurs' orientation toward democracy and to fill the gap in earlier studies, in this book we utilize an original set of data collected in 2006–2007 from a representative sample of private entrepreneurs from five coastal provinces—where the private sector has been most developed—from firms of various sizes and in different business sectors. By utilizing a more inclusive sample and more comprehensive survey measurements, we are able to provide more conclusive findings about the intensity, sources, and behavioral consequences of Chinese private entrepreneurs' support for democracy and democratic change and conversely their orientation to the status quo.

Furthermore, the findings shown in this book shed new light on at least two other important issues related to private entrepreneurs' attitudes toward democracy. First, since the size and power of the private sector in general and private entrepreneurs in particular continue to increase dramatically in China, we expect that the findings about this social class's political attitudes—such as those toward democracy and the current regime—and its political behavior will help us better understand the trajectory and future of political changes, particularly those potentially leading toward democracy. An improved understanding of the political trends in this increasingly influential and dynamic country will in turn assist political leaders in and outside of China to make and implement policies that can better anticipate and cope with future political changes.

Second, our findings about private entrepreneurs' democratic support in China will undoubtedly have significant implications for studies of the role of the private sector in political change in other late-developing countries. Such implications will further contribute to the general theoretical inquiry into the role of capitalists as supporting or opposing forces for democratization in late-developing countries in other parts of the world.

In this first chapter, we will begin by discussing our theoretical approach to and analytical framework for measuring and evaluating the degree of support for democracy and the current regime among China's private entrepreneurs and then describe the empirical data on which this study is based. A brief summary of each chapter will follow.

The Theoretical Context: Economic Development and Political Change

There is a large body of literature on the relationship between economic development and political change, and in particular the role of new social classes emerging as a consequence of economic development. Research on these topics in the Chinese setting has become more common over the past decade. However, there is no definitive consensus in the general or China-specific literature on the causal nature of the relationships among economic development, social change, and political change and on the role of new social classes in these changes.

Relationship between Modernization and Democracy

Scholars have long noted the close correlation between wealth and democracy. Few have questioned this well established relationship, but many have engaged in a long and sometimes heated debate over whether a causal relationship exists between economic development and democratization.

Modernization theory has had enduring appeal, in part because of its clear and intuitive explanation of how economic development leads to political change.[3] In its most basic form, modernization theory argues that countries develop by moving from an agricultural economy to industrialization and then to the development of a large service sector. As a consequence of these structural changes, a greater share of the population moves to urban areas, education levels increase, incomes and standards of living rise, and traditional beliefs and practices are replaced by more "modern" ones based on scientific rationality. These economic, social, and cultural changes in turn provide the basis for the emergence and durability of democratic political systems.

Despite its intuitive appeal, many have questioned whether modernization theory provides a theoretical framework to explain the link between development and democracy. In their test of the main insights of modernization theory, Adam Przeworski and Fernando Limongi found that the level of economic development was not a good predictor of the timing of democratization. The transition to democracy has been attempted at all levels of development, but the prospects for a stable and long-lasting democracy increase in wealthier countries. However, even authoritarian regimes remain stable at high levels of economic development.[4] Although modernization has been challenged on both empirical and theoretical grounds, it continues to guide the thinking of scholars and even policy makers. In particular, it has been the basis for promoting economic development as a precondition for democratization.

The Role of New Social Classes

Scholars looking at democratic transitions tend to focus not only on general economic and social preconditions but also more importantly on the actors who influence the process under certain conditions. These scholars have focused particularly on the formation and influence of new social classes, which are thought to foster political change toward democracy. Drawing on the experience of Europe and European settler countries, scholars have identified the emergence of the bourgeoisie and the urban middle class as key catalysts of democratization. Barrington Moore's oft-cited phrase "no bourgeois, no democracy"[5] succinctly states one of their important roles in a nation's political transformation. From a quite different perspective, Samuel Huntington made a similar observation. His analysis of the dynamics of authoritarian regimes found that their survival is threatened by the "diversification of the elite resulting from the rise of new groups controlling autonomous sources of economic power, that is, from the development of an independently wealthy business and industrial middle class."[6] As these new elites acquired increased wealth and greater autonomy from the state, they were more inclined to demand greater involvement in the political system in order to protect and enhance their private interests. Indirectly, their increased political participation also created space for other groups to gain access to the political arena, further opening the political system.

With the same analytical focus on the role of political actors, some other scholars, however, argue that democratization is not a natural result of economic growth; instead, it is an inherently political process, full of conflict and negotiations among major political forces and leaders. Most recent studies have found that capitalists are not inherently proponents or even supporters of democratization, but under certain sets of circumstances, they can play a decisive role in either maintaining the status quo or facilitating such a political change. They tend to support authoritarian regimes when their material interests benefit from the regime's policies or when they fear that a new regime would adopt policies that would harm their interests, such as higher taxes to pay for new welfare programs or defending the collective bargaining rights of labor, which drive up wages and the cost of production.[7] But when capitalists come to believe that the regime can no longer defend their interests or when they perceive that the strength of the opposition has reached a tipping point, their support for the status quo can change to opposition, thus helping trigger political change. In countries such as South Korea, Brazil, and Mexico, regime change was accompanied by the transfer of capitalists' support from the old regime to the new challengers.[8]

Private Entrepreneurs and Democratization in China

On the basis of the aforementioned empirical and theoretical relationships between economic modernization and democracy, some China scholars have offered optimistic predictions about the advent of democratization in China.[9] Some have given rather precise timetables for such a transition. For example, Henry Rowen relied on straightforward projections of future economic growth to predict that China would be classified as "partly free" on the Freedom House scale of political rights and civil liberties by 2015 and then join the ranks of fully "free" countries by 2025.[10] Shaohua Hu offered an even more optimistic prediction: China would be democratic by 2011 because the main obstacles to democratization, above all the under-developed economy, were breaking down.[11] Many scholars anticipate not only that economic development is leading toward democratization in China but also that private entrepreneurs are likely to be agents of change in that process. Pointing to the fact that the number of private entrepreneurs and their economic and political influence has dramatically increased in recent years, these analysts argue that the entrepreneurs have become potential supporters for or even advocates of democratization.[12] These views were most common in the 1990s, when privatization was first getting under way, and even the party was worried about whether capitalists would push for democratization.

Most recent survey- and interview-based research on China's private entrepreneurs has not supported these optimistic predictions but has been more consistent with comparative studies on the role of private entrepreneurs in democratization in the late-developing countries. In general, these studies demonstrate that private entrepreneurs in China have sided with the current authoritarian state and shunned democracy and democratization. Margaret Pearson argues that contrary to the assumptions of many Westerners, these groups are not likely to push for political change and are not at the forefront of democratization or the emergence of a civil society. Instead, they are content with their cozy relationship with the state, which is built on what Pearson called "socialist corporatist" arrangements designed by the CCP.[13] Drawing on her interviews and a nationwide survey of private entrepreneurs, Kellee Tsai has found that China's private entrepreneurs can hardly be identified as one "unified" or monolithic social class, and most of them do not seem to demand democratic reforms.[14] Using data collected from two surveys of private entrepreneurs from medium and large firms, Bruce Dickson studied the political attitudes of these entrepreneurs. He found that private entrepreneurs were not eager to change the current political system, because they were co-opted by the CCP and heavily dependent on the party-state for their own prosperity. Moreover, he showed that private entrepreneurs have become close allies of the CCP, who strongly support the CCP's rule and its policies.[15] All in all, while a few entrepreneurs may be outspoken supporters of political reform, on the whole China's private entrepreneurs, like capitalists in other late-developing, nondemocratic countries, have been generally unenthusiastic about or opposed to democratization, preferring the authoritarian regime in which they have thrived to the uncertainty inherent in a new and untried political system.

Despite their various insights on the relationship between economic and political change in China, however, these recent studies share at least four potentially serious limitations: (1) most are not based on a representative sampling of private entrepreneurs; (2) they do not take into account either regional variation in levels of development or differences in the size and scope of enterprises; (3) their indicators of both regime support and democratic support for democracy are not theoretically comprehensive and methodologically robust; and (4) they have missed some key individual-level variables explaining entrepreneurs' attitudes toward both the current political system and a potential democratic future. In the sections that follow, we will introduce our theoretical framework and new survey data that are intended to address these theoretical and methodological issues.

State-Led Development and the Role of Capitalists in Political Change

Research on the role of capitalists in the process of political change in China and other countries is not consistent with the conventional wisdom—especially among non-China specialists and Western political leaders—that economic change leads to political change and by extension that capitalists are inherent supporters of democracy. This would seem to offer a puzzle for explanation. However, the contingent role of capitalists in democratization is more consistent with another perspective on the political economy of development. These studies focus on the central role of the state in promoting modernization and the mutual interests of the state and the private sector. The state creates the conditions for the private sector to grow and prosper; to some extent, the state also determines which individuals will be most successful; together, they help shape the political identities and values of capitalists. From this perspective, the lack of support for democratization is less of a puzzle.

This perspective has been most influenced by two related traditions: Alexander Gerschenkron's depiction of the role of the state in late developers and the state-centered paradigm popularized by Peter Evans, Dietrich Rueschemeyer, and Theda Skocpol. Although these two theoretical traditions—

especially the state-centered paradigm—have drawn criticism,[16] both have been continuously applied in various studies of economic and political development in developing countries.[17] Similarly, instead of disentangling the debate over these two traditions, we draw some insights from them to frame our study of private entrepreneurs' democratic support within the context of late development and authoritarian rule.

Late Development and the State

In his seminal collection of essays, *Economic Backwardness in Historical Perspective*, Alexander Gerschenkron first established the critical notion of the state as the leader of economic development in late-developing countries.[18] His insight helped explain socioeconomic development in contemporary developing countries. According to Gerschenkron, the "late developers" are those countries that joined the global tide of development when it was already in rapid motion. As a result, the developing countries, such as China, and newly industrialized countries can be considered later developers or "late late" industrializers,[19] since they commenced their processes of industrialization when economic development was already in rapid motion or had reached maturity in Western Europe and North America. Accordingly, late developers do not follow the early industrializers' "spontaneous" model in their economic development.[20] Gerschenkron's perspective is in sharp contrast with modernization theory, which suggests that the history of the presently advanced countries have "[traced] out the road of development for the [currently] more backward countries." He instead argues that the economic development of the late-developing countries by "the very virtue of their backwardness" will differ fundamentally from that of the early industrialized countries.[21]

Because of such socioeconomic "backwardness," late developers face two key challenges that set them apart from early industrializers. First, all late developers lack capital, a trained work force, and advanced technologies when they initiate major economic-development programs. In addition, as Packenham pointed out, all late developers face international economic conditions that could trap them in unfavorable positions in the transnational division of labor.[22] Second, in order to avoid being left further behind early industrialized countries or losing chances of development altogether, late developers must overcome such socioeconomic backwardness and disadvantages within a shorter time period than that in which early industrialized countries overcame similar obstacles.

Gerschenkron argued that because of these peculiar challenges faced by late developers, the states in these countries play a more important role in the process of socioeconomic development than was the case for early industrializers. This is mainly because late-developing countries need a strong state to meet those challenges effectively under a time pressure. For instance, a late developer needs a strong state to pool a country's resources and mobilize its population to compensate for the inadequate supplies of capital, entrepreneurship, and technological capacity within a constrained timeframe in order to catch up and compete with developed countries. Meanwhile, a strong state is needed to design and coordinate strategies to cope with unprecedented, severe international economic competition.

The Autonomy and Capacity of the State

Contemporary state-centered analysts have developed Gerschenkron's argument for the beneficial role of strong states in late developers into an argument for the inherent autonomy of the state. As Theda Skocpol argues, "states conceived as organizations claiming control over territories and people may formulate and pursue goals that are not simply reflective of the demands or interests of social groups, classes, or society."[23] This kind of autonomy is derived not only from "the basic need to maintain control and order" in crises or major socioeconomic transformations but also from the fact that only organizationally coherent collectivities of state officials, relatively insulated from societal forces, are likely to launch distinctive state strategies in times of major socioeconomic change. "Likewise, collectivities of officials may elaborate already established public policies in distinctive ways, acting relatively continuously over long stretches of time."[24] To Gerschenkron's argument for the necessity of a strong role of the state in major socioeconomic transformation, contemporary state-centered scholars have added empirical and theoretical support, especially by developing the idea of state autonomy. Similar to Gerschenkron, they suggest that the state in a late developer can play an active and decisive role in the nation's social, economic, and political life due to its structural autonomy.

The state-centered paradigm also explores how state capacity affects the realization of policy goals.[25] Among all sources of state capacity, scholars particularly emphasize the importance of the financial and organizational sources for state capacity. The financial resources under the state's control, as Skocpol points out, serve as the critical material base on which the state can fulfill various basic tasks, such as those "to employ personnel, to co-opt political support, to subsidize economic enterprises, and to fund social programs."[26] The organizational resources are considered as a set of cohesive "organizational configurations" within the state apparatus, which together "affect political culture, encourage some kinds of group formation and collective political actions (but not others), and make possible the raising of certain political issues (but not others)"[27] and effectively intervene and coordinate socioeconomic transformations (or reforms).[28]

According to this approach, state capacity may be examined and gauged along two dimensions.[29] One is the cohesiveness of the state as a strategic actor to formulate and implement national policies.[30] The other dimension is the ability of the state to mobilize and guide private firms for the achievement of national goals.[31] In short, these two dimensions together are indicative of the state's ability to formulate and implement policy and to control socioeconomic and political forces in society, including the newly emerged class of private entrepreneurs. Thus, the results of the role played by the state may be in large part gauged along these two dimensions of the state's capacity.

All in all, the combination of Gerschenkron's notion of late development and the contemporary state-centered approach help establish the connection between the socioeconomic conditions of late development and the degree of state intervention in major socioeconomic transformations: that is, the socioeconomic conditions of a late developer necessitate a strong role for the state in its search for rapid socioeconomic development, and the autonomy and capacity of the state facilitate such a strong role. This conceptual connection is important for our study because it largely resonates with the strong role played by the state in China. In order to compensate for the typical disadvantages of a late developer, the Chinese state has needed to play a strong role in leading the unprecedented post-Mao socioeconomic transformation. Moreover, the Chinese state has been to a large extent able to play such a proactive leadership role in initiating and guiding this transformation because it enjoys high degrees of autonomy and capacity.

Compared with many other late developers, the Chinese state is likely to have an even stronger capacity to penetrate society in general, to guide economic transformations, and to create or mold new social classes, because of its control over national financial resources and its monolithic organizational configurations, which is a distinguishing feature of the ruling Leninist party. In addition, as Peter Evans points out, "the historical character of the bureaucratic apparatus must be taken into account in any attempt to explain its capacity, or lack of capacity, to intervene."[32] Thus, the more than half a century of totalitarian and authoritarian rule under the CCP has also reinforced such a strong role and the dominance of the state in China.

Although state capacity has ebbed and flowed in different periods, the CCP has remained largely autonomous throughout the post-1949 period.

For example, although the post-Mao economic reforms proved immensely popular, they were not initiated due to popular pressure. The "household responsibility system" in agriculture, arguably the first step of economic reform, was implemented by Wan Li and Zhao Ziyang in Anhui and Sichuan, respectively. Both were provincial party secretaries at the time, and both later became central leaders. At the beginning of the reform era, Chinese peasants in Anhui and Sichuan spontaneously began to abandon collective farming within the commune system and adopt household farming and small-scale household enterprises.[33] As described by Joseph Fewsmith, "the reform emerged neither from a groundswell of peasant demand for reform, as some romanticized renditions of this period maintain, nor as a coherent program adopted by the top leadership. Rather, it emerged from a highly complex process in which local leaders [e.g., Wan Li and Zhao Ziyang] provided peasants with the opportunity to experiment with reform and then argued, . . . with the central leadership to allow the experiments to continue and eventually to be expanded."[34] In the cities, small-scale enterprises—street vendors, repair shops, delivery services, and so forth—also began to emerge with the permission and encouragement of local and central party leaders.

These key economic reforms involved ongoing interaction between local leaders and central leaders and between the state and society, and both local leaders and societal actors often found creative ways of exploiting ambiguities in what was allowed and what was prohibited.[35] The center did not always play the leading role: many reforms were initiated below and then ratified above. But eventually, without the center's ratification and endorsement, any spontaneous local reform would be unlikely to survive for long or disseminate very far. China's party-state has not always had the capacity to accomplish its policy goals, but it has been autonomous enough to adopt and change policies without explicit pressure from nonstate actors.

Local initiatives for privatization and industrialization were particularly common in the early reform era, when both the size of individual firms and the private sector as a whole were small. Beginning in the 1990s, however, the state assumed a large role with the development of urban coastal areas and the promotion of an export-led growth strategy. As will be described in more detail in Chapter 2, the private sector continued to grow, medium- and large-scale firms emerged, and the state's support for the private sector also strengthened. As a result, success in business became more dependent on the close relations between the state and private sector. Private entrepreneurs benefited from the state's support but also were dependent on the state for easier access to capital and new markets. This dependency attenuated the entrepreneurs' support for democratization but strengthened their support for the current CCP-led regime.

The State and the Social Classes in Late Developers

Consistent with both Gerschenkron's notion of late development and the contemporary state-centered paradigm, some analysts of social classes in late developers argue that through its active and effective interventions in various areas of economic and political life, the state in a late-developing country also helps shape the environment in which new social classes, such as entrepreneurs and the broader middle classes, exist and operate.[36] For example, in the early stage of postwar economic development, the Korean state built government institutions not only for helping indigenous capitalist classes grow, but also for disciplining them in national economic activities;[37] the Taiwanese state implemented a series of policies simply to create and nurture a class of local private entrepreneurs in the early stages of Taiwan's postwar economic transformation, since such a class was almost nonexistent.[38] In short, as Evans, Rueschemeyer, and Skocpol explain, "the organizational arrangements of states, the existing patterns of state intervention in economic and social life, and policies already in place all influence the social interests [of classes] pursued in politics. Some potential group identities are activated; others are not."[39]

Following this theoretical line, some scholars further argue that the new social classes in a late-developing country not only are dependent upon the state for their rise and growth but also share with the state such interests as continuous economic growth and sociopolitical stability (or order).[40] In a late-developing country, therefore, the new class of private entrepreneurs is most likely to support the state and the political system that is sanctioned by the state and under which the state operates rather than support regime change and the uncertainty it would create.

The Political Orientations of Private Entrepreneurs in Late Developers

What do the political orientations of newly emerged private entrepreneurs in a late developer tend to be? As noted earlier, there is a large body of literature on the orientation of capitalists or "bourgeoisie" toward democracy and democratization in general. Some recent studies of capitalists in late-developing countries also emphasize the contingency of the capitalists' orientation toward democratization. As Eva Bellin points out, capitalists in nondemocratic, late-developing societies have been at best "contingent democrats."[41] Most of these studies correctly cite the relationship between the state and entrepreneurs as critical factors determining the latter's orientation toward a political change for democracy. In general, they suggest that private entrepreneurs in a late-developing country not only are dependent on the state for its rise and growth but also share similar values with the state, such as maintaining social stability (even at the expense of political freedom) and promoting high economic growth (even at the cost of economic inequality). In late-developing countries, therefore, the new class of private entrepreneurs is most likely to support the state and the political system that is sanctioned by the state. Consequently, if the political system is undemocratic in that country, private entrepreneurs tend to shun democratization in order to protect their interests and avoid antagonizing the state.

As noted earlier, most recent empirical research (both survey- and non-survey-based) on these issues in China has concluded that China's capitalists are not strong supporters of political change. While the economic reform policies promoted by the CCP have unquestionably fostered rapid and sustained growth, they have also created the kind of close, cooperative relations between state and business that tend to perpetuate authoritarian rule. As a result, these studies have found that China's private entrepreneurs are generally not supportive of efforts to bring about political change and do not hold demonstrably democratic values.[42]

Drawing on the theoretical insights from both Gerschenkron's notion of late development and the contemporary state-centered paradigm and on the basis of the empirical evidence noted above, we assume that the Chinese state plays a critical role in molding the sociopolitical orientations of new social classes in China, including the newly emerging private entrepreneurs. Following this assumption, three propositions for this inquiry can be derived: (1) China's private entrepreneurs tend not to support political changes that may threaten their privileged status or directly challenge the current party-state; (2) because of the close relationship between entrepreneurs and the state and the common values they share, entrepreneurs tend to support the current regime and lack strong democratic values; and (3) such lack of democratic support among private entrepreneurs tends to cause this social class to engage in political behavior that supports the current state rather than promote political reform, especially democratization. These three propositions will be developed in later chapters and tested against the data collected from our survey of private entrepreneurs in the five coastal provinces that account for the lion's share of China's private economy.

Data

The data used in this study come from a survey of private entrepreneurs, which was conducted in five coastal provinces in China where the private sector is most developed: Shandong, Jiangsu, Zhejiang, Fujian, and Guangdong. The survey was implemented beginning in late 2006 and was finished in early 2007. At the time of the survey, China's general sociopolitical environment had several salient characteristics. The fourth generation of the CCP leadership under Hu Jintao had adopted populist policies to "build a harmonious society" (*jiangou hexie shehui*) in order to quell dissatisfaction over worsening socioeconomic inequality and rampant official corruption. The central government increased legal and constitutional protection for the private property rights that are generally seen as important for economic growth but were weakly protected due to lingering Marxist ideology. The party-state stepped up its political repression for the sake of social stability while increasing economic freedom for ordinary citizens. These developments were part of the environment in which the survey was conducted.

The survey was designed to capture firms of different sizes and types of operations and in areas of different levels of development. Respondents in this survey were chosen through a multistage random sampling strategy (see Appendix for details). The goal was to select a random sample of private entrepreneurs that would be representative of the private sector in the five coastal provinces, where the private sector is most developed. Accordingly, the sample included small, medium, and large firms in all industrial sectors, and the counties from which they were selected also varied in terms of their economic development levels.

Like all public opinion surveys that are adequately designed and executed, our five-province survey produces two kinds of results: descriptive and relational.[43] Both kinds of results will be presented in this book. Both can offer at least two general lessons for the study of the political role of private entrepreneurs in China. First of all, although the descriptive results from the survey—such as those dealing with the levels of democratic support and regime support among our respondents—cannot be directly applied to the entire country, they can certainly help to establish some needed statistical baselines against which the findings from other areas of the country can be compared. More important, since about 70 percent of China's private enterprises are in these five provinces, our sample of owners of these enterprises represents 70 percent of the private entrepreneurs in the country. Such a high percentage of private entrepreneurs represented by our sample can certainly strengthen the generalizability of the descriptive results from this survey.

Second, the findings from our five-province survey about the relationships among variables can be directly generalized to other parts of China, especially among private entrepreneurs, since most, if not all, of these relationships are generic in nature.[44] These relationships in this study are mainly those (1) between key socioeconomic characteristics and personal and institutional ties to the state, (2) between these ties to the state and various subjective values and their degree of democratic values, and (3) between state ties and democratic values and the capitalists' political activities and support for the current regime. In fact, some recent empirical studies based on data collected from multiple-locale (as opposed to national) samples have generated insightful, generalizable inferences about patterns of relationships between sociopolitical variables in both urban and rural China. For example, on the basis of a survey carried out in four rural counties, Manion and Jennings identified the patterns of electoral connections and the correlates of political participation in rural China.[45] Drawing on surveys in urban settings, Tang and Chen established the correlations between urban residents' attitudes toward the CCP regime and their evaluations of governmental policies, on the one hand, and some key demographic attributes—such as age, sex, and occupation—on the other.[46] When discussing the generalizability of the data from local samples (single and multiple locale) in the study of contemporary China, therefore, Manion argues that "data from local samples can yield reliable answers, generalizable to a population beyond the sample, to a crucial category of questions—those about *relationships between variables*."[47] In short, our data collected from a local probability sample can yield useful findings regarding the relationships among important variables that are generalizable to the population of private entrepreneurs in these provinces and elsewhere in China.

Précis of the Book

We begin our analysis with discussion in Chapter 2 of the evolution of the new class of private entrepreneurs—which has emerged and grown since the outset of the post-Mao reform in the early 1980s—and the role of the party-state in this historic process. In that chapter, we will first describe the origins and development of the private sector as a whole under the CCP regime. On the basis of this description of the private sector in general, we delineate major paths of the emergence and growth of private entrepreneurs particularly during the post-Mao era. In describing the emergence and growth of private entrepreneurs, we will also show how the CCP's policies helped create this social class and its sociopolitical traits. These lines of analysis are intended to address three important questions: Who are private entrepreneurs in contemporary China—what are their political, social, and economic backgrounds, firm characteristics, and so forth? How has the Chinese party-state created and shaped this social class? What is the relationship between the new class of private entrepreneurs and the party-state?

Chapter 3 examines private entrepreneurs' political embeddedness, that is, their membership and participation in China's most important political and economic organizations. Many private entrepreneurs are deeply embedded in the state: they are members of the CCP, local legislatures, and official advisory bodies. The vast majority of them also belong to the officially organized business associations. In these ways, the state provides access to formal political institutions to a large share of economic elites. In so doing, it expects loyalty and support in return for the privileges and opportunities enjoyed by the private sector. But as we will show in Chapter 5, these types of political embeddedness by themselves do not produce the greater loyalty and support that the state expects.

Chapter 4 analyzes the level of support for democracy and democratization among China's entrepreneurs. We first explain how the empirical measures of such support are designed, based on the results of various measures used in studies of both Chinese and non-Chinese settings. Using these measures designed for this study, we gauge the extent of our respondents' democratic support. We then examine the sources of private entrepreneurs' democratic support. Drawing on the comparative literature on the role of the state in late developers, we hypothesized earlier that the political orientation of private entrepreneurs in China is shaped by the close, symbiotic, and yet asymmetric relationship between private entrepreneurs and the party-state, a connection that is shaped by the party-state's economic reforms and evolving support for the private sector. To test this general hypothesis, we explore the impact of four key dimensions of the state-entrepreneur connection: financial support, institutional ties, value congruence, and policy assessment. The financial dimension is measured by the provision of major financial resources by the party-state to private enterprises; the institutional dimension is determined by the memberships of private entrepreneurs in the Communist Party and in the party-state sponsored organizations; value congruence is gauged by private entrepreneurs' support for the state's leading role in initiating major political changes and for the post-Mao reform led by the state; and the policy assessment is examined through private entrepreneurs' evaluation of major governmental policies. By exploring this hypothesis, we seek to address such critical questions as how the private entrepreneurs' relationship with the state affects their attitudes toward political change and democratization.

In Chapter 5, we offer a more explicit analysis of the intensity and sources of Chinese private entrepreneurs' support for the current political system. One of the most common themes in research on China's private entrepreneurs is that they tend to support the current party-state and to be in favor of the status quo. Our findings point to the same conclusion, but we uncover a more nuanced explanation: private entrepreneurs' subjective values are far more important than their sociodemographic attributes and institutional ties in determining their support for the current party-state. These subjective values include democratic values, life satisfaction, evaluation of the government's policy performance, and perception of official corruption. Only party members who are former cadres are likely to be reliable supporters of the regime when subjective values are also considered; other types of party members and institutional ties to the state do not create support for the regime. Although the CCP expected that integrating capitalists into the party and other political institutions would build political support, its strategy has had limited success thus far; it is beliefs, not institutional ties, that are the most important determinants of regime support. These findings have important implications for the survival of the regime and for the role of private entrepreneurs in a potential political change toward democracy.

In Chapter 6, we study the participation of China's capitalists in both formal and informal channels. These channels include voting in local elections, contacting government officials at various levels, supporting academic activities, petitioning the government individually or collectively, and contacting the news media. The findings about the influences of private entrepreneurs' political participation through both formal and informal channels will help us verify our last proposition, namely, that the low level of democratic support among private entrepreneurs tends to cause this social class to act in favor of the current authoritarian state. Most forms of political behavior are not influenced by democratic beliefs but instead are a result of the capitalists' political embeddedness. The political activities of most entrepreneurs are generally designed to cooperate with the current political system and not instigate political change. However, the respondents' democratic beliefs do influence whether they were satisfied with the results of their activities. Moreover, activities that try to promote political reform, such as supporting academic research on contemporary affairs, are motivated by their sponsors' democratic beliefs. This kind of activity may be unlikely to succeed in the short run and is less common than more supportive activities (such as voting and contacting officials), but it does provide at least an indirect means of voicing an alternative political perspective for the democrats among China's capitalists.

Finally, in Chapter 7, we summarize all major findings about the level, sources, and behavioral impact of democratic support and regime support among private entrepreneurs. We then draw some theoretical implications for the study of the role of China's capitalists in political change and the interaction between the state and these capitalists in this authoritarian late-developing country and discuss some political implications for our understanding of China's political future.

In short, our findings indicate that China's private entrepreneurs are not likely to be agents of democratization; that party membership and institutional ties with the state are not significant predictors of either democratic support or regime support; and that the continuation of regime support is contingent on the government's policy performance and value change among China's private entrepreneurs. This nuanced picture of the political impact of privatization in China unfolds in the remaining chapters.

CHAPTER TWO

The Evolution of the Private Sector in China

THE FORMATION and development of the private sector in China has been a key aspect of the CCP's program of "reform and opening" *(gaige kaifang)*. The introduction of private firms began on a very small scale in the late 1970s, experienced periods of expansion and contraction through the early 1990s, and then underwent rapid growth up to the present. As the private sector grew, its importance to the overall economy—as a source of jobs, economic production, and tax revenue—grew apace. With the CCP focused on producing sustained high growth rates and improved living standards as a fundamental source of legitimacy, its policy toward the private sector evolved over the years. Initially, it tolerated small-scale private firms to fill niches not covered by the planned economy but did not fully or actively promote the growth of the private sector, which was seen by many—particularly within the party—as incompatible with the communist political system. Over time, however, the CCP more fully embraced the private sector. It adapted its policies and even its ideology to encourage and support the private economy. By the beginning of the twenty-first century, the private sector had become the main source of growth, and private entrepreneurs were increasingly integrated into China's political system.

In this chapter and throughout the book, our definition of the private sector largely follows that used in China: firms that are formally registered as "privately managed enterprises" *(siying qiye)* and to a lesser extent the small-scale individual household enterprises *(getihu qiye)*. The survey data introduced at the end of the chapter and examined in detail in later chapters is limited to firms that were registered as *siying qiye* and does not include street vendors and other *getihu*. Although this gives a slightly upward bias in the size of the firms we sampled, we feel that this decision is appropriate because the debate over the role of private entrepreneurs in political change focuses on those who own and manage larger firms. Moreover, Kellee Tsai's research has shown that smaller firms (many of which are not registered) try to avoid interactions with the state rather than engaging it in order to change it.[1] They are also less likely to engage in collective action, making them unlikely agents of political change. We also do not try to determine the ownership status of the many reformed state-owned enterprises (SOEs), some of which remain under state control, some of which are largely private, and still others of which have indeterminate ownership. Limiting ourselves to registered private firms may be an overly strict definition, but in order to do a systematic empirical study, clear and consistent definitions are necessary.

This chapter will provide an overview of the evolution and composition of the private sector in China. This background is necessary to understand the sociopolitical context of private entrepreneurs' orientations toward democracy and the current regime. It will begin with a description of the changing official policy toward the private sector and the debate it generated among central and local officials. This evolution was influenced both by elite politics and the interplay of state-society relations. In the second part of this chapter, we will describe the composition of the private entrepreneurs themselves, showing in particular their various ties to the state. This background is essential for the analysis of later chapters: the interaction between the party-state and private entrepreneurs and the degree of democratic support and regime support among China's new capitalists.

Official Policy toward the Private Sector

The emergence and expansion of China's private sector is an example of "institutional layering," a type of institutional change in which preexisting institutions remain in place while new ones are layered on.[2] In the case of China's private sector, the original planned economy and SOEs were the core elements of the economy, but the CCP allowed a private sector to grow alongside them. Over time, the private sector gradually increased in size and importance. Concomitantly, the level of official support and encouragement also increased incrementally over time. In the early reform period, the CCP intentionally kept the private sector small, and the size of firms was similarly small relative to SOEs. The CCP intended the private sector to supplement, not supplant, the planned economy. Beginning in the

1990s, however, the state provided increasingly stronger official support to the private sector and began to emphasize it as important by itself, not merely as a complement to the planned economy but as a valuable source of new jobs and economic growth.

From the available evidence, it is not clear whether this institutional layering was strategic or evolutionary. China's reform-minded leaders may have deliberately chosen to hide their intentions by giving only limited support to the private sector but intended for it to develop in size and importance in order to prevent opposition from more conservative leaders.[3] Alternatively, reform-minded officials may have come to realize the importance of the private sector only over time. Although there might not have been a long-term and consistent strategy within the party leadership, its intentions during each of the key periods of the reform era were quite evident. The private sector in China did not evolve free of the state's control and intervention. Rather, its emergence and growth were guided or at least heavily influenced by the state.

Regardless of whether the growth of the private economy was an intended or unintended consequence of the early reform efforts, layering the private sector onto the existing planned economy had several important advantages. The first advantage was political: it avoided a direct challenge to politically powerful and economically conservative leaders. It avoided the need to address the problems of central planning in general and SOEs in particular directly and early in the reform era. China's reformers were well aware of the pathologies inherent in the planned economy, such as inefficient and poor quality production, outdated technology, and surplus workers. These problems required an ever greater investment of state resources to subsidize the mostly unprofitable SOEs. At the same time, however, the planning sector was politically powerful, and SOEs were the mainstay of China's economy, providing the bulk of economic production and the best-paying and most prestigious jobs. Its supporters resisted efforts to introduce reforms into the planning system and often had to be replaced or eased into retirement (or, in some cases, pass away) before progress was possible. The incremental reform process that unfolded in China after 1978 sparked often intense conflict among top leaders. A more direct attack on the planned economy would have been even more divisive and politically costly. Rather than confront the central planning apparatus and SOEs early and directly, China's reformers allowed the market economy—of which the private sector was a significant segment—to grow in size and importance until it surpassed the state sector. As Barry Naughton aptly put it, the Chinese economy grew out of the plan.[4]

The second advantage of this institutional layering approach was ideo-logical: private ownership was anathema to many of China's leaders, who believed that capitalism and communism were fundamentally incompati-ble. The CCP eliminated private ownership in the 1950s, soon after con-solidating its hold over the country. Karl Marx summarized the essence of communism as the abolition of private property, and this principle re-mained a central tenet of orthodox communist ideology.[5] Just as replacing the state sector with the private sector would have been politically costly, advocating the wholesale return of private ownership would have been ideologically risky. Throughout the Maoist era (1949–1976), capitalists were designated as class enemies and persecuted during repeated political campaigns. Reformers could not totally ignore that history. Even the grad-ual introduction of small-scale firms triggered harsh criticism from ortho-dox leaders, but the criticism normally did not resonate more widely be-cause the private sector was small and the material benefits it provided were apparent to many. However, in the brief period after the 1989 dem-onstrations in Tiananmen Square and elsewhere, ideologues and planners formed a short-lived tacit coalition against the economic and political re-forms of the 1980s, which they blamed for creating instability. When economic reforms resumed in 1992, the ideological attacks on private ownership became more marginalized although never fully eliminated.

A third advantage of layering the private economy onto the state sector was economic: reformers such as Deng Xiaoping advocated experiment-ing with new economic alternatives before committing to them because of the uncertainty of whether they would be successful. For example, Deng defended the existence of the special economic zones by noting that they were small and separate from the rest of the economy. If they failed, they could simply be disbanded with little cost to the overall economy; but if they succeeded, their innovations could be slowly introduced elsewhere in China. This incremental approach stands in sharp contrast to the "shock therapy" approach to economic reform employed by postcommunist coun-tries in Europe at the urging of American economists such as Jeffrey Sachs. Shock therapy involved the immediate and wholesale privatization of the economy and the elimination of central planning. Although China's reforms began a decade before shock therapy in postcommunist Russia and Eastern Europe, the immediate and severe decline in the Russian economy served to reinforce and justify the incremental approach to eco-nomic reform in China.

Whether it was a deliberate strategy or simply the unintended conse-quence of evolutionary change, the layering of the private economy onto the planned economy allowed it to emerge and expand without posing a direct challenge to the central planners and SOEs or a serious threat of economic dislocation. Initially, the state allowed it to exist without much encouragement or support. Only in the 1990s and beyond did the state actively promote the development of the private sector, through the opening of new privately owned firms and through the privatization of SOEs and collective enterprises. As will be described below, the evolution of China's private sector went through four distinct phases.

1978–1989: Toleration

During the first decade of reform, the private sector was seen as supplemental to the planned economy. China's top leaders were committed to restoring economic growth but were divided on how best to achieve it. While Deng Xiaoping and his lieutenants (especially Hu Yaobang and Zhao Ziyang) favored relaxing the extent of central planning in order to create incentives for more production, conservative leaders like Chen Yun and Li Xiannian insisted on maintaining the primacy of central planning. Zhao Ziyang complained that Chen Yun's views on the planned economy "had not changed since the 1950s. He [i.e., Chen Yun] included the phrase 'planned economy as primary, market adjustments as auxiliary' in every speech he gave."[6] Because even Deng deferred to Chen on economic matters, Chen's opposition to marketization and privatization slowed the reform process. Accordingly, the size of firms was quite limited: private firms were officially described as "individual household [getihu] firms" and were allowed to hire no more than seven workers outside the family. This limit reflected several considerations. First, private firms were to supplement the planned economy but not compete with it. The state would tolerate the private sector but not encourage it. By being kept on a small scale, the private sector would not detract resources from the state sector and would not involve social costs if individual firms failed. Second, the private sector had to be ideologically correct. The limit on the number of workers was based on a comment by Karl Marx, that having more than eight workers was to engage in exploitation.[7] Later in the reform era, this restriction would be lifted, but in these early years, even the promoters of reform justified their actions with an ideological rationale. At a time when class struggle was still fresh in people's minds, it was necessary to avoid the accusation that people were engaging in capitalism or exploitation. Third, getihu were envisioned as one way to provide jobs for people whose family backgrounds and political problems prevented them from getting jobs in the state sector. At least in these early years, getihu were seen as suspicious characters. Some had criminal backgrounds; others had been victims of previous political campaigns. In any event, the private sector they represented was tainted by the people who worked there. Both the state and society viewed *getihu* with suspicion, even scorn.

As Keming Yang argues, in the early reform period, private entrepreneurs prospered not only by taking advantage of areas that were officially approved but also by exploiting what was not explicitly prohibited.[8] Entrepreneurs did not wait for the formal sanctioning of various economic activities but instead pushed ahead into uncertain areas, often with the tacit support, if not outright cooperation, of local officials. In this sense, the growth of the private sector was partially a fait accompli, as changes in central policy caught up to what was already happening at the local level. To take advantage of these gray areas, not only did entrepreneurs have to have entrepreneurial skills in the business arena, but they also had to be equally entrepreneurial in their relations with local officials. Entrepreneurs were required to exert as much energy and creativity in their interactions with the local bureaucracy and the media as they did actually developing and marketing their products. China's capitalists proved adept at taking advantage of the ambiguities and loopholes in central policy. Their individual and largely uncoordinated actions led to the ongoing development of the private sector.

Budding entrepreneurs often had to engage in subterfuge to operate their firms. In the countryside, township and village enterprises *(xiangzhen qiye)* were often officially registered as collective enterprises (meaning that they were owned by the community as a whole and managed by the local government) even though they were for all intents and purposes privately owned and operated. They were known as "red-hat enterprises" because they had the political protection of being officially registered as a collective, even though they were truly private firms. Kellee Tsai refers to these types of practices as "adaptive informal institutions," coping strategies that represent "creative responses to formal institutions that local [state and nonstate] actors find too constraining."[9] Both local officials and private entrepreneurs had a common interest in colluding in this masquerade. Local officials benefited by having new sources of economic development, jobs, and tax revenue at their disposal without the worry of being accused of promoting capitalism, and entrepreneurs could engage as collective firms in activities that were illegal for private firms. In some communities, over 90 percent of township and village enterprises (TVEs) wore a red hat.[10]

As the private sector began to grow, the state created new institutions to monitor and control it. In 1986, it created the Self-Employed Laborers Association *(geti laodongzhe xiehui;* SELA), a mass organization that was normally supervised by the CCP's United Front Department and the government's industrial and commercial management bureaus at the local level. All *getihu* were required to belong to the SELA, and membership was simultaneous with registration of the firm. Like many mass organizations in China, SELA's role was to represent the state's interests, not necessarily the well-being of its members. In addition, because its members were by and large not held in high esteem by either state or society, SELA itself was not a powerful or influential organization.[11] In the late 1980s, a second organization was created for owners of larger private firms, the Private Enterprises Association (PEA). Not only did these firms employ more than eight workers, and therefore did not technically qualify as *getihu,* but more important, they reportedly wanted a separate organization to distinguish themselves from the more unsavory *getihu.*[12] These new business associations coexisted with the All-China Federation of Industry and Commerce (ACFIC), which was created in the 1950s, went dormant during the Cultural Revolution, and revived early in the reform era. Membership in the ACFIC is voluntary and includes both private and state-owned firms. It is generally seen as the most prestigious and influential of the official business associations. (The role of business associations will be examined in more detail in Chapter 3.) All three business associations—SELA, PEA, and ACFIC—are officially sponsored by the state. At the local level, they fall under the supervision of the government's industrial and commercial bureau and the CCP's United Front Department. To make their official status more explicit, they are often headed by current or former officials and share office space with party and government departments.

As the private sector grew in both the number of firms and the size of their operations, ideologically orthodox voices began to question whether these capitalists were compatible with China's communist political system. During the mid-1980s, conservative leaders criticized the illicit activities associated with the small but growing private sector, especially in the special economic zones in south China. In addition to the exploitation of workers that orthodox Marxists opposed, the private sector also contributed to a rise in illegal and decadent activities, including smuggling, gambling, drug use, prostitution, and pornography. These practices had been largely eliminated in the 1950s but were now reappearing along with Deng's reform and opening policies. The special economic zones in particular were targeted for criticism by conservatives such as Hu Qiaomu and Deng Liqun, who warned against the preferential treatment given to foreign investors and the tendency to worship foreign things.[13] These critics warned that economic reform and the turn toward capitalism were risking both the nation's autonomy and the survival of communism in China.

These fears were seemingly realized by the popular demonstrations in spring 1989, when protests against corruption, inflation, and the failure to implement promised political reforms erupted in Beijing and around the country. These protests were led by college students and workers but also drew wider support from most sectors of society. In particular, China's new capitalists seemed to be at the front line of advocating political change. Fleets of motorcycles organized by *getihu* delivered supplies to the protestors in Tiananmen Square. One of China's most famous private entrepreneurs, Wan Runnan, was an outspoken advocate of political reform and democratization. Wan was president and founder of the Stone Corporation, one of China's first successful privately owned electronics companies.[14] During the 1980s, he funded the Social and Economic Sciences Research Institute, a think tank operated by Chen Ziming and Wang Juntao, two leaders of the Beijing Spring protests. Both Chen and Wang were arrested and imprisoned for their involvement in the protests, and Wan fled into exile. Among the orthodox thinkers in the party, these developments were ominous. They raised the prospect of capitalists determined to undermine the communist regime and replace it with a Western-style democracy. What had started as a small-scale supplement to the planned economy suddenly seemed to be a serious threat to the CCP's grip on power. In the aftermath of the demonstrations, conservatives regained the upper hand in policy circles and called for a retrenchment of the economic reforms they believed led to the protests.[15]

1989–1992: Retrenchment and Repression

Days after the imposition of martial law, Deng Xiaoping spoke on the necessity of maintaining the commitment to the reform and opening policies. He told a group of military leaders that his economic reform policies must be maintained and even advanced despite the imposition of martial law. "Our basic proposals, ranging from our development strategy to principles and policies, including reform and opening to the outside world, are correct. If there is any inadequacy for us to talk about, then I should say our reforms and openness have not proceeded well enough."[16] The following week, he told members of the Politburo's Standing Committee, "The first thing for us to do is that we must prevent our economy from declining. We must actively strive for a faster speed within our power."[17]

Deng's confidence in the necessity of continued reform was not shared by other central leaders, who saw the recent demonstrations as a direct consequence of the economic and political reforms of the 1980s. In the aftermath of protests in Tiananmen Square and elsewhere around the country, the CCP blamed "individual and private entrepreneurs who use illegal methods to seek huge profits and thereby create great social disparity and contribute to discontent among the public."[18] Skeptics of reform such as Li Peng, Chen Yun, and Yao Yilin advocated rolling back many of the reforms favored by Deng and implemented by Zhao Ziyang, the former CCP general secretary who was purged during the Tiananmen protests and placed under house arrest. Many *getihu* and private enterprises were forced to close, and even TVEs came under pressure. The starkest symbol of the backlash against reform was the decision in August 1989 to ban the recruitment of capitalists into the CCP. This signified their exclusion from the political system and the conviction of central leaders (other than Deng) of the incompatible interests of the capitalists and the CCP.

With conservatives controlling the propaganda system, Deng and his reform-minded allies were unable to convey their policy preferences to other officials or the general public. Frustrated by the center's conservative agenda and his failure to promote reforms through the central media, Deng traveled to south China in spring 1992. While touring the special economic zones, Deng lauded their achievements as showing the virtues of economic reform and encouraged local leaders to be even bolder in their reform efforts. Although his comments were not initially reported by the central media, his trip received extensive coverage by local media. After a brief delay, the central media also began to report Deng's comments and the successful economic results of the special economic zones.[19] This brilliant tactic by Deng shifted the balance of power in favor of reform, and the private sector experienced explosive growth in the following years.

1992–2001: Encouragement and Support

Although Jiang Zemin was initially reluctant to support Deng's economic reform agenda (Deng reportedly threatened to remove Jiang as CCP general secretary if he did not get on board), throughout the 1990s he championed the rapid expansion of China's private sector. The number of private firms grew dramatically, from approximately 90,000 in 1989 to over 400,000 in 1994 and over 1.5 million in 1999. In addition, the size of the firms also grew: in 1989, China's private firms had an average of 93,000 yuan in registered capital, and by 1999 this had grown to 681,000 yuan.[20] This expansion in the size and scope of the private sector was possible only with the CCP's explicit support and encouragement.

The expansion of the private sector expansion of the 1990s followed the pattern Deng advocated in the 1980s: it favored coastal regions over inland areas. This strategy was based on the coast's comparative advantages—better infrastructure, access to foreign markets, and proximity to sources of foreign investment—and was justified by the slogan "take the lead in getting rich" *(daitou zhifu)*, implying that some areas and some individuals would prosper first before all of China would enjoy the benefits of the reform and opening policies. But whereas private firms in the 1980s were typically small in scale and significance, during the 1990s firms became larger in both regards. As noted above, the average registered capital of private firms increased more than sevenfold during the 1990s. The private sector also became the main source of new jobs, economic growth, and tax revenues. In contrast, the size of the state sector shrank steadily during these years. Whereas it contributed 77 percent of economic production in 1978 when the reform era began, it supplied only 33 percent by 1996.[21] After repeated efforts to make SOEs more efficient and profitable failed, the state began the process of restructuring them. Central leaders adopted the "grasp the large, release the small" *(zhuada, fangxiao)* policy, in which the state would retain control of the largest and most strategically important SOEs but reform, restructure, or close small- and medium-sized SOEs. In some cases, this involved full or partial privatization through public offerings or sales to the firms' managers, staff, and employees. In other cases, the restructuring led to the formation of joint ventures and public-private partnerships, such as shareholding companies and limited liability companies. In still other cases, it led to the bankruptcy and even the closing of many firms. According to one survey, 70 percent of China's SOEs had been partially or totally privatized by 2001.[22] The privatization of SOEs not only shifted more economic activity to the private sector; it also contributed to the larger average size of private firms because the restructured SOEs were typically larger than other private firms. Among the firms in our survey, for example, those that had formerly been SOEs had almost twice as many fixed assets as other private firms (64 million yuan compared with 34 million yuan).

These developments were echoed in official statements of support for the private sector. In the past, the CCP had tolerated the private sector but did not actively encourage it. In 1988, the National People's Congress amended the state constitution to legalize the private sector but required it to operate within strict bounds and remain under the state's control: "The state permits the private sector of the economy to exist and develop within the limits prescribed by law. The private sector of the economy is a complement to the socialist public economy. The state protects the lawful rights and interests of the private sector of the economy, and exercises guidance, supervision and control over the private sector of the economy."

During the 1990s, however, the official support for the private sector grew more explicit and enthusiastic. The 15th Communist Party Congress in 1997 announced that the private sector was now an "important component of a socialist market economy"; accordingly, the CCP would "encourage and guide the non-public sector comprising self-employed and private businesses to facilitate its sound development."[23] In 2000, the Fifth Plenum of the 15th Party Congress announced that "the healthy development of the self-employed and privately-owned businesses . . . [will be] supported, encouraged, and guided."[24] In the years after Deng's southern tour in 1992, the official attitude toward the private sector went from tolerating it as a supplement to the planned economy to promoting it as a necessary feature of China's modernizing economy.

The CCP's vigorous support for the private sector culminated in the "Three Represents" theory first popularized by Jiang Zemin and added to the party constitution in 2002. The "Three Represents" was designed to legitimize the CCP's embrace of the private sector and the incorporation of new elites—in particular private entrepreneurs—into China's political system. More specifically, it removed the CCP's ban on recruiting private entrepreneurs that had been adopted in August 1989 after the repression of popular protests in Tiananmen Square and elsewhere around the country. Whereas the CCP traditionally represented the interests of the "three revolutionary classes"—that is, workers, peasants, and soldiers—in this new era it announced that it represented three distinct sets of interests: first, the "advanced productive forces" in China, a euphemism for the economic and technological elites who were contributing to China's modernization; second, the development of advanced culture; and third, the interests of the vast majority of the Chinese people. The ordering of the Three Represents reflected Jiang's orientation to reform: the elites came first, and the interests of the party's traditional base were subordinate to the priority on rapid growth. While Jiang's elitist strategy succeeded in generating high rates of growth, it also produced growing corruption, inequality, and environmental degradation, which in turn produced large-scale public protests in the mid-1990s and beyond. By the end of Jiang's tenure as CCP general secretary in 2002, these unwanted externalities of economic growth required party leaders to recalibrate the priorities of reform.

2002–Present: Balancing Growth with Equity

Under the leadership of Hu Jintao and Wen Jiabao, the CCP subtly changed its reform strategy. Without abandoning the commitment to the private sector and the growth it created, Hu and Wen placed more emphasis on the parts of society and regions of the country that had not yet prospered under the reform and opening policies. They did not abandon the Three Represents but emphasized the interests of the majority over those of the economic elites, thus reversing Jiang's rankings. Whereas Jiang promoted the promise of achieving a "relatively prosperous society" (*xiaokang shehui*, a term previously promoted by Deng Xiaoping in the 1980s)[25] in which the social and economic elites received more attention from the government, Hu and Wen committed themselves to a "harmonious society" *(hexie shehui)* in which equitable distribution of wealth and sociopolitical stability have been emphasized, at least in the official rhetoric. To pursue this harmonious society, the CCP began to formulate a "scientific development concept," which attempts to address the imbalances of Jiang's pro-growth policies with a concern for balanced growth and sustainable development.

Despite this reorientation of reform priorities, the CCP's commitment to the private sector did not diminish but instead has been continued by the Hu-Wen leadership. The CCP's continued commitment to the private sector has been shown in several ways. First of all, the "Decision on Several Issues Related to Perfecting the Socialist Market Economic System" was approved at the Third Plenum of the 16th Central Committee of the CCP in 2003, which reinforced the party's earlier pledge to support, encourage, and guide the development of the private sector. Specifically, this document called for equal treatment of public and nonpublic enterprises regarding investment, financing, taxation, land use, and foreign trade. It said that "laws, regulations, and policies which constrain the development of the non-publicly owned economy" would be sorted out and revised, and "systemic barriers" into new markets, such as infrastructure and public utilities, would be eliminated.

Second, but equally important, in March 2004, the CCP amended (through the National People's Congress) the state constitution to explicitly protect the private ownership of property, businesses, and wealth. The amended constitution stipulates that "lawful private property is inviolable" and commits the state to "encouraging, supporting and guiding the private economy." While the important principle of protecting and promoting the private sector had been officially adopted by the CCP as a party policy in 2000, this constitutional amendment legalized and perpetuated this principle. Thus, this amendment has been widely described as a critical step in the party's legitimization of the private sector and its protection of private property. Despite this constitutional commitment, actual legislation to protect private property was not approved until 2007. When the bill was first introduced, it was criticized for emulating

Western-style capitalism and ignoring Chinese-style socialism. This example illustrates how ideological concerns remained a stumbling block even though the reform era had been under way for almost thirty years. Although China's leaders have largely abandoned the pursuit of traditional communism, they remain highly sensitive to accusations that their policies violate Marxist ideology. As a result, party leaders continue to search for ideological justifications of their policies within the Marxist framework, even though ideology has little influence over the decisions they make.

Summary

The emergence and development of China's private sector was not a smooth evolution but was dependent on the larger debate among central leaders on the pace and direction of economic reform. Rather than immediately and suddenly replacing the planned economy, the private sector was instead layered on top of it—or, perhaps more accurately, alongside it—in order to mollify critics of economic reform who feared a return to capitalism and the political and ideological costs that such a transition would entail. As the private sector grew larger in size and importance to the economy, the CCP's official posture toward it also changed. Whereas the CCP merely tolerated the private sector in the early reform era, by the end of the Jiang Zemin era it had fully embraced the private sector and even the private entrepreneurs themselves. This full-scale support came with its own costs, however: corruption, inequality, and pollution, to name but a few. The fourth generation of leaders has continued the CCP's support for the private sector but has tried to couple that support with a policy agenda emphasizing balanced development, sustainable growth, and a renewed concern for equity as well as growth. Nevertheless, the private sector is now an ever more important part of China's economy, and the capitalists are an ever more visible and influential part of China's political system.

Challenges in Private Sector Development

Despite the strong rhetorical support, the private sector is still disadvantaged in a variety of ways. First, private firms have a harder time raising capital than do other types of enterprises. Governments at various levels have played a critical role in allocating financial resources among economic sectors and groups in society. As Barry Naughton has observed, as of 2003 almost all the banks and more than 90 percent of the assets of these banks in China were controlled directly or indirectly by the national government and local governments.[26] As a result, bank lending has been determined according to the policies and intentions of the central and local governments. Above all, the lending practices of these banks supported the policy of subsidizing the unprofitable SOEs and collective enterprises, rather than providing direct financial resources to the more profitable and expanding private sector. As Kellee Tsai has pointed out, "the state banking system remains hostage to the socialist legacy of SOEs that require continued subsidization."[27] Private firms are much less likely to receive loans from official state-owned banks, which prefer to loan to SOEs and collective enterprises. SOEs and collectives are backed by the central and local governments, so even if the firm does not pay back their loans, the government is more likely to cover the banks' losses. In contrast, private firms have no such backing, and most find it difficult to receive bank loans without relying on informal connections, paying bribes, or exchanging other types of favors. Among the respondents in our survey, 65 percent reported that obtaining state bank loans was difficulty or very difficult.

Similarly, private firms have difficulty raising capital by issuing bonds, largely because the credit rating industry in China remains undeveloped and heavily influenced by government intervention.[28] Tax policy on investment capital has hampered the private sector. Foreign capital receives incentives for investing in China (such as tax breaks and land use privileges) that domestic capital does not enjoy, creating incentives for "round-trip capital" and fake foreign-invested enterprises. In this creative but deceptive practice, Chinese firms funnel capital through dummy corporations in Hong Kong or elsewhere outside China's borders and then transfer it back into China, giving the appearance of foreign investment and receiving the benefits thereof. On a larger scale, some large Chinese firms are incorporated outside of China even though most of their operations take place within the country. For example, Lenovo is one of China's leading computer and electronics companies and after buying IBM's hardware manufacturing operations acquired a global presence. Although its hardware manufacturing, software production, and research and development mostly take place in China, Lenovo is a wholly owned foreign-invested enterprise headquartered in Hong Kong. As Yasheng Huang describes, Lenovo and other similar cases illustrate the disadvantages that domestic private firms still face in China, the creative responses to those challenges, and the resulting difficulty for analysts to assess the size and contributions of the private sector.[29] The respondents in our survey had almost as much difficulty in obtaining capital as bank loans: almost 60 percent reported that obtaining capital was difficult or very difficult.

In addition to the difficulty in raising capital, private firms also are restricted from entering certain key industries. The state prevents entry of private firms into industries that it deems to have strategic importance, such as energy, transportation, and communication. Other sectors are not officially protected but have other barriers to entry that are difficult to overcome. For example, construction requires a large up-front investment in equipment that most private entrepreneurs cannot meet, given the difficulty in raising capital. Relatedly, sectors such as construction and real estate development require cozy ties with local officials to be successful, and the costs of time and money to wine and dine officials can discourage new entrants into these industries. As will be shown in the next section, privatized SOEs are more likely than indigenously private enterprises to be involved in these industries.

For ambitious private entrepreneurs, the price of ambition can be quite high if they run afoul of the state. Entrepreneurs who challenge or ignore the informal restrictions on the private sector can find themselves in jail and stripped of their property. Sun Dawu was a private entrepreneur in rural Hebei who founded one of the most successful animal feed companies in the country. When he was unable to obtain loans from state banks, he solicited contributions from his employees. More important, he developed a broad-based following for criticizing the government's restrictions on private entrepreneurship in public talks (including a speech at Peking University) and on his company's Web site. These challenges to the CCP's policies led to his arrest and subsequent conviction on the charge of "illegally obtaining public funds."[30] At around the same time, Yang Bin's miraculous success story ended with an eighteen-year jail sentence. He became famously wealthy by growing orchids and other flowers and by 2001 had become the second richest man in China. He achieved such fame that the North Korean government appointed him to direct a planned special economic zone. This appointment apparently was not discussed with or authorized by the Chinese government, which promptly arrested Yang for tax evasion and other economic crimes.[31] Gong Jialong was chairman of Tianfa Group, a large conglomerate with interests in oil, gas, and liquefied petroleum. He claimed to be a successful private entrepreneur, but the local government considered his firm to be state owned. The confusion over the ownership status of the firm and Gong's use of company resources eventually led to his arrest in December 2006.[32] Huang Guangyu, director of Gome Electrical Appliances, a national chain of more than a thousand stores, was detained in November 2008 on allegations of share trading violations and was forced to resign from Gome in January 2009.[33] Because economic crimes are commonly believed to be prevalent in China's business world, arrests are viewed not as indicators of wrongdoing but of poor political connections.

In a variety of ways, therefore, success in business remains dependent on connections with the state. Private entrepreneurs in China do not compete on an even playing field: those with strong political connections and those who previously worked for the state, either as party or government officials or SOE managers, have tremendous advantages in business. The state remains able to channel resources (such as capital and contracts) to privileged entrepreneurs, to restrict access to certain sectors of the economy, and to reward loyal followers and punish perceived threats without restraint. Even those with extensive political ties (such as Gong Jialong) are not immune from punishment when their ambitions run counter to those of the state. For all the CCP's positive rhetoric and publicity about the private sector, the benefits of privatization in China have not been distributed evenly but in ways intended to reinforce the CCP's authority.

The Composition of China's Private Sector

As described in the previous section, the private sector in China began with humble origins, and only over time did it acquire the degree of official support necessary to expand in both size and scope. Whereas the private sector was predominantly comprised of small-scale firms in the early reform period, the CCP's encouragement and support fueled its expansion during the 1990s and up to the present. In this more hospitable environment nurtured by the state, private firms grew in size and operated even in sectors still dominated by state-owned firms, such as steel and mining.

While the growth of the private sector was largely the result of the opening of new firms, it was also due in part to the ongoing reform of SOEs. Party and government leaders recognized early in the reform period that SOEs suffered from chronic inefficiency, unprofitability, and indebtedness, creating a drag on the economy and hampering efforts to modernize the country. Initial efforts to make SOEs more profitable included allowing firms to retain a larger share of their profits; "dual track pricing," which allowed firms to sell at a higher market price after their planned production targets were met; and devolving decision-making authority to managers, which gave them more discretion in deciding what to produce and who to hire and fire. These policies had minimal impact, however. The state was worried about the potential loss of jobs if surplus workers were laid off, a major impediment to making firms more efficient and profitable. Moreover, firms had little incentive to improve their performance because of "soft-budget constraints": they knew that even if they operated at a loss, they would receive loans and subsidies to balance their books. Officials and managers were aware of the problems but were unprepared to apply effective remedies. In the early reform era, actual privatization of SOEs was not even on the agenda.[34]

Beginning in the mid-1990s, SOE reform changed direction. Efforts to make firms more profitable by giving managers more autonomy and incentives were replaced by changes in their corporate structure. As part of the "grasp the large, release the small" policy begun in the mid-1990s, most SOEs were eventually restructured or "reformed," and many were outright privatized. In our sample, 30 percent of the firms had been converted from SOEs. There was significant regional variation in the incidence of SOE conversion, ranging from a high of 42 percent in Jiangsu to a low of 23 percent in Fujian. Private firms that were originally SOEs or part of SOEs are particularly common in certain sectors, such as construction (44 percent), drilling and excavation (42 percent), science and technology (42 percent), and transportation (41 percent), but relatively rare in firms engaged in renting and leasing (18 percent) and cultural and physical education (15 percent). Some capitalists were more likely to own and operate converted SOEs: 41 percent of "red capitalists" (capitalists who are also CCP members) and 60 percent of those who formerly worked as SOE managers operated firms that were originally in the state sector. These types of people are more likely to have the personal connections necessary to arrange for the purchase of SOEs. These insider deals were criticized by the official media for depriving the state of the full value of these converted firms and were similarly resented by those who lacked the same connections and were deprived of the opportunity to buy the restructured firms at such a discount.[35]

Although SOEs are technically owned by the central government, their conversion to private ownership is typically handled by local officials. Whereas the central government prefers to get a higher price for its SOEs, local governments are less concerned about the price because they do not get to keep the proceeds for the sale. Instead, local officials are more concerned about who buys the firms, preferring current management or their cronies. Moreover, local officials stand to personally benefit from these insider deals because they typically involve kickbacks from the buyers. A fairer and more transparent process would be a public auction of the SOE's assets; this would not only set the sale price close to its true value but would also benefit the central government by allowing it to recoup a larger share of its past investments. This is not a very common procedure for several reasons. First, it is often difficult to determine the true value of an SOE's assets because the business's books are not publicly available.

Second, in the absence of public sales, it is hard to determine a market price for an SOE's equipment, inventory, and other assets. Perhaps most important, local officials have little incentive to convert SOEs into private firms by public sale or auction because it is harder to grab a share of the proceeds. As a result of these considerations, only 22 percent of the cases of SOE conversion in our sample were the result of public bidding. More commonly, the original SOE was sold to insiders, either to its top leaders (14 percent) or to its staff and workers as a whole, with the managers having the largest share (17 percent). In 10 percent of the cases, the government invited a specific individual to buy the firm. These arrangements are prone to corrupt sweetheart deals, as the government agrees to sell the firm for a fraction of its true value, instantly enriching the lucky individuals who are part of this corrupt transaction (including the local officials, who often get kickbacks from the grateful buyers).

Just as many current private firms have their origins in the state sector, so too did many of China's capitalists begin their careers working in the CCP and government bureaucracies and SOEs. Although popular images of China's private entrepreneurs suggest an emerging new class of capitalists, the reality is rather different. The main beneficiaries of the reform and opening policies have been those with close ties to the party-state. In fact, the CCP has encouraged its members to "take the lead in getting rich" by "plunging into the sea" *(xiahai),* a euphemism for going into private business. These individuals were able to take advantage of networks of political connections, access to capital and other scarce resources, and superior information, all of which are necessary to succeed in business.[36] Most private entrepreneurs in our sample had previous work experience in the state sector. A slight majority (51 percent) formerly worked in SOEs, either as managers (15 percent), specialists and technicians (18 percent), or regular staff or workers (18 percent). These people had extensive experience in business before joining the private sector, giving them a distinct advantage over those going into business for the first time.

A large proportion of the respondents (19 percent) were former party and government cadres at various levels. Before formally joining the private sector, many local officials were directly or indirectly involved in industrial and commercial operations as a way of boosting the local economy as well as enriching themselves and their families. These cozy ties between China's capitalists and the party-state have been blamed for the corruption that has arisen unabated during the reform era.[37] About half of these respondents also had previous experience in SOEs, giving them both political ties and business experience. In total, 63 percent of the respondents in our sample had previous work experience in SOEs, in the party and government bureaucracies, or both.

Less than half of the private entrepreneurs in our survey have occupational backgrounds that do not involve the state sector. They include former *getihu* (30 percent), farmers (18 percent), workers in joint ventures and foreign-invested enterprises (9 percent), and migrant workers (5 percent).[38] People from these backgrounds do not have the same advantages as those with more extensive official connections and management experience. Consequently, they generally operate smaller firms and are less likely to belong to the official business associations and the CCP. They lack not only the official connections but also the social status and economic clout needed to wield much political influence.

In short, China's capitalists by and large have previous professional experience that gives them the political ties that are essential for success in business. This is especially important in an environment where the economy is not well regulated and where fundamental aspects of doing business, such as enforceable contracts and property rights, are not well established. As we will demonstrate in later chapters, this previous experience also generated connections with the current regime that influence the political beliefs and behavior of these capitalists.

Conclusion

In this chapter, we have provided a brief overview of the emergence, development, and evolution of the private sector in China. This process was driven by a combination of local initiative and central policy. Local officials and private entrepreneurs did not wait for official approval before opening private firms but instead found ways to work around existing policies. When central policy had not yet authorized these activities, they adopted informal practices, such as "wearing a red hat"—that is, registering private firms as collective enterprises—to formally comply with central policy while in practice going well beyond it. Although these convenient fictions were successful in getting the private sector under way, they also inhibited its growth. Private firms had to remain relatively small in size and few in number to avoid drawing attention from higher-level officials. Even where local party and government officials supported the private sector, they could not risk retaliation from above for being too far in front of changes in official policy. The lack of central support, in short, limited the scale and scope of the private sector in the early reform era. The shift toward active support and encouragement in the years after 1992 allowed the private sector to expand ever more rapidly.

As the size of the private sector grew, its importance to the state rose accordingly. It has become the main source of job creation, economic growth, and increases in tax revenue. With the CCP focused on economic growth as its key task, it has gradually embraced the private sector as a necessary partner. It has changed its official rhetoric to demonstrate its support, encouraged its members and officials to go into the private sector, and co-opted successful entrepreneurs. These close ties between the state and the private sector are the result of institutional ties, previous professional experience, and common interests. Whereas the popular conception of capitalists portrays them as supporting democratizing reforms and posing an inherent threat to authoritarian regimes, this has not been the case in China. As later chapters will demonstrate in more detail, China's capitalists are more inclined to be allies of the state than agents of change.

CHAPTER THREE

Political Embeddedness among China's Capitalists

CHINA'S PARTY-STATE uses different means to integrate itself with the private sector. In some cases, it co-opts capitalists by bringing them into key political institutions, above all the CCP. More commonly, it encourages those already in the party to "plunge into the sea," that is, to leave their state jobs and go into private business. Furthermore, it uses officially sponsored business associations to serve as an institutional bridge between private business and the state. These business associations provide their members with access to decision makers and in some cases to political appointments, which is itself an important indicator of political embeddedness. In each of these ways, the party-state provides opportunities for private entrepreneurs to be embedded in the state. These different indicators of political embeddedness are interrelated in two ways. Empirically, membership in the CCP and the ACFIC are crucial for being nominated or appointed to government posts. Conceptually, these different indicators of embeddedness are like overlapping circles: an entrepreneur can possess one or more types of embeddedness (see Figure 3.1). The more types of embeddedness entrepreneurs possess, the more deeply they are embedded in the party-state.

Political embeddedness not only conveys political privileges, such as access to decision makers, but also signifies economic opportunities. As will be shown below, politically embedded capitalists operate larger and more profitable firms and have been in business longer than those who are not embedded. In short, the political embeddedness of China's capitalists signifies their membership among the political and economic elites of their communities. In addition, the CCP gives political access to only the best

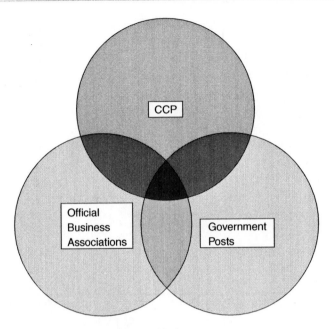

Figure 3.1.   Layers of Political Embeddedness

connected and most politically trustworthy capitalists. For these reasons, the key finding in this chapter is that the presence of private entrepreneurs in China's political system is not a harbinger of democratization. Instead, their presence indicates that the party-state carefully screens those who are allowed to participate and uses access to formal institutions as a means of generating political support. Rather than pose a challenge to the party's supremacy, therefore, the political embeddedness and political activism of China's capitalists helps support CCP rule.

The Chinese Communist Party

Despite three decades of economic reform and social change, the most important fact of the Chinese political system remains that the country is ruled by a Leninist party, the CCP. The party remains the entry point for access to political appointments and government jobs. As we will see later in this chapter and in Chapter 6, connection with the party is a primary factor explaining many forms of political participation. Therefore, the place to begin in analyzing political behavior among China's capitalists is the CCP.

The CCP has been deeply ambivalent about the inclusion of capitalists into China's political system. On the one hand, it needed their cooperation in the pursuit of the party's key task in the post-Mao period—that is, economic modernization—and also wanted to prevent them from becoming agents of political change. As Jowitt describes the strategy of inclusion, the CCP wanted to avoid "the possibility that the increasing social heterogeneity of socialist society, in the form of an increasing range of articulate social audiences, might express itself as an articulated plurality of political-ideological definitions." The CCP therefore co-opted capitalists in "an attempt to prevent that plurality by revising the regime's format and its relationship to society from insulation to integration."[1] On the other hand, many in the CCP were concerned that integrating capitalists, a group previous pilloried as class enemies, would undermine the CCP's ideological and organization integrity. Even if the CCP needed to expand its political and social base, not all CCP leaders were convinced that co-opting capitalists was necessary or wise.

For more than a decade after the tragic end of the popular protests in Tiananmen Square and elsewhere throughout the country in 1989, the party maintained a formal ban on recruiting capitalists. Hard-line leaders were convinced that allowing capitalists into the CCP was incompatible with the party's ideological traditions, and those fears were heightened by the public support for student demonstrators by high-profile capitalists such as Wan Runnan, one of the founders of the Stone Corporation, an early leader in China's electronics industry. On a smaller scale, individual proprietors *(getihu)* showed their support and sympathy for student demonstrators by providing food, money, and logistical support with their fleet of motorcycles known as the "Flying Tiger Brigade." Despite the formal ban, which lasted from 1989 until 2001, local officials quietly co-opted capitalists into the party. They recognized that they needed the support of the private sector to provide the jobs, tax revenues, and economic growth that was a principle component of the CCP's claim to legitimacy and the career prospects of individual officials. As the years passed and the hard-liners gradually faded from the scene, opposition to the political inclusion of China's capitalists began to wane even among central party elites. In 2001, Jiang Zemin formally announced his "Three Represents" theory, which claimed that the CCP represented the interests not only of workers and farmers—its traditional mass base—but urban economic elites as well. This became the justification for formally lifting the ban on recruiting capitalists into the CCP and for incorporating them into the formal political system more generally.[2]

By 2006, when our survey was conducted, the ban on recruiting capitalists had been lifted for several years, and the number of red capitalists was steadily growing (see Figure 3.2). Among all respondents in our survey, nearly 38 percent were party members. This is a much higher percentage than among the population as a whole, where roughly 6 percent of the population belongs to the party. This higher concentration of party members among the business community reflects two important facts: first, the CCP recognizes the importance of the private sector, both for economic growth and the CCP's survival as the ruling party; and second, most red capitalists were in the party before going into business. Although the co-optation of capitalists has been an increasingly important dimension of the CCP's party-building strategy, most red capitalists were previously employed as party and government cadres or worked in SOEs, either as managers, technicians, or as regular workers. In other words, most capitalists in China, and especially red capitalists, came out of the state sector. They were already embedded in the state before going into business.[3] This connection to the state can be seen in the firms themselves: 41.3 percent of the red capitalists' firms were originally SOEs, but only 24.3 percent of firms owned by non–party members started out as SOEs. As will be shown throughout this book, this background of state embeddedness makes these business enterprises more supportive of the political status quo and less inclined to seek political change.

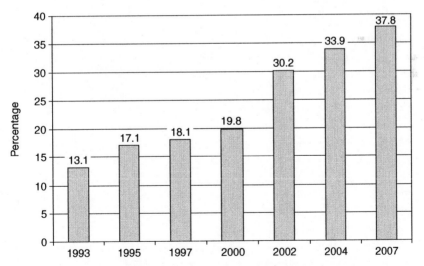

Figure 3.2.   Growth in Red Capitalists, 1993–2007 (Percentage of CCP Members among China's Private Entrepreneurs)

Note: Data for 1993–2004 come from surveys organized by the All-China Federation of Industry and Commerce; data available from the Universities Service Centre of the Chinese University of Hong Kong; data for 2007 comes from authors' survey.

Who are the red capitalists? In many ways, the political and social characteristics of red capitalists are similar to those of party members as a whole. For one thing, they are overwhelmingly male: men outnumber women in our survey by almost nine to one, but the percentage of men who are party members is even higher—92.3 percent of red capitalists are men. (By comparison, about 82 percent of all party members are men, and this proportion has changed little for several decades.) Put differently, a businessman has about a two in five chance of being a red capitalist, all else being equal, but a businesswoman has only a one in four chance. Red capitalists are also better educated than other capitalists. About 33 percent of red capitalists have college degrees, compared with just under 20 percent for non–party members. Conversely, 30.7 percent of non–party members have only a middle school education or less, compared with just 17.2 percent of red capitalists. The higher education levels of red capitalists reflect the CCP's recruitment strategy. Whereas it used to focus on the "three revolutionary classes"—workers, peasants, and soldiers—as its base of support, it now increasingly recruits the elites of society into the party. At least two-thirds of new recruits each year have a high school education or above, and college campuses have become a primary source of new party members. The CCP's general emphasis on education standards is also reflected in the profile of red capitalists.

Red capitalists are the economic elites of the private sector. According to our survey, red capitalists tend to operate larger and more lucrative firms than do non–party members: firms operated by red capitalists have more workers (368 to 140), more fixed assets (70.9 million yuan to 26.2 million yuan), more annual sales (73.8 million yuan to 26.2 million yuan), and more after-tax profits (4.6 million yuan to 1.9 million yuan). This size advantage is true in most types of firms: of the nineteen industrial sectors identified by the state statistical bureau, red capitalists had larger firms in fifteen of them, accounting for 94 percent of the firms in our sample. As a consequence of their larger size, red capitalists also pay more taxes than do non–party members. This is a key motive for the CCP's increasing integration of capitalists, especially those with large firms: it relies on the private sector to produce new jobs and new growth and to provide a growing share of local tax revenue.

Red capitalists are more prominent in some sectors of the economy than in others. For example, red capitalists represent 45.6 percent of those who own and operate excavation firms, 47.7 percent of construction firms, and 54.8 percent of science and technology firms. These are lucrative sectors that also require large start-up costs in equipment, technology, and human capital (i.e., education, especially for science and technology firms), and party members generally have better connections with banks and government offices that allow them to mobilize these kinds of resources. In contrast, party members are relatively underrepresented in sectors with smaller-scale operations, such as wholesale and retail stores, hotels, and restaurants. In these sectors, less than 30 percent of owners and operators are CCP members.

Party membership varies not only by sector but by region. Approximately 43 percent of respondents from Shandong and Zhejiang and a remarkable 51 percent of those from Jiangsu reported being party members. In contrast, 25.3 percent from Fujian and only 20 percent from Guangdong were party members. This difference is due to both supply and demand: fewer non-CCP respondents in Fujian and Guangdong had applied to join the CCP (7.9 and 6.7 percent, respectively, compared with 24.6 percent in the other three provinces), and the CCP had tried to recruit fewer of them to join the party (34.5 and 21.8 percent, respectively, compared with 39.8 percent in the other provinces). This low level of party membership among capitalists in south China, especially in Guangdong, will be repeated in other forms of political participation discussed later in this chapter and elsewhere in the book; in particular, capitalists in Guangdong were consistently less involved in politics than were those from provinces to the north.

Despite these figures, most respondents in our survey did not acknowledge that party members have advantages when it comes to business. Red capitalists were most likely to acknowledge the advantages of membership (41.3 percent), but even they were ambivalent: almost 60 percent said that party membership was not necessarily advantageous. Non–party members were even more skeptical. Among those who had applied to join the CCP, almost 70 percent said that it was not necessarily an advantage; and among those who had not applied to join, a remarkable 86.2 percent said that party members did not necessarily have advantages in business. This undoubtedly explains why so few of the capitalists in our sample who were not party members had applied to join (only 14 percent): CCP support for the private sector has become so strong and consistent that capitalists do not need to join the party in order to reap the benefits. According to local party officials responsible for party building in the private sector, private entrepreneurs who actively seek to join the party hope to obtain a political appointment, such as to local people's congresses; most other entrepreneurs have little interest in joining the party.[4] Moreover, party membership brings obligations that many capitalists find unwelcome and unhelpful to their business interests: the CCP will scrutinize their operations more rigorously, expect them to pay more taxes and comply with other laws, and mobilize them to make more charitable contributions. For private entrepreneurs with limited political and economic ambitions, the costs of party membership often outweigh the benefits.

In addition to encouraging its members to join the private sector and recruiting private entrepreneurs into the party, the CCP also builds ties to the private sector by other means of traditional party building, including creating party organizations in private firms and also recruiting workers from within the firms. In our sample, 30.7 percent of the firms had party cells.[5] The CCP has not put equal effort into creating party cells in all firms but instead concentrates on the largest firms and those run by red capitalists. This makes the work of party building easier and more efficient: large firms have more workers and are therefore more likely to have more party members among the workforce, and red capitalists are more likely than non–CCP members to be willing to allow party cells in their firms. Of the firms in our sample, 69.3 percent of those with above average fixed assets (42.7 million yuan) had party cells, compared with only 24.6 percent of firms with below average fixed assets. Among firms run by red capitalists, 56.6 percent had party cells, compared with only 15.2 percent of firms run by non–CCP members. The same pattern is apparent for workers joining the party: 40.2 percent of respondents said that workers in their firms had joined the party in recent years, but it was more likely in large firms than in smaller ones (76.5 percent compared with 34.5 percent) and in firms run by red capitalists than in those run by non–CCP members (64.1 percent compared with 26.1 percent). In its party-building efforts, the CCP is clearly targeting large firms and those where it will most likely be successful.

The characteristics of party members described above come into sharper focus in a multivariate analysis, which allows us to analyze the importance of each individual characteristic while holding the rest constant (see Table 3.1). Compared with the rest of the capitalists in the sample, party members are much more likely to be older and better educated and slightly more likely to be male. As noted above, this is consistent with the CCP's overall preferences in recruitment. Party members are also more likely to operate larger firms and privatized SOEs. The level of development is not a significant predictor of party membership, but which province the capitalists live in does matter: capitalists in Shandong, Jiangsu, and Zhejiang are more likely to be red capitalists than are those in Fujian and Guangdong, even when other variables are held constant. These consistent results reveal the strategy of the CCP's efforts to integrate the party and the private sector.

Table 3.1 Determinants of CCP Membership among Private Entrepreneurs (OLS Regression Analysis)

	b	*SE*	β
Age	0.012***	0.001	0.186
Level of education	0.112***	0.015	0.170
Gender	0.064*	0.032	0.042
Ex-SOE	0.112***	0.022	0.107
Firm size (natural log of fixed assets)	0.024***	0.006	0.087
Level of development (per capita GDP)	−0.001	0.001	−0.022
Jiangsu[a]	0.021	0.033	0.018
Zhejiang[a]	−0.002	0.032	−0.002
Fujian[a]	−0.151***	0.033	−0.122
Guangdong[a]	−0.179***	0.033	−0.147
Constant	−0.537***	0.079	
N	1,981		
R^2	0.159		
Adjusted R^2	0.154		

[a] Shandong is the reference point.
*p<.05   ***p<.001

Business Associations

In addition to party building in the private sector, the CCP uses other institutional ties to monitor and interact with private entrepreneurs. These institutional ties exhibit a corporatist logic. Philippe Schmitter's oft-cited definition of corporatism is useful here:

> Corporatism can be defined as a system of interest representation in which the constituent units are organized into a limited number of singular compulsory, noncompetitive, hierarchically ordered and functionally differentiated categories, recognized or licensed (if not created) by the state and granted a deliberate representational monopoly within their respective categories in exchange for observing certain controls on their selection of leaders and articulation of demands and supports.[6]

Although corporatism as a theoretical framework has been criticized on various grounds,[7] it has been frequently used in studies of state-society relations in countries in East Asia, Europe, and Latin America.[8] Distinct from pluralism[9]—another theoretical approach to the study of state-society relations—corporatism emphasizes the formalized (or institutionalized) connection between the state and societal groups and the important role of the state in such a connection. First, in the corporatist model, societal groups are formally incorporated by the state into a set of state-guided and/or controlled organizations (e.g., labor unions and business associations) at national and local levels. As Paul Adams puts it, the "corporatist model generally assumes a *formal* or *legal* system of relationships between the state and societal groups."[10]

Second, corporatism as a theoretical approach emphasizes and elaborates the vital role of the state in shaping state-society relations. According to this approach, the state should not be viewed merely as an "umpire or referee" among societal groups.[11] Instead, the state plays an active and even intrusive role "not only in intermediating between societal groups, but also in choosing which groups were to be represented and how representation would take place."[12]

Furthermore, to cope with the variation of state-society relations in different sociopolitical and cultural settings within the general corporatist framework, some scholars of corporatism have classified these relations into two general categories. In the state corporatist framework, the state plays a more dominant role in shaping its relationship with society. In this framework, typically the state directly or indirectly creates and controls major societal groups or organizations by, for instance, financing, staffing, and giving policy guidelines to these organizations. These societal organizations are used by the state as tools to achieve national goals defined by the state. This framework of state-society relations therefore can be also characterized as a "top-down" model: that is, political influence runs from the state to societal organizations. State corporatist arrangements have often been identified with authoritarian regimes, such as those in southern Europe, Latin America, and East Asia, especially during the early postwar period.[13]

Conversely, in the societal corporatist framework, the state plays a less dominant role in influencing and guiding its relations with society. Rather than single-handedly creating and controlling societal organizations, the state in the societal corporatist framework often plays an active role in facilitating the emergence and operation of (as opposed to creating and controlling) societal organizations. Instead of serving as "transmission belts" of the state's decrees, societal organizations serve as institutionalized forums for mutual interactions and continuous negotiations between the state and the organizations. Thus, this framework of state-society relations can be considered as a dual-direction—top-down and bottom-up—model; that is, political influence is mutually exchanged between the state and societal organizations. Consequently, societal corporatist arrangements have often been found in democratic systems or transitional systems moving toward democracy, such as those in Western and northern Europe.[14]

Both state corporatism and societal corporatism as theoretical approaches have been employed in the inquiry into state-society relations in post-Mao China. Some analysts argue that societal corporatism best explains the state-society relations in post-Mao China.[15] They contend that societal groups have gained more influence on and autonomy from the state as the result of social and economic liberalization brought about by the post-Mao reform. On the basis of their research in the 1990s, for example, Jonathan Unger and Anita Chan found that at local levels, some societal "associations are coming under increasing pressure from below to represent and lobby on behalf of their assigned constituencies, similar to some of the peak corporatist associations in Beijing." Thus, the authors concluded that state-society relations in contemporary China were moving from "state corporatism" toward "societal corporatism."[16] In a similar fashion, Joseph Fewsmith suggested that societal organizations "have moved away from the narrow 'transmission belt' function they had in Maoist China to take on a role of articulating, at least to some degree, societal interests." Business organizations and other societal groups may pursue their own interests that are different from those of the state and in fact "have forced the state to seek a new accommodation with society."[17]

In contrast, some other China analysts believe that state corporatism is more suitable a model to explain state-society relations in reformist China.[18] In general, these observers argue that the current party-state still firmly adheres to the cardinal principle of one-party domination/control of society; the Leninist organizational and policy-making legacy still significantly influences the party-state's management of its relations with society. Thus, these scholars suggest that as a theoretical model, state corporatism is more appropriate than societal corporatism for our understanding of current state-society relations in China, since the former emphasizes the dominant role of the state. As Margaret Pearson suggests, "by assuming the existence of a strong state at its core, state corporatism does not obscure the fundamental hierarchy of power between state and society."[19] That is, the state dominates society through its powerful political and bureaucratic mechanisms. For example, Kenneth Foster found ample evidence of the dominant role of the state in his study of business associations in Yantai: "nearly all business associations there were created at the initiative of state and party officials, and . . . they are in essence appendages of government or party organizations. Over the past two decades, these associations have accordingly functioned more as new parts of the local administrative system than as new sites of state-society engagement."[20]

The suitability of state corporatism as a theoretical framework for state-society relations in post-Mao China is also determined by the fundamental nature of the current political system—that is, a one-party authoritarian regime. Despite post-Mao economic and political liberalization (as opposed to democratization), authoritarianism remains intact and continues to constrain state-society relations. In this nondemocratic system, the state attempts to dominate societal groups for its own survival. In China, bottom-up nonpolitical societal organizations (e.g., sport and hobby clubs, cultural associations, business sectoral associations, and alumni associations) are allowed to exist to the extent that they do not become involved in politics but are subject to the state's intervention and control.[21] Any bottom-up political societal organizations (e.g., parties, independent labor unions, and student unions) are prohibited with almost no exception. In short, although China is not a clear-cut example of state corporatism, the concept still helps us to understand the institutionalized links between the state and societal groups—including business associations.

Since the onset of the post-Mao economic reform, business associations have grown in size and, to a certain extent, in number as well. Thus far, there are two broad categories of business associations: state-sanctioned (official, *guanfang*, or semiofficial, *ban guanfang*) business associations and self-organized/managed *(zizhi zuzhi)* associations/clubs. The state-sanctioned trade associations include the ACFIC and PEA, while self-organized/managed associations are too numerous and localized to name many specific ones (e.g., Wenzhou Chamber of Commerce, *Wenzhou Shanghui*).

The ACFIC is the most prestigious of the officially sanctioned business associations. It was originally created in 1953 as part of the CCP's effort to build a united front in the years after it came to power. It ostensibly represented former capitalists during the transition to socialism during the 1950s. It was suspended during the Cultural Revolution and reestablished in 1977. Its members include both state-owned and private firms, and they are typically the most politically, economically, and socially prominent people in the industrial and commercial sectors. Along with the eight so-called democratic parties, themselves relics of the pre-1949 period and also designed to illustrate the CCP's united front approach to governing, the ACFIC is able to nominate people to belong to local people's congresses and political consultative conferences.[22] This is an important asset for controlling which capitalists get appointed to official posts, as will be shown in the next section.

The PEA was created at the national level in 1986, and local chapters formed in later years. The state had previously created SELA to manage the small-scale enterprises that emerged in the early reform era. As time went on, private firms grew large in size, exceeding the limit of eight workers that was allowed by the state. Larger private firms wanted to distinguish themselves from the *getihu* that belonged to the SELA and to have their own organization, and the PEA was established. Over time, the distinction between *getihu* and other private firms began to dissolve, and the offices of SELA and PEA were merged in many communities.

In addition to these two large-scale business associations, there is a growing number of associations organized by the capitalists themselves. These tend to be smaller, often industry specific and even locality specific, and are not part of a nationwide hierarchy, as are the ACFIC and PEA. Although they are not formally part of the state structure, their members overlap considerably with those of the state-sponsored organizations. More important, some of them maintain close ties with the state and at least informally interact extensively with the party and government officials.[23]

There are several major differences between these two categories of organizations. First, and most obviously, they differ in terms of their ties with the party-state. The ACFIC and PEA come under the jurisdiction of the government's industrial and commercial bureau and the CCP's United Front Department. Although not formally state organizations, their offices are often in the government compound, their leaders are usually leading officials in the local industrial and commercial bureaus and United Front departments, and a substantial portion of their budgets is provided by the state. In contrast, self-organized/managed associations are formed and managed by individual entrepreneurs themselves. Although these organizations are registered with the state as "social organizations" *(shehui tuanti)*, they do not usually receive state funds. In addition, state-sanctioned organizations are formally included in the state's policy-making and implementing process, whereas the self-organized/managed organizations are not formally included in that process. Using Stepan's inclusion-exclusion spectrum of state corporatism,[24] one can say that state-sanctioned associations are included in the official policy-making and implementation channels, whereas self-organized/managed associations are neither totally included nor excluded but tolerated by the state (in the middle of the inclusion-exclusion spectrum). Despite the difference in their ties with the party-state, both categories of organizations are required by the state to conform to the cardinal principle of one-party rule. No doubt, the state's scrutiny of such political conformity is more institutionalized and routinized for state-sanctioned organizations than for self-organized/managed ones.

Second, these two types of organizations are distinct in their practices of membership recruitment. Membership in the PEA is often conferred simultaneously with the firm's registration with the local Industrial and Commercial Management Bureau, which is the government's agency for monitoring and regulating private enterprises. In contrast, the membership recruitment of self-organized/managed organizations is primarily voluntary. Entrepreneurs join these organizations mainly for their specific business and social purposes (e.g., concerns with a specific business sector) on the basis of their self-interests. Membership in the ACFIC is also voluntary and tends to attract the owners and managers of the largest firms.

Third, the two kinds of organizations are different in organizational structure. State-sanctioned organizations are hierarchically organized. For example, the ACFIC at the national level has authority over its branches, the Federations of Industry and Commerce (FICs), at the provincial level, which have power over FICs at local levels. In addition, the ACFIC and all FICs are subject to the leadership of the party organizations and governments at their respective levels. In contrast, due to the lack of national leadership and coordination, self-organized/managed groups are more horizontally organized—that is, each of them is independent of and equal to one another. The Wenzhou chambers of commerce are particularly noteworthy in this regard: in an otherwise hierarchical political system, Wenzhou merchants have created a network of chambers to coordinate activities around the country.[25] Moreover, self-organized business associations are usually organized locally and by professional sector.[26] In short, the structure of state-sanctioned organizations is more monolithic and hierarchical than that of self-organized/managed organizations.

Fourth, in terms of the organizations' size, state-sanctioned organizations have a much larger membership than do self-organized/managed organizations. According to the 2004 nationwide survey of private entrepreneurs conducted by the Industrial and Commercial Management Bureau (ICMB) and ACFIC, about 80 percent of private entrepreneurs were members of the ACFIC and/or PEA, while only about 40 percent of them belonged to various self-organized/managed organizations.[27] There are at least two possible reasons for this gap. One is obviously that the membership in PEA is almost automatic upon the registration for a business license, as mentioned above. Another reason is that entrepreneurs have more of an incentive to join state-sanctioned organizations, which are officially authorized to "represent" entrepreneurs and also enjoy secure financial and staff support. As a result, these organizations are more prominent and appealing to entrepreneurs.

Finally and most important, both categories of organizations have been organized to assist entrepreneurs in engaging in legitimate economic activities. Nonetheless, state-sanctioned organizations are also formally charged by the state with ideological and political functions, such as conducting "ideological education" among entrepreneurs and implementing policies and decrees of governments at various levels. According to Central Document No. 15 issued by the Central Committee of the CCP in 1991, for example, the ACFIC and its local branches are required to educate members about the correctness and importance of the CCP's one-party leadership *(dangde yiyuanhua lingdao)* as well as other CCP cardinal principles.[28] In contrast, self-organized/managed organizations do not have responsibility for political education and indoctrination, although they must obey the CCP's authority, as must all other societal groups. Rather than engage in political work, most of these organizations are formed to address specific business issues in certain business sectors or specific localities.

In sum, the Chinese party-state strategy to institutionalize its external links with new capitalists follows a corporatist logic in two ways. One is to create, control, and support state-sanctioned organizations and include them in the formal policy-making and policy-implementing process. These organizations are embedded "within the system" *(tizhi nei)* and treated by the state as the core of the institutionalized connection between the party-state and private entrepreneurs. The other strategy is to tolerate self-organized/managed organizations and to keep them outside of the formal policy-making and policy-implementation process. These organizations are considered "outside of the system" *(tizhi wai)* and are treated by the state as being on the periphery of the institutionalized connection between the party-state and private entrepreneurs. The two strategies are both designed to harness the connections of the party-state with capitalists as a whole, but the two kinds of organizations are treated differently. More important, the growing number of self-organized business associations, with varying degrees of autonomy from the state, indicates that China does not have a full-blown corporatist system, even though the CCP continues to pursue a somewhat corporatist-like strategy. As time goes on, the corporatist model is becoming less useful for understanding state-society relations in China and government-business relations in particular.

Members of the ACFIC and PEA have very similar profiles (see Table 3.2). They are slightly older than the average respondent in our survey and more likely to be better educated. They are more politically embedded than nonmembers: a higher percentage of ACFIC and PEA members are red

Table 3.2 Key Characteristics of Members of Various Business Associations (Average Values and Difference of Means)

	All entrepreneurs	ACFIC	t	PEA	t	Self-organized business association	t	Not a member of any business association	t
Political embeddedness									
Member of business association (%)		64.49		59.86		39.07		18.94	
Member of CCP (%)	37.96	42.85	−6.82***	39.10	−3.24**	41.03	−3.11**	22.16	6.21***
CCP organization in firm (%)	30.66	39.37	−12.55***	34.60	−6.83***	40.03	−8.10***	8.36	9.75***
Individual characteristics									
Average age	43.08	43.83	−6.36***	43.48	−3.94***	43.57	−2.72**	41.44	4.15***
Gender (% male)	88.41	89.55	−2.25*	88.61	−0.68	87.06	1.19	85.60	1.70
Level of education									
Middle school or below (%)	25.72	22.21	4.87***	23.82	2.80**	20.03	4.84***	36.31	−4.89***
High school (%)	49.93	50.96	−0.86	48.98	1.64	50.43	−0.16	47.48	1.28
College (%)	24.35	26.83	−3.97***	27.20	−4.87***	29.54	−5.26***	16.20	3.55***
Firm characteristics									
Average fixed assets (million yuan)	42.77	52.05	−3.53***	55.74	−2.81**	57.50	−2.48*	7.17	2.49*
Average annual sales (million yuan)	43.14	55.07	−3.83***	59.44	−3.29***	58.75	−2.39*	10.47	2.56*
Average number of workers	225.3	281.56	−2.66**	289.25	−2.35*	235.15	−0.3	69.81	2.13*
Years in business	7.92	8.40	−6.47***	8.19	−4.46***	8.35	−3.96***	6.74	4.58***
Ex-SOE (%)	30.31	32.68	−3.05**	31.9	−2.26*	35.02	−3.54***	22.43	3.47***

*p < .05   **p < .01   ***p < .001

capitalists and have party cells in their firms. A higher percentage of their firms were former SOEs, another indicator of their political ties. Their firms also tend to be larger than the average firm, in terms of fixed assets, annual sales, and number of workers, and have been in business longer. On all these measures, membership in the officially sponsored business associations signifies both the capitalists' stronger political ties with the party and their economic accomplishment.

Members of self-organized business associations have many of the same characteristics as ACFIC and PEA members but with a few key differences. First, fewer entrepreneurs in the sample belonged to these kinds of business associations. Second, members of self-organized business associations are most likely to have party cells in their firms and most likely to run firms that are former SOEs. Third, most of them also belong to the FIC or PEA, and 64 percent of them belong to both. Rather than seeing self-organized business associations as autonomous organizations, therefore, it is important to recognize that their members are very closely tied to the CCP and the government.

In contrast, those who do not belong to any business association have the opposite characteristics. They are younger and less well educated; they are less likely to be red capitalists or have party cells in their firms; and they tend to operate smaller firms and have been in business fewer years. Whether by their own choice or by an unwritten state strategy, these types of entrepreneurs lack the institutional ties that other entrepreneurs enjoy.

Private Entrepreneurs in Government Posts

A very public manifestation of the CCP's integration of private entrepreneurs into the political system is their selection for local legislative and consultative bodies, specifically people's congresses and political consultative conferences. As the national "legislative" body, the National People's Congress (NPC) is considered, at least in theory, the highest organ of the state. In reality, however, the NPC and its local branches have been controlled by the CCP and, in general, dominated by the administrative apparatus of the government at various levels. Whereas deputies to people's congresses at the county and township levels are directly elected by the eligible individual voters, deputies above the county level are indirectly elected by deputies at lower levels. Elections of people's congress deputies are closely monitored and controlled by CCP organizations at various levels. As a result, almost all candidates and all elected deputies have been scrutinized and approved by the party.[29] In other words, those who become people's deputies, including private entrepreneurs, are included or co-opted by the party into this "legislative" body under the condition that they are supportive of the party line.[30]

As a "consultative" body within the one-party system, the Chinese People's Political Consultative Conference (CPPCC) is supposed to have such functions as "political consultation, democratic supervision, and political participation." Even according to the CPPCC constitution, however, all these functions are carried out firmly under the CCP leadership and should not contradict the party's leading role. The CPPCC and its local branches serve as part of the CCP's united front strategy to rally support from people of all walks of life for its economic and political policies and programs. More important, members of the CPPCC and its branches are all appointed by the leaders of previous sessions of these organizations with the approval of CCP organizations at various levels. In other words, members of the CPPCC and its branches owe their membership to the leaders of these organizations and ultimately to the party leadership at various levels, rather than to citizens. Consequently, CPPCC membership among private entrepreneurs also results from the CCP's strategy of including or co-opting capitalists.

Rather than risk having capitalists push for political change from the outside, the CCP has brought large numbers of capitalists into these bodies at the local, provincial, and national levels. Among deputies to the NPC and CPPCC, which met in tandem in spring 2008, were over 200 private entrepreneurs, a sharp increase from the 130 who were deputies to these same bodies in 2003.[31] Nationwide, over 9,000 entrepreneurs have been elected to people's congresses (PC) at the county level and above, and 30,000 have been elected to people's political consultative conferences (PPCCs).[32] Among the respondents in our survey, 18.2 percent were members of PCs, and 20.7 percent were members of PPCCs at various levels.[33]

The Chinese media have given much attention to entrepreneurs who serve in PCs and PPCCs at various levels.[34] Some of China's most prominent—and most wealthy—entrepreneurs have been elected or selected for high-ranking posts, including the following:

Zhang Yin   (born 1957, number 2 on the 2007 Hurun list of richest Chinese)[35] is general manager of Hong Kong's Nine Dragons Paper Industries, the richest woman in China, and the richest self-made woman in the world.[36] Starting out reprocessing waste (recycled) paper for resale in Hong Kong, she then expanded to California to become the top U.S. exporter of waste paper to China (which imports half the world's exportable waste paper for domestic reprocessing); her business is now one of the largest paper manufacturers in the world.[37] Her father was a Red Army officer, and she used his connections to open government doors. Since 2003, she has been a deputy to the CPPCC, where she sparked controversy by speaking out on behalf of her own interests. She has advocated amending the Labor Contract law to exempt labor-intensive companies from signing permanent contracts with their workers, lifting the duty on imported pollution-control equipment, and lowering the rate for the highest income tax bracket.[38] Although she was criticized for making proposals that were obviously in her self-interest, as a rich industrialist in a polluting, labor-intensive industry, others saw her honest promotion of self-interest as a breakthrough for the CPPCC.[39]

Li Shufu   (born 1963, number 198 on the Hurun list) is chairman of Zhejiang's Geely Automobiles. From a peasant background, Li started out making refrigerators, expanding his business into motorcycles,[40] and then establishing the first independent car manufacturer in China, with plans to expand production abroad.[41] Li has advocated the creation of auto standards specific to China, in order to spur domestic innovation and give China an edge in competing with foreign brands. Li has been a deputy of the Taizhou City People's Congress and a CPPCC deputy since 2003.

Liu Yingxia   (born 1972, number 497 on the Hurun list) is general manager of Heilongjiang Xiangying Group, whose businesses include real estate, water supply, and road construction. Liu is known as one of the youngest wealthy women in China (number 40 on the Hurun list of women).[42] In the CPPCC since 2003, she has advocated creating a level legal and policy playing field for private firms, especially in industries where the government has traditionally had a monopoly.[43] Although a member of the "new social stratum," she started out in the People's Liberation Army (PLA) at age fifteen before becoming an entrepreneur.[44] With this background, she has stated that the new social stratum (i.e., private entrepreneurs and other urban professionals) should be concerned about rising inequality and about being "rich and responsible," abiding by the law and giving something back to society.[45]

Wang Jianlin   (born 1954, number 148 on the Hurun list) is president of the Dalian Wanda Group, a property development business that includes the domestic Wanda Cinemas line. With plans for rapid expansion of his cinema business, Wang has opposed piracy,[46] and he has shown concern for the development of small- and medium-sized enterprises, in particular by advocating more bank loan opportunities for them.[47] Like Liu Yingxia, Wang is a former soldier who wants entrepreneurs to stay in touch with common people;[48] he has thus supported changes in the tax laws to encourage charitable contributions.[49] Wang joined the CCP in 1996 and has been a CPPCC deputy since 2008.

Nan Cunhui   (born 1963, number 397 on the Hurun list) is chairman of the Zhejiang Chint Group (based in Wenzhou), which manufactures electronic products, and his concerns relate to manufacturing. Nan wants China to rely less on copying imported technologies, since continuing to do so will make China lag behind foreign competitors.[50] Instead, the government should find ways to encourage investment in research and development by domestic manufacturers. Nan believes that innovation can be encouraged if the government makes it a policy to purchase domestic products, and he gives the negative example of a road construction project that explicitly required construction equipment that was imported or produced by foreign companies in China.[51] If the government procured only domestic products, there would be favorable demonstration effects, enhancing the value of domestic brands. Nan was elected to the Ninth NPC in 1998 and reelected in 2003 and 2008. In 2003, he was also appointed as vice chairman of the Zhejiang Provincial FIC, the local chapter of the ACFIC. Although apparently not a CCP member, he has actively sought out contacts with party members in Wenzhou and has supported party building in private enterprises.[52]

Zhu Yicai   (born 1964, number 78 on the Hurun list) is chairman of the Jiangsu Yurun Group, which is involved in real estate and best known for being a giant in meat processing. Being in the food industry, and with ambitions to build the largest meat-processing plant in Asia,[53] Zhu has spoken out about food-safety controversies, advocating stricter criteria for giving market access to food processors and banning the illegal operation of small producers.[54] Zhu has also supported corporate social responsibility, specifically government-given tax preferences and priority in purchasing to firms that not only donate to charity but have a favorable impact on their operating environments, including job creation.[55] He has been an NPC deputy since 2003 and has also served in the Jiangsu provincial PC and as vice-chair of the Jiangsu Provincial FIC.

Zhou Xiaoguang   (born 1962, number 44 on the Hurun list of richest women) is chair of the Zhejiang Neoglory Group, a leading costume jewelry manufacturer.[56] She is known for having paid for an ad that ran for twenty days on local television in Yiwu, which she represents, to solicit local opinions and proposals to be conveyed to the NPC.[57] As a manufacturer, she has spoken out against the "monopolistic merger and acquisition" of local firms by foreign ones, especially in the manufacturing sector, where (she claims) nearly all the leading players are foreign-funded firms, seeing this as an issue of China's "sovereignty and economic security."[58] Zhou has also advocated passage of laws to control the import of foreign plant and animal species, which could disrupt China's native ecosystem if left unregulated.[59] Since 2003, she has served simultaneously as a PC deputy for Yiwu municipality, Zhejiang province, and the NPC.

These profiles indicate the types of prominent capitalists the CCP has selected for various official posts. It tends to favor people with long-term ties with the party who are less likely to pose a challenge to the party's policy agenda. Rather than be potential agents of change, they have proven to be dependable supporters of the status quo. To better understand the political impact of capitalists in China's political system, we will explain the CCP's strategy and process for selecting deputies to local people's congresses and political consultative conferences.

Local People's Congresses

The legislative branch in China's political system is widely seen as less powerful than either the party or the executive branch at all levels. Although this remains the case today, the emphasis on creating a modern legal system has also meant that the legislative branch has become more active and in some aspects more powerful. At the local level, PCs provide some degree of supervision over local government officials. During their annual meetings, local PCs review work reports by the local government and appraise the work of local officials. In some cases, they have vetoed the local governments' work reports and have dismissed incumbent officials from their positions. In an even more activist role, they have rejected the party's nominees for government posts and elected alternative candidates. In their investigations, they may make inquiries to government agencies on behalf of their constituents or as part of their own investigations. These more active roles have indicated a degree of political reform often overlooked in the study of Chinese politics.[60]

Despite these significant changes, the power of the PCs remains inferior to that of the party and government. In part, this is because of the limited period of time the PCs meet in full session, typically only a few weeks each year. More important, the party has prevented PCs from becoming a truly representative institution by controlling who is selected as its deputies. According to election regulations, candidates can be nominated either by the CCP, the eight so-called democratic parties, the local branch of the ACFIC, other official organs, and by groups of ten or more voters. A local election commission makes the decision on the final list of candidates. This election commission is controlled by local party officials, thus ensuring that all candidates are screened and approved by the party before they are presented to the voters. (The voting behavior of China's capitalists will be examined in more detail in Chapter 6.) Moreover, only township- and county-level PCs are directly elected by voters. Above those levels, PC deputies are selected by the lower-level body (for instance, deputies to the NPC are selected by provincial PCs). Many of the people nominated and elected as PC deputies are also party or government officials, further reducing the independence of the legislatures. Moreover, the chair of local PCs is also party secretary at that level, and the NPC chairman must be a member of the Politburo Standing Committee. In each of these ways, the party has restricted the ability of PCs to either represent public opinion or supervise the government.

The CCP is the main gatekeeper to formal political participation within China's political system, and it clearly favors its own members. Even when it does not directly nominate candidates, its election committees approve nominations from other individuals and groups. Not surprisingly, the data from our five-province survey showed that capitalists with official ties were more likely to be PC deputies than those not connected to the state (see Table 3.3). Our data also indicate that red capitalists account for 71.1 percent of those capitalists elected to local PCs, ACFIC members account for 84.8 percent, and 61.8 percent belong to both (not shown in the table). Another measure of political embeddedness is whether entrepreneurs have a party cell in their firms: whereas 30.7 percent of all firms in the sample had party cells, more than twice as many firms run by PC deputies had party cells. In fact, PC deputies were more likely to have party cells than were red capitalists as a whole. These details demonstrate the CCP's desire to select only the most politically dependable capitalists for legislative posts.

Although the PEA and self-organized business associations do not have the special status of the ACFIC (which is identified in the election law as the equivalent of one of the eight democratic parties), their members are also overrepresented among PC deputies. In our sample, almost 75 percent of PC deputies are PEA members, and 52.5 percent of them belong to self-organized business associations. This is lower than for ACFIC and PEA members but much higher than the percentage of entrepreneurs who

Table 3.3 Key Characteristics of PC and PPCC Deputies (Average Values and Difference of Means)

	All entrepreneurs	PC		PPCC	
			t		*t*
Percentage of sample	100.00	18.21		20.70	
Political embeddedness					
CCP membership (%)	37.96	71.31	−16.18***	37.78	−1.06
Party org in firm (%)	30.66	62.87	16.09***	50.62	10.62***
Firm characteristics					
Firm converted from SOE (%)	30.31	43.09	−6.14***	37.10	−3.54***
Average number of workers	225.30	598.37	−5.40***	293.95	−7.02***
Average fixed assets (million yuan)	42.77	14,305.66	−7.55***	6,361.95	−4.52***
Average annual sales (million yuan)	43.14	13,767.40	−7.86***	6,924.37	−4.14***
Years in business	7.92	9.23	−5.81***	9.38	−7.16***
Individual characteristics					
Gender (% male)	88.41	92.66	−2.94***	92.66	−1.57
Average age	43.08	46.44	−9.71**	44.74	−5.17***
Level of education					
Middle school or less (%)	25.72	20.22	2.62**	19.35	3.39***
High school (%)	49.93	46.54	1.53	44.47	2.44**
College (%)	24.35	33.24	−4.47***	36.18	−6.38***
Province					
Shandong (%)		21.23	−1.72	25.33	−2.48**
Jiangsu (%)		26.10	−4.98***	33.26	−7.5***
Zhejiang (%)		25.44	−4.18***	10.99	5.25***
Fujian (%)		10.42	4.42***	22.85	−1.14
Guangdong (%)		6.53	6.81***	9.46	6.18***

**p<.01   ***p<.001

belong to no business associations (only 3.1 percent). These are not exclusive categories: entrepreneurs can and do belong to multiple business associations, both those sanctioned by the state and those organized by the members themselves. Of the PC deputies who belong to self-organized business associations, 89 percent also belong to the ACFIC, 85 percent belong to the PEA, and 68 percent belong to both. The group least likely to be PC deputies is capitalists who do not belong to the CCP nor to a business association: less than 1 percent of these fiercely independent capitalists were PC deputies. They were presumably the least well connected and therefore the least trustworthy of the capitalists. They may also be the least politically inclined; in other words, their low numbers may signify apathy as much as exclusion.

PC deputies are drawn from the economic elites of their communities. Our data show that they own the largest firms: whether measured by the number of workers, the amount of fixed assets, or sales volume, their firms are more than twice as large as the average of all firms in the sample. They are also more likely to operate firms that were former SOEs, another indication of both their economic elite status and their preexisting ties to the state. Their firms have also been in business longer than average. In all of these ways, we can see how capitalists who are PC deputies are local economic elites.

Our data also indicate that there is tremendous regional variation in the pattern of where capitalists are selected for seats in local PCs. In the three northernmost provinces (Shandong, Jiangsu, and Zhejiang), a higher than average proportion of capitalists in our survey were PC deputies, but in Fujian and especially Guangdong, it was much less commonplace that capitalists would be a PC deputy. This is consistent with the pattern found for red capitalists above: capitalists in south China are generally less politically active than in the north.

In short, access to local PCs is largely controlled by the formal political and business associations. Members of the CCP and ACFIC vastly outnumber the capitalists with weak political ties.

People's Political Consultative Conferences

A peculiar feature of the Chinese political system is the presence of PPCCs. These bodies meet in tandem with the PCs at all levels and are designed to allow party and government officials to discuss policy issues with nonstate actors. They are described as essential parts of the "consultative democracy" that China's leaders claim they want to develop. As its name suggests, the PPCC is a consultative body, and its recommendations are not binding on the party or the state. It is therefore more of an honorary than authoritative institution, but membership on it still connotes elite status. In some cases, PPCC deputies are economically or socially influential; in other cases, it is a sinecure for retired officials, allowing them to be in the flow of policy discussions but removed from the actual decision making. Because of this symbolic status, it is a common way of integrating nonofficials into the formal political institutions without having to actually share power with them.

The selection of PPCC deputies is done not through popular elections but by nominations from the CCP, the eight so-called democratic parties, the ACFIC, and a few other privileged groups. Deputies are chosen in a three-step process of "consultation and recommendation" designed to select people "who represent all areas and various sectors of society in China, have social influence and are capable of participating in the deliberation and administration of state affairs."[61] Local notables consult with members of the organizations to which they belong, with members of other organizations, and with the local party committee (Step 1). After this consultation, they recommend a name list, which is then evaluated and finalized by the party (Step 2). This list is then voted on by the incumbent members of the PPCC to determine who will serve on the next one (Step 3).[62] Because candidates for PPCCs are approved by the party in advance and then selected by the outgoing PPCC members, they are typically politically embedded and socially prominent individuals who represent the local elites more than society at large.

Among private entrepreneurs, those selected as PPCC deputies are typically already among the political and economic elites of their communities. In our survey, a large percentage of PPCC deputies—37.8 percent—were party members (see Table 3.3). This is lower than the percentage of PC deputies (of whom more than 71 percent were red capitalists), but that is to be expected because the PPCC is supposed to allow officials to consult with a wider spectrum of society. Moreover, firms run by PPCC deputies are more likely than the average in our sample to have party cells, but they are less likely than PC deputies and red capitalists to have party cells. This suggests that the CCP is willing to consult with capitalists regardless of their relationship to the CCP but is more discriminating in whom they trust with political power—the PC deputies. Membership in different business associations is a more important determinant of the political ties of PPCC deputies. A remarkable 91.9 percent of PPCC deputies in our sample belonged to the ACFIC, exactly 70 percent were PEA members, and slightly less than half (48.4 percent) belonged to self-organized business associations. As these numbers show, membership in the PPCCs is largely determined by individuals' membership in other political and economic associations. As was the case for PC deputies, the least politically embedded entrepreneurs—that is, those who do not belong to either the CCP or any business association—are much less likely to be appointed to the PPCC: less than 2 percent of these independent entrepreneurs in our sample were PPCC deputies.

The entrepreneurs selected for the PPCC not only are politically connected but are also drawn from among the economic elites of their communities. Their firms are larger than the average size in our sample but not as large as those of PC deputies. In short, PPCC deputies are more politically embedded and economically privileged than the sample as a whole but less so than PC members.

Multivariate Analysis of PC and PPCC Memberships

Being either a PC or PPCC deputy signifies acceptance as part of the political elite, but this status is not independent of the other indicators of political embeddedness discussed above: membership in the CCP and the official business associations. The easiest way to show this relationship is through a multivariate analysis, which allows us to see the impact of single variables when others are held constant. In this analysis, we want to test several hypotheses.

First, we expect that the more closely connected to the party-state entrepreneurs are, the more likely they are to be PC and PPCC deputies. Here we use the indicators of political embeddedness described earlier: membership in the CCP, ACFIC, and PEA. Existing ties to the state make entrepreneurs more dependable regime supporters and therefore more likely to be trustworthy in government posts. In other words, some forms of political embeddedness, specifically membership in the CCP and ACFIC, make another form of embeddedness—the holding of a government post—more likely.

Second, we expect that the CCP favors economic elites among the capitalists who participate in formal political institutions, so that the larger the firm owned and operated by the respondents and the longer they have been in business, the more likely they will be PC or PPCC deputies. Similarly, those whose firms were former SOEs will also be favored because they have strong ties to the state.

Third, we believe that for most forms of political participation, older and better educated people are more likely to participate than others, and we expect that relationship to hold true here as well. As is true in most countries, China's political system is predominated by men, and China's capitalists are also predominated by men, so we expect that men will be more likely than women to be selected as PC deputies.

Finally, we include several control variables to account for contextual factors: the local per capita GDP of the county-level units included in our survey and dummy variables for four of the five provinces represented in our survey, with Shandong as the reference point.

As can be seen in Table 3.4, the survey results mostly are consistent with our expectations.

PC Deputies. Among the measures of political embeddedness, CCP membership stands out as the largest determinant of being a PC deputy. Even when other factors are considered, CCP membership remains the most important criterion in the selection of PC deputies, as seen by its beta coefficient, which is the largest of all the variables in our model.[63] Similarly, membership in the ACFIC is also a significant factor. In contrast, membership in the PEA and self-organized business associations was not statistically significant when membership in other organizations was controlled for.

Economic elite status is also a good predictor of who are PC deputies. Owners of larger firms (measured by fixed assets)[64] and of converted SOEs were more likely than others to be PC deputies. However, the length of time that a firm has been in operation was not significant. Even though firms owned by PC deputies were on average 1.6 years older than other firms, when other variables were held constant, this factor alone was not significant. Capitalists among PC deputies represent the elites of their communities, not necessarily the business community as a whole.

Among capitalists' individual traits, age, gender, and level of education are all positive, but only age is statistically significant—that is, the older the respondents are, the more likely they are to be chosen as a PC deputy, but education and gender are not significant factors when other variables are held constant; a test for a curvilinear relationship between education and the probability of being a PC deputy was negative.

The contextual variables show that the local context also matters. The level of economic development was not by itself a significant variable, but the local setting was: respondents living in Fujian and Guangdong were less likely to be PC deputies than those in Shandong (the reference point for the other provinces), Jiangsu, and Zhejiang, although the difference is only statistically significant for Fujian when other factors were controlled for.

In sum, these results reveal a deliberate strategy for which capitalists are chosen to be PC deputies: they are politically embedded and economically

Table 3.4 Determinants of People's Congress and People's Political Consultative Conference Deputies (OLS Regression Analysis)

	PC deputies			PPCC deputies		
	b	SE	β	b	SE	β
Institutional ties						
CCP member	0.168***	0.020	0.212	−0.073***	0.021	−0.088
Party cell in enterprise	0.101***	0.022	0.120	0.095***	0.024	−0.108
ACFIC member	0.067***	0.019	0.085	0.175***	0.020	0.217
PEA member	0.023	0.019	0.030	0.040*	0.021	0.051
Self-organized business association member	0.012	0.019	0.015	−0.006	0.021	−0.007
Economic elite status						
Firm size (natural log of fixed assets)	0.028***	0.006	0.125	0.014*	0.006	0.059
Ex-SOE	0.047*	0.019	0.057	0.019	0.020	0.022
Years in business	0.002	0.002	0.031	0.008***	0.002	0.010
Individual and firm characteristics						
Age	0.005***	0.001	0.090	0.003*	0.001	0.051
Gender	0.018	0.026	0.015	0.004	0.028	0.003
Education	−0.002	0.013	−0.004	0.030*	0.014	0.055
Local economic and political context						
Level of development (per capita GDP)	0.000	0.001	−0.013	−0.004***	0.001	−0.152
Jiangsu[a]	0.058*	0.026	−0.064	0.023	0.028	0.024
Zhejiang[a]	0.027	0.027	0.027	−0.175***	0.029	−0.173
Fujian[a]	−0.099***	0.030	0.090	−0.028	0.032	−0.024
Guangdong[a]	−0.046	0.027	0.050	−0.071*	0.028	−0.074
Constant	−0.144	0.086		0.054	0.092	
No. of observations	1,666			1,631		
R^2	0.221			0.191		
Adjusted R^2	0.213			0.183		

[a] Shandong is the reference point.
*$p < .05$ ***$p < .001$

influential and as a result more likely to support the status quo and less likely to pose a threat to the CCP.

PPCC Deputies.   To analyze the factors that determine which capitalists are most likely to be selected to become PPCC deputies, we use the same multivariate analysis as for PC deputies. Among measures of political embeddedness, ACFIC membership stands out as the most important factor, with the largest beta coefficient. PEA membership also has a positive impact but one that is much smaller than for ACFIC. CCP membership makes it less likely that a capitalist will be selected, all else being equal, which is consistent with the descriptive finding that most PPCC deputies were not red capitalists. This may be a form of affirmative action to allow elites who are not party members to be selected for this consultative body. However, the party is still closely tied to the firms of PPCC deputies: those with party cells are more likely to be selected.

PPCC deputies are more likely to be drawn from the economic elites of the community, as noted above. Among the respondents in our survey, PPCC deputies were more likely to have a higher level of fixed assets and have been in business longer than nondeputies. Although in the bivariate analysis above we showed that a higher percentage of owners of ex-SOEs are PPCC deputies than are owners of other types of private firms, the effect of being an ex-SOE is not statistically significant when other variables are held constant. Other measures of political embeddedness and economic elite status are more important explanatory variables.

Among individual characteristics, PPCC deputies are more likely to be older and better educated than nondeputies. Although men are more likely than women to be PPCC deputies (21.2 percent compared with 16.7 percent), gender is not a statistically significant variable when other individual characteristics are controlled for. In this case, it is age that makes the difference: women in the sample were on average three years younger than men but were equally well educated.

The local context was also an important determinant of being a PPCC deputy, as it was the case for PC deputies. Although the level of development was not a statistically significant determinant for being a PC deputy, it is for PPCC deputies; those from more prosperous areas were less likely to be PPCC deputies. Once again, capitalists in Guangdong are less likely than those in Shandong, the northernmost province in our sample, to be PPCC deputies. More surprisingly, the coefficient for Zhejiang is large, statistically significant, but negative. This seems to run contrary to our hypothesis that capitalists are more politically active in more northern provinces. We suspect that our basic hypothesis is correct but that being a PPCC deputy is the exception to the rule. Because it is generally seen as a largely symbolic but politically inconsequential body, those interested in politics are likely to seek other avenues. As we will show in later chapters, other types of political participation are consistent with the general hypothesis regarding regional variation.

Among the respondents in our survey, PPCC deputies are distinguished by their status in the economic elites of their communities. Elite status, along with the particular features of the local context, seems to be the most influential determinant of who is chosen to be a deputy. In short, the CCP selects the people least likely to pose a threat to the political status quo for official posts such as local PCs and PPCCs.

Conclusion

China's capitalists have become an increasingly prominent component of its political system, but this is not occurring in a vacuum. On the contrary, the CCP has devised a clear strategy for including capitalists—especially those who are deemed dependable and trustworthy by the party—into the regime. On the one hand, the CCP encourages its members to join the private sector and simultaneously recruits successful entrepreneurs into the party. These "red capitalists" provide one important means of integrating the CCP and the private sector. On the other hand, the CCP uses corporatist-style techniques for including some capitalists while excluding others. State-sanctioned business associations provide an institutional link between the state and business, giving members an opportunity to engage with policy makers on business-related issues. Private entrepreneurs also have the opportunity to be appointed to government posts, especially local PCs and PPCCs. Obtaining a government post is not solely the result of the entrepreneurs' own initiative, however; in order to gain access to these privileged positions, entrepreneurs must first gain the support of the CCP and the official business associations. The party-state carefully screens who gains access to the political arena and rewards its own members.

These indicators of political embeddedness show how systematically capitalists are integrated by the CCP into the key political and economic institutions in China. As would be expected in most countries, politically embedded capitalists in China are also prosperous capitalists: they operate firms with more workers, larger assets, and higher sales volumes than do those without institutional ties to the state. In other words, those who have prospered the most under the current policies are also most likely to be embedded in the existing political institutions. Their ties to the state serve to reinforce the current regime rather than pose a challenge to it. They have little incentive to be agents of political change. These insights will be further explored in later chapters, which look at levels of regime support and the motivations for engaging in other types of political activities.

CHAPTER FOUR

The Level and Sources of Capitalists' Democratic Support

I N THIS CHAPTER, we address several critical questions regarding the level and sources of support for democracy among China's newly emerging private entrepreneurs. Do these entrepreneurs support democratic values and institutions, as many people and policy makers in the West have expected? If so, how strongly do they support democracy, and why do they support it? By answering these questions, we hope to shed some light on the potential role of China's new capitalists in democratization.

In order to put the findings from our survey in a broad theoretical and political context, we will first examine the previous findings about democratic support among private entrepreneurs in China as well as in other late-developing countries. We will then discuss the measurement of democratic support used in this study and present the results of democratic support among private entrepreneurs based on our five-province survey. Finally, we explore some key sources of entrepreneurs' attitudes toward democracy and democratization.

Early Findings about the Level of Capitalists' Democratic Support

Comparative studies of capitalists in late-developing countries in Latin America, the Middle East, and East/Southeast Asia argue that the attitudinal orientation of capitalists toward democratization in those late-developing countries is influenced by their dependence on the states as well as by their perceived threat from the lower classes.[1] As Eva Bellin has said, capitalists are "contingent democrats" at best.[2] The findings from these studies indicate that, contingent on their dependence on the state and the perceived threat from other classes, capitalists support democratization in some developing countries but not in others. Within one country and over time, capitalists may change their attitudes toward democratization in response to variations in their dependence on the state and their perceived threat from other classes. For example, Bellin found that capitalists supported democratization in Korea by the mid-1980s and in Brazil by the late 1980s but did not support such a political change in Indonesia, Singapore, and Syria.[3] Peter H. Smith showed that capitalists within Argentina, Chile, and Uruguay shifted their attitudes from anti- to pro-democratization in the late 1970s.[4] According to these scholars, the degree of capitalists' dependence on the state is one of the most critical determinants in explaining the variation in their orientations toward democratization across and within countries.

In contrast to the aforementioned studies of capitalists in other late-developing countries, analyses of this new social class in China are anchored in two different theoretical approaches, which therefore lead to two conflicting findings about political attitudes of this social class. On the one hand, some studies, which are directly or indirectly informed by modernization theory, argue that modernization inevitably brings about unprecedented socioeconomic changes, such as industrialization, urbanization, value shifts, and new social classes (including the middle class and private entrepreneurs).[5] These studies suggest that all these changes promote democratization. Based on aggregate data or anecdotal evidence, these studies also found that new middle classes and private entrepreneurs—which emerged during the post-Mao economic modernization—supported democracy and had or would serve as the harbingers of democratization in China, since these new classes inherently were supportive of such democratic principles as free competition, rule of law, and constrained government.[6] For instance, Ronald Glassman argues that China's "capitalist businessmen . . . have come to realize that bureaucratic decrees usually lead to red-tape impediments rather than legal guarantees" for the operation and growth of their business;[7] therefore, the capitalists demand political changes toward a democratic system in which their interests can be protected by the rule of law and can flourish in a free market. Moreover, on the basis of his analysis of aggregate data, Yongnian Zheng suggests that "Some connections between capitalism and political changes embedded in Western democracies have already taken shape in China";[8] he argues that Chinese capitalists have begun to show some nascent signs of support for democratization in their opinion and behavior.

On the other hand, some other studies emphasize the critical role of the state in guiding economic development and shaping new social classes during economic modernization in China.[9] They argue that the CCP uses a corporatist strategy to both cooperate with private entrepreneurs and to monitor and control their activities. Because the state and the private sector have a common interest in promoting economic growth, according to these analysts capitalists tend to shy away from democratization, because such a political change could threaten the very existence of the current regime and thereby jeopardize their economic interests. Based on survey data and systematic interviews, these studies also found that China's private entrepreneurs tended to be less enthusiastic about democracy and democratization. For example, Margaret Pearson observed that entrepreneurs were not likely to initiate demands for democratization but might "lend support if others take the lead in pressuring for economic and political change."[10] The evidence from Bruce Dickson's studies of private entrepreneurs of large firms indicated that these capitalists shared similar views on key political issues with government officials and were very reluctant to promote democratization.[11] Kellee Tsai has recently found that although China's private entrepreneurs can hardly be identified as one "unified" or monolithic social class, most of them do not seem to demand democratic reforms.[12]

Some recent survey studies carried out by China-based scholars have confirmed these aforementioned findings. Drawing on data from a survey of private entrepreneurs conducted by the Chinese Academy of Social Sciences in two southern Chinese cities (Guangzhou and Wenzhou), for instance, Ao Daiya found that about 70 percent of respondents were not in favor of such democratic principles as the political rights to demonstrate and to petition the government.[13] In agreement with the government's view, according to this analyst, private entrepreneurs believed that mass demonstration and petitioning could disrupt social stability. Having examined data from a survey of the private entrepreneurs in five cities (Beijing, Shanghai, Guanzhou, Nanjing, and Wuhan), Zhang Chunmin found that most respondents strongly favored social stability and the status quo over political changes or reforms, because any major changes could jeopardize their "economic prosperity and social advancement."[14]

In summary, the empirical findings about capitalists' orientations toward democracy and democratization in China are mixed. One group of studies—which are mostly based on aggregate data or anecdotal evidence and often date from the 1990s—suggested that private entrepreneurs would serve as the harbingers of democratization in China. The other group of studies—which are mostly based on survey data or systematic interviews—found that China's capitalists tended to shy away from democratization. The findings about capitalists' support for democratization from both Chinese and non-Chinese settings, as described above, provide some important empirical baselines against which the findings from our survey can be compared. Although it is unfeasible to compare the results from our survey with those from earlier studies on a one-to-one basis, a comparison between them in a general sense will help us better understand where China's capitalists stand on democracy and democratization in the broad theoretical and empirical contexts.

The Measurement of Democratic Support

The findings from the earlier survey-based studies mentioned above have many important insights regarding capitalists' attitudes toward democracy and democratization. Nonetheless, the measurements used in these studies to gauge such attitudes suffer from several shortcomings. Some of these earlier studies utilized questionnaire instruments that did not directly tackle the attitudes toward democratic political systems or democratization itself. As a result, these studies had to infer capitalists' attitudes toward democracy from the indirect questionnaire instruments.[15] Other studies adopted highly abstract, though direct, survey questions to measure support for democracy among China's capitalists.[16] These questions raise the threat of invalid responses from respondents, who tended to confuse democracy as defined by classical liberalism with the one propagandized by China's party-state. In short, these shortcomings often resulted in highly indefinite and inconclusive findings about the orientation of China's private entrepreneurs toward democratization.

In order to help rectify these shortcomings in the earlier studies and more accurately gauge private entrepreneurs' support for democracy, we draw on the conceptualization and operationalization of democratic support, which have been used in several survey-based studies of democratic support in various countries. Specifically, to investigate the level of support for democracy among China's new capitalists, we conceptualize such support based mainly on that developed by Gibson and his associates.[17] This conceptualization summarizes various writings on democratic values,[18] and it has been successfully utilized in several survey studies in former Soviet societies and post-Mao China.[19] Such a conceptualization suggests that the "democratic citizen is one who believes in individual liberty and who is politically tolerant, . . . who is obedient but nonetheless willing to assert rights against the state, who views the state as constrained by legality, and who supports basic democratic institutions and processes."[20]

Following this conceptualization and drawing on our field observations in China, in this study we utilize a multidimensional variable to measure support for democracy by China's private entrepreneurs. This variable encompasses three conceptual subdimensions of democratic values that we believe are critical for democratization in China: (1) support for competitive elections, (2) support for a multiparty system (vs. the current one-party rule), and (3) the valuation of individual liberty (vs. order). In our five-province survey of private entrepreneurs, each of these subdimensions is measured by two to three specific questions.

Support for Competitive Elections

Most scholars of democracy consider competitive, multicandidacy elections to be the imperative process for a functioning democratic system.[21] They believe that only through this kind of institutionalized process can government be based on popular sovereignty and serve the common goal. As Samuel Huntington contends, a contemporary democratic system is one in which "its most powerful collective decision makers are selected through fair, honest, and periodic elections in which candidates freely compete for votes and in which virtually all the adult population is eligible to vote."[22] Moreover, to many political analysts, it is inconceivable that any democratization can be initiated and succeed without widespread support for competitive elections. Therefore, they define the belief in competitive elections as an essential component of democratic values held by the general public, which should be acquired in a transition from a totalitarian or authoritarian regime to a democratic system.[23] Following the procedural definition of democracy popularized by Schumpeter and Dahl, Huntington notes that "open, free, and fair" elections "are the essence of democracy, the inescapable sine qua non."[24]

It is even more relevant to tap into the level of support for competitive elections in China, because Chinese traditional political culture has been deemed to be inherently nondemocratic. It is argued that the traditional culture has a strong tendency toward a totalitarian system in which a "wise-and-able" sage rules the country with "the mandate of heaven" rather than the mandate of the people. Some observers of Chinese politics even suggest that these basic cultural predispositions remain remarkably consistent.[25] In addition, there has not been any popular competitive election of government leaders beyond the local level in China. Support for competitive elections would therefore indicate support for popular sovereignty in the selection of government leaders, a change from the current practice of appointment from above for most government posts.

To measure support for competitive election, we employed two items in our survey. One refers to the multicandidate election of key government leaders at various levels, while the other relates to expansion of competitive elections of leaders from the local level (i.e., governing committees in villages and urban neighborhoods) to higher levels, such as governments of townships and counties. The results from the two items are reported in Table 4.1. The vast majority of our private-entrepreneur respondents supported multicandidate elections (80 percent) and expansion of the current local elections of government leaders to higher levels (77 percent).

Support for Multiparty Competition (versus One-Party Dictatorship)

Scholars of democracy have also argued that free multiparty competition—as opposed to one-party or one-person dictatorship—is one of the most important democratic institutions, because such a competition facilitates the openness and inclusiveness of any democratic system.[26] This kind of competition provides citizens with open, meaningful channels for the aggregation and articulation of their diverse interests, and more important, it helps make the ruling party accountable to ordinary citizens. In general, therefore, popular support for the idea of multiparty competition is considered an important condition for the emergence and maintenance of a democracy.

Support for multiparty competition is even more critical for the emergence of a democratic system in China, since the current political system is characterized as one-party rule in which multiparty competition is prohibited. For more than a half century, the CCP has relentlessly promoted among the population the ideas that the CCP is the only legitimate

Table 4.1   Support for Competitive Elections

	% prodemocratic
Key leaders of the government at various levels should be elected through multicandidacy elections. (Agree)	80.4 (2,053)
Elections for local government at the village level could be expanded to townships/towns and districts/counties. (Agree)	76.6 (2,039)

Note: The nature of the "prodemocratic" responses is shown in parentheses. Numbers in parentheses are total observations.

organized political force in China and that multiparty competition can undermine the stability and unity of the country.[27] Given this adamant antagonism to multiparty competition in China as well as the crucial role of multiparty competition in democratic politics, we consider it important to know whether China's capitalists accept the presence of multiple parties competing for power.

To measure support for multiparty competition, we utilized two items in our survey. One was designed to gauge respondents' support for multiparty competition; the other was intended to detect their views of the current one-party rule. As shown in Table 4.2, only a small minority of our respondents supported multiparty competition (28 percent) and opposed the current one-party dictatorship (13 percent). These results suggest that an overwhelming majority of private entrepreneurs do not support multiparty competition. In reality, the CCP has always dominated and controlled all important aspects of the political life of the country, including elections at almost all levels, despite the presence of several so-called democratic parties, which are not truly opposition parties but at best serve consultative roles in policy making. Thus, rejection of multiparty competition seems to imply consent to the current one-party political system.

Valuation of Individual Liberty (versus Order)

There are at least two distinct propositions on the valuation of political freedom by the citizens in transitional societies, such as the former Soviet Union and the People's Republic of China. On the one hand, a group of scholars who studied such valuation in the former Soviet Union assumed that "democracies require citizenries committed to liberty even when there is a prospect for disorder."[28] When designing instruments to measure the level of mass support for democracy in the former Soviet Union, therefore,

Table 4.2 Support for Multiparty Competition

	% prodemocratic
A one-party system promotes economic, social, and political development in China and is most suitable to China's current circumstances. (Disagree)	13.2 (2,062)
If a country has multiple parties, it can lead to political chaos. (Disagree)	28.4 (2,061)

Note: The nature of the "prodemocratic" responses is shown in parentheses. Numbers in parentheses are total observations.

these scholars hypothesized that respondents who support democracy as a set of political institutions and principles should choose liberty over order. Moreover, Gibson and his associates suggested that even within a political culture that has a "penchant for order" (i.e., the Soviet political culture), democratic supporters should be more likely to choose liberty over order.[29] In short, this theoretical approach suggests that the preference for political liberty over order is almost unconditionally positively related to support for democratic institutions and principles.

On the other hand, with emphasis on the uniqueness of Chinese political culture, some China analysts suggest that the Chinese conceptualize and prioritize certain democratic principles quite differently than their counterparts in some other societies, especially in the West. Specifically in terms of the relationship between social order and democracy, Chinese political culture tends to assume that "democracy should be conducive to social harmony [or order]."[30] Moreover, Chinese political culture emphasizes social order and collective interests over individual rights and liberty. As Pye has pointed out, most Chinese "accept completely the need for order."[31] Some findings from earlier survey studies of urban China also support this proposition.[32] In contrast to the view that the Chinese culture is inhospitable to democracy in general, Andrew Nathan suggested that "China's political culture today is different from what it was earlier in this century" and also pointed out the evidence from some recent survey studies indicating the emergence of democratic culture in today's China.[33] Furthermore, Wm. Theodore De Bary even argued that Chinese culture is not inherently incompatible with some key democratic values, such as individual rights.[34] The uniformity and continuity of Chinese political culture in general and its influence on democratic values remain much debated.

In addition to the cultural factor, material interests could also prompt Chinese private entrepreneurs to favor social order over individual liberty. This is because these interests—such as the growth of the private sector and protection of private property—could be harmed by social disorder, which could be caused by the masses' exercise of individual liberties through various forms of political participation (e.g., mass demonstration). As Xiao Gongqin suggests, the Chinese private entrepreneurs will therefore resist democracy if democracy might bring about chaos.[35]

To explore these two propositions, we fashioned two questions that postulated a conflict between individual freedoms—such as the rights to demonstrate and organize—and social order and one question that probes the absolute obedience to authority, which relates to the valuation of individual rights and sovereignty. Table 4.3 reports the responses of Chinese private entrepreneurs. On the one hand, less than one-third of private entrepreneurs favored such individual liberties (vs. social stability) as the right to demonstrate (17 percent) and the right to organize (32 percent). These findings support one of the two propositions mentioned above—that is, when political freedom is pitted against potential social order, Chinese entrepreneurs decisively choose the latter. On the other hand, a majority of the respondents (60 percent) were willing to defer to the decision-making authority of government leaders almost unconditionally. This result reinforces the findings from the other two questions in this category. These results suggest that most capitalists are less likely to champion such individual liberties as the right to demonstrate and the right to organize and are more likely to defer to the authority of government leaders.

Summary Indicator of Democratic Support

How strongly do private entrepreneurs in China support basic democratic values and institutions? The answer to this question according to our analysis is twofold. On the one hand, an overwhelming majority of private entrepreneurs support competitive elections of leaders. On the other hand, most private entrepreneurs do not support or accept multiparty competition in Chinese politics and do not support ordinary citizens' rights to engage in public demonstrations and form nongovernmental organizations (even though many enterprises have formed their own organizations) if asserting those rights would potentially disrupt social order.

The contradiction between these two findings prompted us to suspect that questions about support for competitive elections actually measured

Table 4.3   Support for Individual Liberty and Sovereignty

	% prodemocratic
Public demonstrations can easily turn into social disturbances and impact social stability and should be forbidden. (Disagree)	17.3 (2,064)
Social harmony will be damaged if people form nongovernmental organizations. (Disagree)	31.9 (2,057)
Government leaders are like heads of family, and their decisions should be obeyed. (Disagree)	39.9 (2,053)

Note: The nature of the "prodemocratic" responses is shown in parentheses. Numbers in parentheses are total observations.

a political value dramatically different from or even unrelated to what the other questions were designed to measure. To verify this suspicion, we ran a factor analysis of all seven questions (as listed in Tables 4.1, 4.2, and 4.3). The results of the analysis indicated that there were two separate factors among these seven questions (see Table 4.4): one (shown as Factor 2)

Table 4.4   Factor Analysis of the Questions on Support for Competitive Elections, Multiparty Competition, and Individual Liberty and Sovereignty

Items	Factor 1: Multiparty competition and individual liberty	Factor 2: Competitive elections
A one-party system promotes economic, social, and political development in China and is most suitable to China's current circumstances. (Disagree)	.732	
Public demonstrations can easily turn into social disturbances and impact social stability and should be forbidden. (Disagree)	.703	
If a country has multiple parties, it can lead to political chaos. (Disagree)	.678	
Forming various kinds of nongovernmental organizations can easily damage social stability. (Disagree)	.663	
Government leaders are like heads of family, and their decisions should be obeyed. (Disagree)	.612	
Elections for local government at the village level could be expanded to townships/towns and districts/counties. (Agree)		.861
Key leaders of the government at various levels should be elected through multi-candidacy election. (Agree)		.853

Note: Figures are factor loadings of .25 or larger from the varimax-rotated matrix for all factors with eigenvalues greater than 1.0. To capture a collective profile of a respondent's democratic support, the first five items were combined to form an additive index ranging from 5 (indicating the lowest level of democratic support) to 25 (indicating the highest level of democratic support). The mean of the interitem correlations of this index is .33; the reliability coefficient (Cronbach's alpha) among the items in the index is .74.

includes the two questions about competitive elections, while the other (Factor 1) consists of the remaining five questions (two for multiparty competition and three for individual liberty). These results confirmed our suspicion—that is, what the two questions about competitive election actually measured was significantly different from what the other questions tackled among our respondents.

Given the recent trends in local elections in China, one can see why there was such a distinction between the two questions regarding competitive elections and those about multiparty competition and individual liberty. The current electoral system is "competitive"[36] to the extent that there is supposed to be more than one candidate for each government and PC post, but nominations are firmly controlled by the CCP, and most candidates are CCP members. However, the law allows single-candidate elections for the most important government leaders, and this escape clause is the norm throughout China.[37] Therefore, asking respondents if they supported competitive elections is likely to prompt them to consider the current policy of the party-state, rather than a completely competitive electoral system that is beyond the control and manipulation of any single political party. In contrast, the other five questions clearly directed respondents to think about political norms and systems (i.e., multiparty competition and individual liberty) that are dramatically different from the incumbent one-party authoritarian system. In other words, the two questions about competitive elections deal with the current CCP-controlled electoral system that is "competitive" only in a very limited sense, while the other five questions tap into democratic norms that are fundamentally distinct from the norms and institutions advocated by the CCP regime. Thus, in the Chinese context, questions about competitive elections are conceptually and empirically different from questions about multiparty competition and individual liberty. To capture a collective profile of private entrepreneurs' attitudes toward democracy as a political system distinct from the current CCP regime, therefore, we combine only the five questions about multiparty competition and individual liberty (vs. order) to form an additive index as the collective measurement of democratic support. This index is used in the statistical analyses below and in the chapters that follow.

All these findings suggest that while most private entrepreneurs like to check individual leaders through competitive elections under the current one-party system, they do not seem to be eager to support and participate in fundamental political change toward a democratic system characterized by multiparty competition and individual liberty. Moreover, the findings confirm some earlier studies by both U.S.-based scholars and China-based scholars, noted earlier, that suggested that China's capitalists tend to be conservative and status quo–oriented and hence are not likely to serve as the harbingers of democratization in China.

Determinants of Democratic Support

As we discussed in Chapter 1, the socioeconomic conditions of late developers often necessitate a strong role for the state in the quest for rapid socioeconomic development, and the autonomy and capacity of the state facilitate its leading role. For these reasons, the Chinese state has played the leading role in the unprecedented post-Mao socioeconomic transformation, thus compensating for the typical disadvantages of a late developer. Moreover, as shown in Chapters 2 and 3, the party-state in China—with its unchallengeable (or almost absolute) political power and pervasive administrative institutions—has actually been able to lead this socioeconomic transformation and to create and mold China's capitalists during the transformation. Following this theoretical line (explained in Chapter 1) and on the basis of the aggregate evidence of the role of the state in the evolution of China's capitalists (delineated in Chapters 2 and 3), we have hypothesized that capitalists' orientation toward democracy and democratization is shaped by the capitalists' dependence on or their alliance with the party-state. To test this general hypothesis, we explore the impact on capitalists' attitudes toward democracy of four key aspects of their relationships with the state—financial, institutional, value, and policy—based on the data from our five-province survey.

Financial Dependence on the State

When trying to explain political phenomena in general, one may recall two oft-cited definitions of politics. According to Harold Lasswell, politics is about "who gets what, when, and how."[38] To David Easton, politics can be understood as the "authoritative allocation of values."[39] These two definitions suggest that politics is the process engaged in by the government and people to decide which groups or members of society receive social values, which are always deemed, at least in a relative sense, scarce. Moreover, these definitions imply not only that the allocation of social values itself is politics but that the results of such an allocation have political consequences. These definitions not only are applicable to the study of politics at the general level but also are useful for analyzing the political impact of the allocation of specific social values—that is, financial resources—by the states among private enterprises in late-developing countries. As John Zysman contends, "money is not only a medium of exchange but also a means of political and social control: it is one way of deciding who gets what."[40] Thus, how the state decides on the allocation of financial resources certainly has a significant impact on the political attitudes of those who receive and those who do not receive such resources. In this section, we examine how the allocation of bank credit by the Chinese party-state influences the views of China's capitalists about democracy.

In general, all states (or national governments) in either early- or late-developing countries try to "deploy whatever financial resources [they do] enjoy" through whatever "authority and organizational means" they have to achieve their national goals, such as economic reform and development.[41] Thus, some states—especially those so-called developmental states—in the late-developing countries have played a more "intrusive" or "proactive" role than their counterparts in their intervention in financial markets. For example, in the East Asian newly industrialized countries (NICs), the states wielded their monopolistic power over financial institutions such as central banks to channel resources toward the achievement of their national goals, such as economic development.[42] In South Korea, the government gave long-term credit to "selected firms at negative real interest rates in order to stimulate specific industries" during the country's postwar economic takeoff.[43] Similarly, in Taiwan, the government chose "certain sectors as deserving high priority for expansion" when making decisions on the allocation of financial resources through banks or other channels.[44] In general, this active intervention in financial markets by the states in late-developing countries was carried out to achieve high economic efficiency and growth (according to the criteria set by the state) as well as to guarantee the political and ideological conformity of major business elites.[45]

As described in Chapter 2, the party-state in China has also played a decisive role in allocating financial resources among different economic sectors and groups, albeit with some problematic consequences of the allocation for economic development.[46] During the early post-Mao reform years, the lending practices of banks very much embodied the intention of the central and local governments to buffer and save SOEs and some collectively owned enterprises from the negative consequences of economic competition (e.g., bankruptcy and employee layoffs). Beginning in the late 1990s, the central government began steadily moving the system toward a profit- and service-oriented financial entity.[47] As a result of the government's efforts, bank credit has become more accessible to nonstate sectors, such as private enterprises. Although most private entrepreneurs—especially those of small and medium firms—have complained about the difficulties getting long-term or short-term bank credit,[48] the number of private entrepreneurs receiving loans from banks (which are still controlled directly or indirectly by the national government and local governments) has gradually increased since the mid-1990s. As Figure 4.1 indicates, the percentages of private entrepreneurs who received bank loans increased from 11 percent in 1993 to 34 percent in 2007. The size of these loans may fall short of the firms' capital needs, requiring them to continue to rely on family, friends, and informal sources, such as private banks and pawn shops. Nevertheless, private entrepreneurs' improved access to bank loans corresponded with the government's efforts to shift the orientation of the banking system from mainly rescuing SOEs to making profits and providing services to both state and private sectors.

To gauge our respondents' access to loans from state-dominated banks (vs. other sources), we asked them two questions. One was about the major financial sources from which they acquired the funds to start their businesses. The other question dealt with the major financial sources from which they usually received loans for their business operation and expansion (after the business start-up period). The results from these two questions indicated that about 25 percent of respondents received loans from state-run banks to start their businesses, and about 34 percent of respondents acquired loans from state-run banks to operate and expand

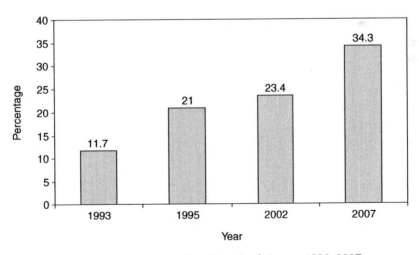

Figure 4.1.   Private Entrepreneurs Receiving Bank Loans, 1993–2007
Note: Data for 1993, 1995, and 2002 come from surveys organized by the All-China Federation of Industry and Commerce; data available from the Universities Service Centre of the Chinese University of Hong Kong. Data for 2007 come from our five-province survey.

their businesses.[49] These two questions are combined to form an additive index of access to bank loans, which is used in the statistical analysis that follows.

On the basis of our assumption that the way resources are distributed affects how the recipients view politics, we expect that the allocation of financial resources among private entrepreneurs by China's party-state may influence entrepreneurs' views of democracy. Specifically, we hypothesize that those who receive loans from state-dominated banks tend to be less enthusiastic about democracy and democratization, both of which could threaten the party-state and the status quo. To test this proposition, we examine the bivariate correlation between the index of our respondents' access to financial resources (state banks vs. private sources) for their firms and the index of support for democratic values and institutions. The results of this analysis are shown in Table 4.5.

As expected, those private entrepreneurs who received loans from state-dominated banks either for opening or for operating/expanding their businesses were less likely to support those democratic principles and institutions that we have identified earlier in this chapter. As Table 4.5 shows, most of the bank-loan recipients (about 57 percent) had the lowest level of democratic support, while almost half of the non-bank-loan recipients had the highest level of such support. In addition, the overall correlation between the index of democratic support and the index of access to bank loan was negative and moderately strong (gamma = −.65). This result highlights the difference between bank-loan recipients and non-bank-loan recipients in democratic support. Those who received bank loans were less likely to support democracy.

Table 4.5   Support for Democracy and Acquisition of Loans from State-Dominated Banks

Receiving bank loans	Level of support for democracy			
	Low	Medium	High	Total
Receiving (%)	56.6	33.6	9.8	100
Not receiving (%)	14.6	36.7	48.7	100
		gamma = −.65*		

Note: The index of support for democracy (see Table 4.4) is trichotomized into three categories: low, medium, and high, with cutoff points of 5–12 (low), 13–17 (medium), and 18–25 (high). The index of the receiving of bank loans is dichotomized into two categories: receiving and not receiving.
*$p < .05$

Political Embeddedness with the State

In Chapter 3, we described the CCP's strategy for interacting with the private sector. At the individual level, the CCP encourages its members to join the private sector and also co-opts private entrepreneurs into the CCP. At the institutional level, the CCP has created official business associations to provide a bridge between the state and the private sector. In this section, we examine these connections between the state and private entrepreneurs and the impact of these connections on entrepreneurs' views of democracy. Our analysis draws on Alfred Stepan's typology of inclusionary and exclusionary poles of the state-corporatism spectrum.[50] According to this typology, the state plays a decisive role in determining which societal groups and members will be included in or excluded from the corporatist institutional arrangements that are sanctioned and dominated by the state. Those included are supported and nurtured by the state and are expected to obey the state's policies, while those excluded are suppressed and even banned by the state. Still, in the middle, some societal groups are more or less tolerated by the state, but the state always stands ready to intervene in and ban these groups if they challenge or threaten the state. All in all, the state plays a preponderant role in shaping its relations with certain societal groups and molding political views held by the members of societal groups through such inclusionary and exclusionary strategies.

On the basis of this corporatist model and the inclusion-exclusion typology, we analyze in this section the effects of two dimensions of the institutional connections between the party-state and China's capitalists. One dimension deals with the internal institutional inclusion of private entrepreneurs into the party-state, which is reflected in entrepreneurs' memberships within the party and governmental institutions at various levels. The other dimension refers to the external institutional links between the party and the private entrepreneurs, which are mainly manifested as membership in various business organizations. As we explained above, moreover, the connections along these two dimensions are expected to exert a significant impact on private entrepreneurs' views of democracy and democratization.

Memberships in the Party and Government.   The membership of entrepreneurs in the CCP and in governmental institutions at various levels is one aspect of their inclusion in China's party-state. Using Stepan's inclusion-exclusion typology of corporatism, we identify the CCP's strategy of co-opting capitalists into its own organization and into the

government as a strategy of "inclusion." As Dickson argues, the co-
optation of new members is "a key dimension of the policy of inclusion
that allows Leninist parties to adapt" to a changing sociopolitical environment and to achieve their new national goals, such as socioeconomic
reforms.[51] Since the onset of the post-Mao reform, the party-state has
gradually but surely opened the doors of the party and the government to
new social and economic elites, such as capitalists. The purpose has been
to mobilize and channel these new forces for economic development and
to strengthen the CCP's legitimacy. Moreover, as we explained above,
these institutional connections, shaped by the CCP's strategy of inclusion,
are expected to influence private entrepreneurs' views of democracy and
democratization.

First of all, we expect that among capitalists, those who are already
party members are most likely to oppose democratic principles, such as
multiparty competition in politics. This is because being "embedded"
within the CCP provides them with tangible benefits, such as more direct
protection of their business interests, easier access to loans, and other opportunities for their business to prosper.[52] Any democratic change toward
multiparty competition could jeopardize their vested interests. Thus, we
expect that in our sample, "red capitalists" are less likely than non–party
members to support democratic values and institutions. To test this expectation against our data, we first run a cross-tabulation between party
membership and the index of democratic support.

The results of this bivariate analysis (Table 4.6) support our expectation: those who were party members were less in favor of democratic
values and norms. For instance, only 12 percent of the respondents with
party membership registered a high level of democratic support, while
50 percent of them had a low level of such support; conversely, 38 percent of respondents without party membership expressed a high level of

Table 4.6   Party Membership and Democratic Support

Party membership	Level of support for democracy			
	Low	Medium	High	Total
Member (%)	50.1	37.7	12.2	100
Nonmember (%)	22.7	39.1	38.2	100
		gamma $= -.23$*		

Note: The index of support for democracy (see Table 4.4.) is trichotomized into three
categories: low, medium, and high, with cutoff points of 5–12 (low), 13–17 (medium), and
18–25 (high).
*$p < .05$

democratic support, whereas 22 percent of them had a low level of such support. Although these results support our hypothesized correlation between party membership and support for democratic values and norms, it should be noted that the correlation was quite weak, though significant, as indicated by the value of gamma (-.23). Such a weak correlation might have resulted from influences of other related factors on democratic support. One such factor might be membership in self-organized/ managed organizations among party members. Our survey revealed that about 44 percent of party-member capitalists also joined these organizations. As a result, membership in self-organized/managed organizations might also exert an impact on party members' view of democracy. This kind of effect of membership in self-organized/managed organizations, along with other potential factors, will be further examined in the multivariate analysis that follows.

The other aspect of the internal institutional inclusion of private entrepreneurs into the party-state, as mentioned above, is membership in different governmental institutions at various levels. As discussed in Chapter 3, there are two major kinds of governmental institutions into which the party-state has tried to co-opt capitalists, PCs and PPCCs. Although neither the NPC nor the CPPCC, along with their local branches, can be totally dismissed as rubber-stamp institutions due to the increasing assertiveness of their members in recent years,[53] in this section we focus on the impact of membership in these organizations on capitalists' attitudes toward democracy and democratization. The CCP has called on PC deputies and members of the CPPCC among private entrepreneurs not only to express their opinions but more importantly to convey and explain policies and regulations of the party and government to their fellow private entrepreneurs.[54] As a result, those who are elected under the CCP's scrutiny to the NPC (and its branches) and appointed by the party to the CPPCC (and its branches) are more likely to accept and be able to convey the party line, including principles of economic growth and one-party rule. In addition, as mentioned in Chapter 3, members of both institutions owe their membership, along with sociopolitical privileges that come with the membership, to the party-state. Thus, we expect that those who are members of either PCs or PPCCs at various levels will tend to be less supportive of democratic values and institutions.

To explore this expectation, we conducted an analysis of the correlation between the combined memberships of the NPC and the CPPCC and their subnational branches, on the one hand, and the index of democratic support, on the other hand (see Table 4.7). Consistent with our expectation, the results from this bivariate analysis show that among members of these

Table 4.7   Support for Democracy and Government Membership

Government membership (PC and PPCC)	Level of support for democracy			
	Low	Medium	High	Total
Member (%)	39.9	47.2	12.9	100
Nonmember (%)	12.0	48.5	39.5	100
		gamma = −.45*		

Note: The index of support for democracy (see Table 4.4) is trichotomized into three categories: low, medium, and high, with cutoff points of 5–12 (low), 13–17 (medium), and 18–25 (high). Government membership includes either or both of memberships in the NPC (and subnational PC) and the CPPCC (and subnational CPPCC).
  *$p < .05$

government institutions, about 40 percent had a low level of democratic support, while only 13 percent expressed a high level of such support; in contrast, among nonmembers, about 40 percent strongly supported democratic values, while only 12 percent did not care very much for democracy. This preliminary finding is consistent with anecdotal evidence from interviews of private entrepreneurs who were either deputies to PCs or members of the CPPCC. For instance, Wang Jianhua, a deputy to the People's Congress of Beijing, said that "as a people's deputy, I will not only express demands and suggestions from the private sector, but also convey important policies of the party and government to private entrepreneurs." Xue Guanchen, a newly appointed member of Beijing's CPPCC, told an interviewer that "I will serve as a bridge between the party and private entrepreneurs, and try to be a good assistant to the government in managing the private sector."[55] These examples clearly indicated the willingness of private entrepreneurs who were people's deputies and CPPCC members to operate under the CCP's one-party rule and to support it.

Memberships in Business Associations.   As described in Chapter 3, the CCP has adopted at least two broad corporatist strategies to institutionalize its external links with capitalists. One is to create, control, and support government-sanctioned organizations and include them in the formal policy-making and policy-implementing process. These organizations are embedded "within the system" *(tizhi nei)* and are treated by the state as the core of the institutionalized connection between the party-state and private entrepreneurs. The other strategy is to tolerate self-organized/managed organizations, some of which are also able to participate in the policy process. These associations are self-organized but not necessarily autonomous because they interact closely with party and government officials, and some even share office space with local chapters of the ACFIC. To be effective, most organizations in China seek to be politically embedded, rather than autonomous. The two strategies are both designed to integrate the party-state with capitalists as a whole, while the two kinds of organizations are treated differently, as mentioned above. Consequently, we expect that those who belong to government-sponsored business associations are less likely to support democratic values. This is because these associations are supervised by the CCP's United Front Department, and their members are more likely to be exposed to the party's cardinal principles, which include the leading role of the party and oppose the need for fundamental political change toward democracy. For instance, according to a study of owners of large and medium privately owned enterprises, most of the owners believed that government-sponsored organizations, such as the ACFIC and the PEA, represented the government's views.[56] However, we anticipate that members of self-organized business associations are more likely to support democratic values and norms, since these organizations are formed on a voluntary base, are run on the basis of member equality, and do not engage in the ideological education of the party line. These two expectations are explored against the data from our five-province survey.

To explore the hypothesized correlations between business association memberships and support for democratic values and norms among private entrepreneurs, we ran cross-tabulations between membership in government-sponsored and self-organized associations, on the one hand, and the democratic-support index, on the other. The results of the cross-tabulations (Table 4.8) show that, as expected, membership in official business associations was negatively associated with democratic support (see the upper portion of the table), while membership in self-organized associations was positively correlated with such support (see the lower portion of the table). For instance, about 50 percent of members of self-organized associations professed a high level of democratic support, while only about 14 percent of them reported a low level. Among members of official business associations, however, only about 22 percent showed a high level of democratic support, while almost 37 percent of them showed a low level. This finding supports an earlier study suggesting that "the interests of membership [in government-sanctioned organizations] may in fact lie more with the preservation of the authoritarian one-party state than with democratization."[57] That said, however, it should be noted that the negative correlation between membership in official business

Table 4.8   Support for Democracy and Business Association Memberships

Official business associations	Level of support for democracy			
	Low	Medium	High	Total
Member (%)	36.5	41.6	21.8	100
Nonmember (%)	18.1	48.2	33.8	100
		gamma = −.15*		

Self-organized business associations	Level of support for democracy			
	Low	Medium	High	Total
Member (%)	13.7	36.4	49.9	100
Nonmember (%)	51.3	37.3	11.3	100
		gamma = .69*		

Note: The index of support for democracy (see Table 4.4) is trichotomized into three categories: low, medium, and high, with cutoff points of 5–12 (low), 13–17 (medium), and 18–25 (high).
*$p < .05$

associations and support for democratic values and norms was quite weak (gamma $=-.15$), though statistically significant (at the .05 level), in this bivariate analysis. Such a weak correlation might have resulted from the fact that a substantial number of the members of these associations also joined self-organized business associations. They might be more attached to and hence more influenced by the latter. This speculation will be further explored in the multivariate analysis that follows.

In sum, the party-state has adopted a corporatist strategy of inclusion or co-optation of capitalists in its political structure. As shown above, this strategy has had two dimensions. One deals with the internal institutional inclusion of private entrepreneurs into the party-state, which is reflected in the memberships of entrepreneurs in the party and governmental institutions at various levels. The other dimension refers to the external institutional links between the party and the private entrepreneurs, which are mainly manifested as the memberships of various business organizations. The institutional connections along these two dimensions exert a significant impact on private entrepreneurs' views of democracy and democratization. The results from the bivariate analyses presented above showed that those who were members of the party, who were NPC or CPPCC deputies, and who were members of state-organized/managed business organizations tended to be less supportive of democratic values and norms as defined in this study. This would seem to vindicate the CCP's strategy of inclusion. However, an alternative explanation is also consistent with these findings: the CCP selects for inclusion those individuals who do not exhibit strong support for democracy or democratization. Because there is an obvious selection bias toward whom the CCP recruits into the party and appoints to political posts, it is likely that those with prodemocratic beliefs are intentionally excluded. In contrast, the correlation between democratic values and self-organized business associations, where membership is voluntary, is quite high, suggesting that prodemocratic values may lead them to join such organizations. In short, the exact cause-and-effect relationship between democratic values and various indicators of political embeddedness is complex and varied. The correlation between them, however, is clear: the beneficiaries of inclusion are not strong supporters of democracy and not likely to be agents of change. The political implications of this finding are examined in more detail in Chapter 5.

Value Congruence with the State

As we discussed in Chapter 1, in late-developing countries, the state often plays a decisive role in the emergence of new social classes. These new social classes tend to share common values with the state, such as continuous economic growth and sociopolitical stability (or order). In a late-developing country, therefore, the new capitalist class is most likely to support the state and the political system through which the state operates.[58]

Moreover, compared with the states of many other late-developing countries, the party-state in China has an even stronger capacity to create, mold, and in some cases control new social classes—such as private entrepreneurs—due to its monopoly of national financial resources, as described above, and its party-state organizational structure, which gives it a monopoly over political organization. The new capitalist class in China, therefore, not only economically and politically depends upon the party-state to promote and protect its interests but also is likely to have similar views on fundamental values and principles (e.g., social order and stability under the one-party rule) that are sanctioned and advocated by the party-state. Consequently, the more that the values of capitalists are congruent with those of the party-state, the less enthusiastic they should be about democratic values and norms, which directly contradict party-state sanctioned values and principles. In this section, we explore this expectation based on the data from our five-province survey.

Value congruence can be measured by private entrepreneurs' subjective orientations toward, or their support for, the party-state's leadership position and its most salient sociopolitical programs. Specifically, we focus on two sets of subjective orientations among our respondents: their views of the state's leading role in initiating major economic and political changes and their assessment of the post-Mao political reform led by the state. These orientations, we believe, serve as the foundation of the value congruence between the current party-state and capitalists. The measurement of these orientations and the hypothesized relationships between them and democratic support are discussed in the sections that follow.

Support for State Leadership in Economic and Political Change. Should the state alone initiate major economic and political transformations, or should societal actors also be involved in the process? The current party-state has relentlessly tried to legitimize and advocate among the population its monopoly position of initiating and leading major social, economic, and political changes in China. Are the capitalists in agreement with the party-state on such a monopoly position? If so, what is the effect of this agreement? Some analysts suggest that in China, those who believe that the party-state should initiate such changes tend to support the status quo, oppose expanded popular participation in the policy process, and hence side with the current political regime. Consequently, these people are less likely to support democratic values and institutions.[59] On the basis of this argument, we expect that there is a negative relationship between support for the state's leading role in economic and political changes, on the one hand, and support for democratic values and institutions, on the other.

To measure private entrepreneurs' view of the state's leadership role, we used two straightforward statements:

1. Measures to further promote political reform should be initiated by the party and government, not by society.
2. Measures to further promote economic reform should be initiated by party and government leaders, not by society.

Respondents were asked to rate each of these two statements on a five-point scale, where 1 is "strongly disagree" and 5 is "strongly agree." These two items were combined to form an additive index of the view of the state's leadership role in reforms, which is used in the bivariate and multivariate analyses that follow. Table 4.9 shows that a majority of the sampled private entrepreneurs (60 percent) either agreed or strongly agreed that promoting economic and political reforms is the responsibility of the party-state rather than that of ordinary citizens. This finding is consistent with that from Dickson's earlier study of large and medium private entrepreneurs: most of them are willing to defer to the party-state

Table 4.9   View of the State's Leadership Role in Economic and Political Reforms

	Strongly disagree (%)	Disagree (%)	Not clear (%)	Agree (%)	Strongly agree (%)
1. Measures to further promote political reform should be initiated by the party and government, not by society.	2.1	16.2	21.6	35.2	24.9
2. Measures to further promote economic reform should be initiated by party and government leaders, not by society.	1.9	17.2	21.4	41.3	18.2

for any economic and political changes.[60] But where those earlier studies did not examine the link between support for state leadership with support for democracy, our study allows us to do so.

To explore the hypothesized relationship between democratic support and belief in the state's leadership role in reforms, we examine the correlation between the index of such a belief and the index of democratic support. As shown in Table 4.10, as the level of belief in the state's leadership increases, the level of democratic support decreases. For example, although a majority of the entrepreneurs who did not support the state's leading role in reforms registered a high level of support for democratic values, only 10 percent of those with a strong belief in the state's leading role had such a level of democratic support. In contrast, this negative relationship between belief in the state's leading role and democratic support was also quite strong as indicated by the overall correlation between the two indexes (gamma = −.62).

Evaluation of Political Reform.   The other dimension of value congruence between the party-state and capitalists is the latter's view of post-Mao political reforms. It is erroneous to say that China has not undergone meaningful political reform since the late 1970s. Led and designed by the party-state, political reforms in the post-Mao era have never been intended to change the CCP's one-party rule. Instead, they have been designed to strengthen party rule, not to make the political system more democratic. The central themes of the post-Mao political reforms have been rationalization and legalization.[61] Specifically, party leaders have gradually abandoned the practices of class struggle and

Table 4.10   Support for Democracy and Belief in the State's Leading Role
in Reforms

State's leading role in reforms	Level of support for democracy			
	Low	Medium	High	Total
Low (%)	19.6	23.9	56.5	100
Medium (%)	32.1	58.1	9.8	100
High (%)	48.3	41.2	10.0	100
		gamma $=-.62$*		

Note: Both indexes of support for democracy and belief in the state leading role in
reforms are trichotomized into three categories: low, medium, and high.
  *$p < .05$

continuous revolution of the Mao era, rationalized the party and governmental apparatus, strengthened so-called socialist legality, and loosened control of the personal (if not political) life of Chinese citizens. Despite the fast and drastic economic reforms led by the state, however, the CCP has not taken any significant deepening of political reform that would fundamentally change the political system. Quite to the contrary, in recent years the party-state has been more vigorous in stressing the need for political stability—instead of further political reform—as the foremost political priority. Thus, we hypothesize that those who consider the current pace of the political reform to be appropriate or already too fast are less likely to have democratic values.

In our survey, we tapped into the evaluation of the state-led political reform by asking our respondents to answer a straightforward question: "What do you think of the pace of political reform?" To this question, respondents were offered five choices: "too slow," "slow," "appropriate," "fast," and "too fast." A majority (about 56 percent) of our respondents believed that the pace of political reform was either appropriate or too fast. In other words, most of our respondents seemed to be politically conservative, wanting at least to maintain the political status quo, and they were in agreement with the party-state on the pace of political reform.

To explore the hypothesized relationship between the evaluation of the state-led political reform and support for democracy, we ran a cross-tabulation between the index of democratic support and the perceived pace of political reform. The results of this analysis (Table 4.11) are consistent with our expectation—that is, those who believed that the current pace of political reform was adequate or too fast were less likely to sup-

Table 4.11   Support for Democracy and Satisfaction with the Pace of
Political Reform

	Level of support for democracy			
Perceived pace of political reform	Low	Medium	High	Total
Too slow (%)	19.6	26.2	54.2	100
Appropriate/too fast (%)	58.7	34.8	6.6	100
		gamma $=-.68^*$		

Note: The index of support for democracy (see Table 4.4) is trichotomized into three categories: low, medium, and high, with cutoff points of 5–12 (low), 13–17 (medium), and 18–25 (high). The question about perceived pace of political reform is dichotomized: "too slow" and the combination of "appropriate" and "too fast."
$^*p < .05$

port a democracy, which could bring about multiparty competition and hence threaten the status quo. Specifically, about 60 percent of the respondents who considered the pace of political reform adequate or too fast showed little or no support for democracy, while only about 7 percent of them were strongly supportive of democracy; in contrast, almost 55 percent of those who judged the pace too slow had strong support for democratic values and norms, while only about 20 percent registered a low level of support for such values and norms. This relationship between the perceived pace of political reform and democratic support was also substantiated by a strong correlation coefficient ($\gamma=-.68$).

All in all, the bivariate statistical results presented above showed that there is strong value congruence between China's capitalists and the party-state, as measured by entrepreneurs' belief in the state's leadership role in major sociopolitical changes and their assessment of the pace of party-led political reform. More important, the results also indicated that such value congruence exerted a negative impact on entrepreneurs' support for democratic values and norms.

Policy Evaluation

Many studies in comparative politics have found a significant positive relationship between individual citizens' assessment of public policies and their support for the current political regime, even though researchers debate the measurement of both variables.[62] The population's evaluation of government policies is also considered the citizens' assessment of the "outputs and performance of the political authorities."[63] Similarly, several recent studies of popular support for government policies and initiatives in China also suggest that citizens' evaluation of government performance in major policy areas is significantly and positively associated with their support for the current regime led by the CCP.[64] We assume that such a "generic" relationship between support for the government's major policies and support for the current political regime and the status quo, which has been verified in earlier studies of general populations, should also be applicable to private entrepreneurs' political attitudes. On the basis of these arguments, therefore, we infer that in our sample of private entrepreneurs, those who have a high evaluation of government policies are less likely to support political change, such as democratization, since such a change would shatter the status quo and consequently disrupt government policies and initiatives. In other words, we expect that there is a negative relationship between support for democracy and support for the government policy performance.

In our survey, we asked our respondents to evaluate government policy performance in twelve specific socioeconomic areas as follows:

1. Controlling inflation
2. Providing job security
3. Narrowing the gap between rich and poor
4. Improving housing conditions
5. Maintaining social order
6. Providing adequate medical care
7. Setting fair tax regulations
8. Providing welfare to the needy
9. Combating pollution
10. Fighting official corruption
11. Protecting entrepreneurs' legal rights
12. Promoting growth of enterprises.

The relevance of these policy areas to our sample was assessed in several interviews of private entrepreneurs conducted prior to the administration of the formal survey. The results from these presurvey interviews indicated widespread interest among interviewees in each of these policy areas.

The relevance of these items for the evaluation of government policy performance has also been shown by some earlier field observations. From a systemic perspective, for example, Tang and Parish noted that since the beginning of the post-Mao reforms, the sociopolitical base of the relationship (or what they call "social contract") between the state and the population has been transformed from citizens' acceptance of Maoist idealist goals to constant evaluations by them of government policies dealing with their daily socioeconomic life.[65] In this context of a changing social contract, Tang and Parish identified fifteen areas of the "government's outputs" about which the public in urban China was concerned during the late 1990s. Furthermore, among these fifteen areas, the public was most worried about inflation, housing, medical care, official corruption, and social (or community) order.[66] In addition, according to some more recent field studies in China, private entrepreneurs were mostly concerned with tax regulations and protection of their legal rights and properties.[67] Thus, we added some items in our questionnaire, which were unique to private entrepreneurs, such as those regarding establishment of fair tax regulations (Item 7), protection of private entrepreneurs' rights (Item 11), and promotion of a private economy (Item 12). In short, earlier findings from field observations by China scholars indicate that the policy issues covered in our list of questionnaire items above are at the core of the public's and entrepreneurs' concerns.

For each of the questionnaire items listed above, respondents were asked to "grade" the government's policy performance based on the grading scheme commonly used in China's schools, that is, on a five-point scale, where 1 is very poor and 5 is very good. In order to capture a collective profile of the respondents' evaluation of government policy performance, the twelve items were then combined to form an additive index, ranging from 12 (indicating very poor policy performance) to 60 (indicating excellent policy performance). This index is employed in the bivariate and multivariate analyses that follow.

Table 4.12 presents the evaluations by our respondents of government policy performance in the twelve areas. At least two important findings stand out from these evaluations. First, our respondents in general gave quite decent "grades" for government policy performance in most of the twelve socioeconomic areas tackled in our survey. Specifically, the mean scores for nine of the twelve areas were well above "passing grade" (or point 3). In other words, most of the sampled private entrepreneurs were somewhat contented with the government performance in most socioeconomic areas. This general impression was also supported by the mean score of the entire twelve-item index for the evaluation of government policy performance, 38.58, which was slightly higher than the midpoint (35) of the index scale (from a minimum of 12 to a maximum of 60).

A second important finding from the results presented in Table 4.12 is that private entrepreneurs evaluated government policy performance variably across the twelve policy areas, although their overall assessment was quite positive. For example, our respondents gave a below-passing grade (below 3) for policy performance in the areas of fighting official

Table 4.12   Evaluation of Government Policy Performance

Item	Mean score (1–5)	SD
1. Fighting official corruption	2.80	.998
2. Narrowing the gap between rich and poor	2.87	.914
3. Combating pollution	2.87	975
4. Providing adequate medical care	3.02	.937
5. Providing welfare to the needy	3.21	.834
6. Providing job security	3.23	.806
7. Establishing fair tax policy	3.28	.835
8. Improving housing conditions	3.38	.852
9. Maintaining social order	3.40	.926
10. Protecting entrepreneurs' legal rights	3.42	.816
11. Controlling inflation	3.55	.795
12. Promoting growth of private enterprises	3.62	.803
Entire index (12–60)[a]	38.58	

[a]The mean of the interitem correlations of this set of items is .44; the reliability coefficient (Cronbach's alpha) among these items is .91. Statistically, therefore, this set of items is considered highly reliable.

corruption, narrowing the gap between rich and poor, and combating pollution, while they gave the highest score to promoting growth of private enterprises. These nuances suggest that private entrepreneurs appreciated the party-state's promotion of the private sector where they have benefited the most but meanwhile shared concerns with the general population over rampant corruption, the increasing rich-poor gap, and the deteriorating environment.[68]

To examine the hypothesized impact of private entrepreneurs' policy evaluation on their support for democratic values and norms, we then conducted an analysis of the correlation between the indexes of democratic support and policy evaluation (see Table 4.13). Consistent with our earlier expectation, the results from this analysis show that about half of those who evaluated the government's performance as doing poorly showed a high level of democratic support, while only 15 percent registered a low level of such support; in contrast, among those who gave high evaluations to government policy performance, more than half (55 percent) had low support for democracy, while only 5 percent expressed a high level of democratic support. All this supports the pattern of the hypothesized relationship: the higher China's capitalists evaluated the government's policy performance, the lower their democratic support.

Table 4.13   Support for Democracy and Evaluation of Policy Performance

Policy evaluation	Level of support for democracy			
	Low	Medium	High	Total
Low (%)	14.6	37.6	47.8	100
Medium (%)	34.2	43.4	22.4	100
High (%)	54.7	40.0	5.3	100
		gamma = −.62*		

Note: Both indexes of support for democracy and evaluation of policy performance are trichotomized into three categories: low, medium, and high.

*p < .05

Control Variables

In addition to financial, institutional, value, and policy congruence as the explanatory variables specified above, we suspect that there are some other factors that might also be related to democratic support. Treated as control variables in this analysis, these factors include several key sociodemographic attributes, state employment background, and the size of enterprise.

Sociodemographic Attributes.   A large body of literature on democratic societies has established that some key sociodemographic variables— such as gender, age, and education—affect people's democratic values. More important, the findings from recent survey studies conducted in China and former Soviet societies also indicate a significant relationship between these sociodemographic variables and citizens' support for democracy in those nondemocratic societies.[69] This is mainly because in both democratic and nondemocratic societies, sociodemographic attributes may affect people's political socialization processes, which in turn have a strong and lasting impact on their attitudes toward such important political issues as democracy and democratization. Thus, we suspect that these attributes may also influence private entrepreneurs' belief in democratic values and institutions.

State Employment Background.   Some early studies of private entrepreneurs in China found a correlation between entrepreneurs' previous employment in a government unit (e.g., SOE, government agencies, or state-run cultural and social organizations) and their attitudes toward sociopolitical issues, although these early studies disagree on the direction of such correlations. These studies generally argue that state employment experience/background creates closer personal connections between the private entrepreneur and the current party-state and its officials at various levels and brings about unique behavioral patterns of "getting things done" in business; in turn, these connections and behavioral patterns affect entrepreneurs' views of sociopolitical issues. For example, David Wank found that former state employers among private entrepreneurs had an advantage of knowing government officials and operation procedures and hence tended to have a smoother experience dealing with the government.[70] Consequently, those with previous employment with the state tended to have more positive views of the state in general and its policies dealing with the private sector in particular. In contrast, Kellee Tsai found that "entrepreneurs formerly employed by the state [were] more likely to expect the government to bear primary responsibility for employment, education, retirement services, and environmental protection. This may be because former state employers are accustomed to receiving more services from the government."[71] Whereas Wank found that former state employees have advantages over those without state-employment backgrounds and hence were less likely to complain,[72] Tsai found that "former state employees are more likely than entrepreneurs with other types of backgrounds to report operational difficulties" in their business.[73] Their previous backgrounds in the state sector made them expect more from the state, and their strong political connections allowed them to be more demanding. On the basis of these earlier studies, we speculate that our respondents with a state employment background might not be very enthusiastic about the democratic system, since such a system may threaten the current party-state, on which they rely for the advancement of their own business and personal interests.

The Size of Enterprise.   Previous research in China has found that the size of firms is a significant factor influencing the political behavior and attitudes of their owners.[74] This is largely because the economic resources and social influences of firms vary with their size, and such a variation of these resources and influences inevitably has an impact on their relations with the government. According to some recent field observations by Chinese scholars, large firms pay more taxes and create more jobs, and even more important, they contribute more "'soft' money to government projects."[75] Thus, governments at various levels usually try to accommodate large enterprises in order to secure tax revenues, employment opportunities for local residents, and soft funds for their local projects. Consequently, these large firms usually have much better relations with governments and their officials. Furthermore, these large firms in turn also receive more benefits from governments and their officials, such as easier access to bank credit and relaxation of environmental regulations. Ole Odgaard therefore suggests that large firms are more likely to utilize their private ties with the government and its officials to advance their own business and individual interests.[76] On the basis of these observations, we infer that owners of larger firms in our sample will be less supportive of democracy and democratization, since a change to a democratic system would jeopardize their relations with the government and adversely affect their firms.

The Local Socioeconomic Context. The local socioeconomic context here includes two dimensions: (1) the local level of economic development, measured by per capita GDP of each county; and (2) local multifaceted social conditions, operationalized by the proxy of respondents' residence in each of the five surveyed provinces. In terms of the impact of economic development, one of the central arguments of modernization theory suggests that as modernization unfolds in a society, the levels of the individual's income, education, socioeconomic mobility, and freedom valuation markedly increase. All these attributes in turn facilitate democratic values among people and hence promote democratization in a nondemocratic society and strengthen the democratic institutions.[77] On the basis of this argument, we expect that the local level of economic development should be positively associated with private entrepreneurs' orientation toward democracy. In addition, it is commonly assumed that the multifaceted social conditions unique to each province may influence our respondents' views about social and political issues, since these conditions—along with the sociodemographic factors mentioned above—are likely to affect people's political socialization processes. Thus, we suspect that residence in a particular province, as the proxy of the multifaceted social conditions unique to that province, might have an impact on our respondents' attitudes toward democracy.

Results of the Multivariate Analysis

Table 4.14 presents the results of the multiple regression model (ordinary least squares [OLS]) for democratic support among our respondents, which includes all independent variables and the control variables specified above. Several major findings from these results are summarized and highlighted below.

Table 4.14 Multiple Regression of Democratic Support among Private Entrepreneurs

	Dependent variable: Democratic support[a]		
	b	SE	β
Independent variables			
Bank loan[b]	−.272*	.137	−.052
Official business association member[c]	.108	.218	.013
Self-organized business association member[c]	.270	.181	.038
CCP member[c]	−.131	.190	−.018
PC/PPCC deputy[c]	.172	.205	.023
Support state's leading role in initiating reforms[d]	−.450***	.043	−.255
Satisfaction with pace of political reform[e]	−.898***	.120	−.188
Evaluation of government's policy performance[f]	−.112***	.013	−.242
Control variables			
Gender[g]	−.542*	.265	−.050
Age	−.020	.012	−.044
Education[h]	.099	.133	.021
State employment background[i]	.099	.152	.017
Firm assets (log.)	.182**	.057	.090
Local socioeconomic context			
Level of development (per capita GDP)	−.005	.006	−.019
Location[j]			
Jiangsu	.309	.283	.038
Zhejiang	.380	.273	.045
Fujian	.042	.315	.004
Guangdong	.590*	.296	.069
Constant	18.043***	1.167	
R^2	.240		
Adjusted R^2	.230		
N	1,371		

[a] To capture a collective profile of private entrepreneurs' attitudes toward democracy, we combine all five items included in the two subdimensions (i.e., multiparty competition and individual liberty) to form an additive index. The mean of the interitem correlations of this set of items is .33; the reliability coefficient (Cronbach's alpha) among these items is .74.

[b] An additive index of receiving loans from state-run financial institutions for both starting and operating business.

[c] Not member = 0; member = 1.

[d] To measure Chinese private entrepreneurs' perception of government's role in reforms, we asked respondents to assess the following two statements on a five-point scale: "Government should take the leading role in political reform"; "Government should take the leading role in economic reform." These two items were combined to form an additive index of a respondent's perception of government's role in reform.

[e] The responses about perceived pace of political reform is on a five-point scale, ranging from 1 (*too slow*) to 5 (*too fast*).

Table 4.14   (continued)

---

^f To measure the evaluation of the government's policy performance, we combined the twelve items to form an additive index. The mean of the interitem correlations of this set of items is .44; the reliability coefficient (Cronbach's alpha) among these items is .91.

^g Male = 0; female = 1.

^h Middle school and below = 1; high school = 2; postsecondary professional training = 3; four-year university education = 4; graduate education = 5.

ⁱ Not having state employment background = 0; having state employment background = 1.

^j Shandong is used as the base category for comparison; each of the other provinces is a dummy variable.

*$p < .05$ **$p < .01$ ***$p < .001$

First of all, with a few exceptions, the results from this comprehensive statistical model support most of the hypotheses and the results from the bivariate analyses that have been presented in this chapter. In terms of the impact of financial support, as we expected, those who received loans from state banks were less likely to support democratic values and institutions. In terms of the influence of value congruence, those respondents who had a strong belief in the state's leadership role in sociopolitical changes and who were satisfied with the pace of political reform were less likely to support democratic values and institutions. As for the consequences of policy congruence, those who gave a higher score for government policy performance in major socioeconomic areas were less supportive of democratic change. More important, each of the above-mentioned independent variables (i.e., bank loan, belief in the state's role in reform, evaluation of the government policy performance, and perceived state role in political change) exerted an independent impact on the dependent variable—support for democracy—even after controlling for one another and a group of control variables. In other words, the impact of each of these independent variables on democratic support was very robust.

Second, as an exception to our earlier expectations, the results in Table 4.14 show that none of the variables for political embeddedness (i.e., memberships in official business associations, self-organized business associations, or the CCP and roles as PC or PPCC deputies) were statistically significant in this multivariate analysis. Not only did the coefficients fall short of statistical significance, for two of the indicators of political embeddedness—PC/PPCC deputies and members of official business associations—the sign was also in the wrong direction (positive when we expected it to be negative). As we have noted earlier in this chapter, the bivariate correlations between these memberships on the one hand and democratic support on the other were somewhat weak, although statistically significant (at the .05 level). The results from the multivariate analysis further confirm that the impact of these independent variables on democratic support were too weak to be sustained when other independent and control variables were taken into account. Such weak effects of membership in the main political and economic organizations seem to indicate that the CCP's corporatist strategy has had a minimal impact on private entrepreneurs' orientation toward democracy: membership alone has not swayed their political orientation. Moreover, the impact of the political memberships is also muted by more powerful variables included in this multivariate analysis, such as receipt (or nonreceipt) of a bank loan, belief in the state's role in reform, evaluation of the government's policy performance, and perceived state role in political change.

Third, among the control variables included in this multivariate analysis, only gender and a firm's size (measured by its fixed assets) proved to have a significant impact on private entrepreneurs' democratic support. Specifically, those who were male or ran larger firms, all else being equal, were more likely to support democratic values and institutions. It should be noted that the positive relationship between firm size and entrepreneurs' democratic support contradicts our earlier expectation made based on observations of earlier studies of China's capitalists. We suspect that this positive correlation may reflect a changing trend—that is, further growth of large firms has been increasingly restricted by the government's existing regulations and policies, which were helpful in launching new firms but now constrain their expansion. Thus, owners of these firms might prefer a more democratic system that could help them break these constraints.

However, the other control variables—such as age, education, state employment background, and local socioeconomic conditions—did not have an independent impact on respondents' democratic support. It is worth mentioning that private entrepreneurs' state employment background did not influence their democratic support in a meaningful way. Perhaps this background no longer gives private entrepreneurs as many advantages as it had during the late 1990s when many state employees had "plunged into the sea" of the private sector with the state's encouragement. Now, many of those with state employment backgrounds have plunged into the sea after being laid off by their former state employers.[78]

Finally, as the standardized coefficients (i.e., beta in Table 4.14) indicate, among the independent variables, both belief in the party-state's leading role in sociopolitical changes and evaluation of the party-state's policy performance had the most powerful impact on private entrepreneurs' attitudes toward democratic values and institutions. In other words, value and policy congruence between the state and capitalists play the most important role in shaping capitalists' orientations toward a democratic system.

Summary and Conclusion

Throughout this chapter, we have attempted to address two closely related questions: How strongly do China's capitalists support democracy? And why do they support or not support it? To answer the first question, we have found that, on the one hand, an overwhelming majority of private entrepreneurs support competitive elections of leaders and, on the other hand, most entrepreneurs do not support or accept multiparty competition in Chinese politics and are not in favor of ordinary citizens' right to engage in public demonstrations and form nongovernmental organizations. Thus, China's private entrepreneurs are not likely to serve as agents of potential democratization.

To answer the second question regarding the sources of entrepreneurs' orientation toward democracy, we have examined different effects of the four types of congruence or connections (i.e., financial, institutional, value, and policy) between the party-state and private entrepreneurs. We found that private entrepreneurs who received loans from the state-controlled banks, strongly believed in the state's leadership role in economic and political reforms, highly evaluated the government's policy performance, and perceived the pace of political reform to be appropriate or too fast—in other words, those who highly supported the current party-state—were less supportive of democracy. Conversely, the party-state's institutional connections with private entrepreneurs had only a slight influence on entrepreneurs' attitudes toward democracy, but that influence was not as strong as the influences exerted by the financial connections, value congruence, and policy evaluation. The different types of memberships we examined—in the CCP, local legislative and advisory bodies, and state-sanctioned and self-organized business associations—had mixed and minimal effects on the democratic beliefs of China's private entrepreneurs when the other determinants of democratic support were held constant.

These findings generally support one of the central hypotheses we laid out in Chapter 1; that is, the close relationship between the party-state and capitalists—embodied by their financial, institutional, value, and policy congruence—causes China's capitalists to be less supportive

CHAPTER FIVE

Regime Support among China's Capitalists

I N THE PREVIOUS TWO CHAPTERS, we have discussed private entrepreneurs' institutional connections with the party-state (Chapter 3) and their orientation toward democracy and democratization (Chapter 4). The findings presented in those chapters indicated that the party-state made relentless efforts to incorporate entrepreneurs into its institutional framework, and most entrepreneurs were willing to be embedded in such a framework. In addition, these findings showed that most capitalists were not supportive of democratic values and institutions. Given the private entrepreneurs' institutional connections with the party-state and their orientation toward democracy, what attitudes do they have toward the current party-state itself? On the basis of the previous findings on institutional connections and democratic support, we will in this chapter explore capitalists' attitudes toward the regime and the main sources of these attitudes.

In general, many studies have argued that regime support (or political support) within the population is crucial for the functioning and persistence of any form of government.[1] In democratic systems, it is quite obvious that the level of political support significantly influences both the functioning and the stability of governments (especially in crises), because democratic governments can exist and operate only with the consent of the people.[2] In nondemocratic systems, while order is usually maintained by coercion and/or monolithic ideologies, the prolonged absence of political support may eventually bring about political instability and even "revolutionary alteration of the political and social system."[3] Such political instability and revolutions, for example, were witnessed in the former

Soviet Union and Eastern European countries in the late 1980s and the early 1990s.[4] In general, therefore, as Inglehart has argued, "societies with legitimate authority systems [i.e., ones enjoying popular support] are more likely to survive than those without them."[5]

From these arguments about popular political support, we can infer that there is a significant negative relationship between support for the incumbent regime and support for political change. In other words, those social groups that have a low level of support for the current political regime are more likely to advocate a fundamental political change, while those that have a high level of such support are more likely to support the maintenance of the status quo. In order to study the role of private entrepreneurs in political change in China, therefore, we must understand their attitudes toward or support for the current party-state. In this chapter, we will first gauge the level of regime support among China's capitalists and then explore several key determinants of their support, including capitalists' political embeddedness in the state (discussed in Chapter 3) and their attitudes toward democratic values and institutions (explored in Chapter 4). Finally, we will highlight the implications of our findings.

Level of Regime Support among Chinese Capitalists

In order to operationalize the concept of regime support (or regime legitimacy), many scholars in political science have identified several major components of the concept. For Lipset, regime legitimacy is tied to affect for the prevalent political institutions in a society.[6] David Easton sees regime legitimacy (or "diffuse support" in his original term) as affect primarily for values, norms, and institutions of the regime.[7] Combining these two approaches, Muller and Jukam locate three major operational components for the concept of regime legitimacy or regime support: (1) "affect tied to evaluation of how well political institutions conform to a person's sense of what is right"; (2) "affect tied to evaluation of how well the system of government upholds basic political values in which a person believes"; and (3) "affect tied to evaluation of how well the authorities conform to a person's sense of what is right and proper behavior [or conduct]."[8] In general, therefore, support for the current regime represents a person's value conviction that the existence and functioning of the current political regime conform to his or her moral or ethical principles about what is right in the political sphere. It is believed that citizens are linked to the regime by their attitudes toward it, which stem from their assessment of the fundamental values, norms, and institutions of the government. Consequently, we believe that support for the current regime indicates the value congruence between private entrepreneurs and the regime. Furthermore, we believe that this value congruence serves as the foundation of the tie between the current party-state and private entrepreneurs in China.

Following Muller and Jukam's operationalization of regime legitimacy,[9] as described above, we measured support for China's current political regime among private entrepreneurs by asking our respondents to assess seven items (or statements) as follows:

1. I believe that the Chinese Communist Party represents my interests.
2. I believe that the National People's Congress represents and articulates the interests of the majority of the population.
3. I believe that the military is capable of defending the country.
4. I trust the police are able to enforce laws impartially.
5. I believe that the courts are impartial.
6. I support my country's political institutions.
7. I feel that my personal values are the same as those advocated by the government.

Specifically, Items 1–6 are together designed to detect a respondent's evaluations of the political authorities and major political institutions in terms of whether the authorities have functioned and wielded their power in accordance with the respondent's sense of fairness and basic interests. Item 7 is intended to measure the affect for the values/norms that the regime has promoted. Respondents were asked to assess each of these seven statements on a five-point scale, where 1 stands for strong disagreement with the statement and 5 refers to strong agreement with it. These seven items were combined to form an additive index of a respondent's support for the current regime.[10]

Table 5.1 shows the distributions of these seven items designed to capture capitalists' support for the current regime. The overall results from these distributions revealed that a clear majority of our respondents supported the current political regime.

Although it may seem that these questions would elicit pre-programmed and politically correct responses, in fact the responses were not uniform. The percentages of those who either agreed or strongly agreed with the seven individual statements (which collectively measure regime support) ranged from a low of 63 percent for Item 5, regarding court impartiality, to a high of 94 percent for Item 2, about confidence in the armed forces; 86 percent of the respondents expressed overall support for the current

Table 5.1 Distribution of Regime Support among Private Entrepreneurs

	Positive responses[a] (%)	Mean	SD	N
1. I believe that the Communist party represents my interests. (1–5)	75.7	4.01	.834	2,055
2. I believe that the National People's Congress represents and articulates the interests of the majority of the population. (1–5)	84.4	4.16	.724	2,057
3. I believe that the military is capable of defending the country. (1–5)	93.7	4.40	.618	2,063
4. I trust the police are able to enforce laws impartially. (1–5)	64.5	3.80	.924	2,060
5. I believe that the courts are impartial. (1–5)	63.3	3.79	.916	2,059
6. I support my country's political institutions. (1–5)	86.0	4.17	.697	2,059
7. I feel that my personal values are the same as those advocated by the government. (1–5)	68.6	3.88	.825	2,029
Entire index (7–35)[b]	—	28.17	4.503	2,006

Note: Respondents were asked to assess each of these seven statements on a five-point scale, where 1 stands for strong disagreement with the statement and 5 refers to strong agreement with it.

[a]The percentage of positive responses is the combination of the percentages of those who "agree" and "strongly agree" with the questionnaire statement.

[b]The seven items above were combined to form an additive index to capture a collective profile of respondent's regime support, ranging from 7 (indicating the lowest level of regime support) to 35 (indicating the highest level of regime support).

political institutions (Item 6), but only 69 percent felt that their personal values were shared by the government (Item 7).

These results from individual items were also reinforced by the fact that the mean score of this regime support index was 28, well above the midpoint (21) of the 7–35 scale. This summary score for the index suggested that the respondents in our sample offered quite strong support for the political regime as a whole, or most of them considered the current regime legitimate. All in all, the results from our survey support those from recent empirical studies suggesting that, in general, China's private entrepreneurs tend to be supportive of the party-state and in favor of the status quo, but also that this support was not uniform.[11] Our goal in the remainder of this chapter is to explain that variation in the level of regime support.

Sources of Regime Support among Chinese Capitalists

What explains the level of regime support among Chinese capitalists? To answer this question, we focus on two primary explanatory (independent) variables—private entrepreneurs' political embeddedness in the party-state and their subjective orientations toward several important political issues, such as those toward democracy. In general, we assumed (1) that regime support among private entrepreneurs is influenced by both their relationship to the party-state and certain key subjective orientations and (2) that these political ties and subjective orientations influence capitalists' regime support even independently of some key demographic and socioeconomic contextual factors.

Political Embeddedness

As we discussed in Chapter 3, the CCP has tried to incorporate through various channels entrepreneurs into its institutional framework, and most entrepreneurs were willing to be embedded in one way or another. In general, we assume that the closer capitalists are tied to the state, the more likely they are to support the incumbent regime. Specifically, our first hypothesis is that "red capitalists" (i.e., capitalists who are CCP members) are more likely to support the regime than capitalists who are neither CCP members nor interested in joining the party. Furthermore, we expect that regime support will be higher among party members who were previously employed by the state—either as party and government officials or as SOE managers—than among those who were not employed by the state, since the former tended to have stronger and more extensive connections with the state apparatus.

Our second measure of political embeddedness is membership in the ACFIC, an officially sponsored business association. Membership in this association is voluntary and includes state-owned, privately owned, and mixed ownership firms. Membership in this organization signifies membership in the economic elite. This organization is embedded "within the system" *(tizhi nei)* and treated by the state as the core of the institutionalized connection between the party-state and private entrepreneurs. Thus, we expect members of the ACFIC to be more likely than nonmembers to support the regime. As mentioned in Chapter 3, among our respondents, 64.5 percent belonged to this organization.[12]

In sum, we expect that the closer capitalists are tied to the state, the more likely they are to support the incumbent regime. This has also been a key rationale for the recruitment of entrepreneurs into the CCP and

CCP-controlled organizations and for its encouragement of party members to "take the lead in getting rich" by going into private business.[13]

Subjective Orientations: Political and Social Values

Drawing on earlier studies of both Chinese and non-Chinese settings, we examine whether certain political and social values enhance or undermine regime support among China's capitalists. Specifically, we expect that the strength of democratic values and perceptions of the severity of official corruption will be negatively correlated with regime support, while respondents' satisfaction with their economic and social status and their evaluation of the state's policy performance will be positively correlated with it. The logic behind these hypothesized relationships is described below.

Democratic Support.   There is a broad consensus among China scholars that the party-state has to a large extent relaxed its control over citizens' private lives during the post-Mao reform era but also that this post-Mao regime remains far from democratic. The CCP has by no means given up its insistence on one-party rule nor has it ceased its harsh repression of political dissidents.[14] Overall, the current regime's norms and practices have thus far worked against most democratic norms and principles investigated, such as elections with multiparty competition and rights of free speech, demonstration, and assembly. Thus, we hypothesize that those who support democratic norms and institutions are less likely to support the current undemocratic regime.

As we described in Chapter 4, while private entrepreneurs like to check individual leaders through competitive elections under the current one-party system, they do not support fundamental political change toward a democratic system characterized by multiparty competition and individual liberty. Moreover, our findings support the arguments from some earlier studies that private entrepreneurs are not ready to support and participate in political changes favoring democracy.[15] Accordingly, we expect that democratic values will be negatively related to the respondents' regime support.

Perception of Official Corruption.   The rapid expansion of the private sector in China and the high economic growth rates it has fostered have also been accompanied by increasingly severe official corruption. Corruption has ranked at or near the top of the list of China's worst problems in most public opinion polls.[16] The general perception is that corruption among China's party and government officials is widespread and getting worse, both in terms of the monetary value of the cases and the level of officials involved.[17] Although some businessmen view bribes and other forms of official corruption as a regular part of doing business, others find it unacceptable, because they are less able to afford the bribes, have less access to decision makers, or believe corruption is morally objectionable. More fundamentally, if capitalists come to believe that the state's commitment to economic development and the accumulation of private wealth is outweighed by the predatory demands of local officials, their support for the current regime may drop. As has been the case in other countries, growing discontent with corruption will likely compel China's capitalists to withdraw support for the current regime.[18]

Many theorists of democracy suggest that while a democratic system does not guarantee the eradication of corruption committed by officials, it does provide citizens with some effective mechanisms to hold officials accountable and hence to prevent corruption. A democratic system in China, as Yan Sun argues, could offer at least two meaningful mechanisms to check and prevent official corruption: "media exposure and periodic removal of corrupt officials through democratic processes," such as free election of leaders and impeachment.[19] Moreover, as Melanie Manion has recently found in her study of local democracy in rural China, the existence of democratic institutions such as democratic elections is associated with less perceived corruption, because these institutions "can be expected to constrain leaders."[20] Since the current regime operates against these democratic principles and institutions, we expect that those who perceive that official corruption is widespread and getting worse are less likely to support the current regime.

As seen in Table 5.2, the capitalists in our survey were relatively sanguine about the severity and prevalence of corruption in their communities. Most respondents thought that corruption was less severe than in the past, at least locally, and almost two-thirds thought that only some officials were corrupt. Given the conventional wisdom that corruption is widespread and getting worse, these may seem unusual findings, but they are consistent with responses to a separate question in the survey. Asked to evaluate the government's performance at combating official corruption, about 36 percent answered "poor" or "very poor," 40 percent answered "fair," and 24 percent answered "good" or "very good" (this question is left out of the index evaluating the government's performance to avoid multicollinearity).

Table 5.2   Perceived Severity of Corruption

	Getting better	About the same	Getting worse	Total
Compared with the past, is corruption in your county or city:	52.8	34.5	12.5	100 (2,066)

	Very few officials are corrupt	Some officials are corrupt	Most officials are corrupt	Total
How widespread do you think corruption and bribe taking are in your county or municipal government? Would you say:	17.6	63.1	19.0	100 (2,066)

Note: Numbers without parentheses are percentages, while those within parentheses are the totals of observations.

Life Satisfaction.   It has been argued by many scholars of democracy that individuals' satisfaction with or assessment of their social and material lives is related to stability of established democracies. As Samuel Barnes and his colleagues note in their empirical study of five democracies, "it is widely believed that a happy people give rise to a tranquil polity, and that the roots of political violence are often to be found in individual frustration."[21] Ronald Inglehart further points out that personal life satisfaction, as a cultural variable, is necessary for the development as well as maintenance of a democratic system.[22] More important, this argument has been supported by the finding from Chen and Zhong's study of an urban area in China that those who were satisfied with their social and material lives tended to be more likely to support democratic values and institutions.[23]

Overall life satisfaction not only creates stability in democratic regimes; it can have a similar impact on authoritarian regimes as well. In his discussion on the link between life satisfaction and democratic stability, Inglehart also argues that "the same cultural factors that stabilize and sustain democracy can also stabilize authoritarian regimes," but he does not test this possibility.[24] Following a similar logic, Finifter and Mickiewicz found that "higher satisfaction with one's own life resulted in decreased receptivity to change" in their empirical study of former Soviets' attitudes toward political change in 1989. Specifically, the results of their analysis showed that people who were more satisfied with their life tended to be more likely to support the current political regime but less likely to support democratic changes in which such key democratic norms as free speech and competitive elections were advocated.[25]

Although these arguments concern different types of regimes, they agree that high levels of life satisfaction are correlated with support for the incumbent regime, regardless of whether it is democratic or authoritarian. Accordingly, we expect that the level of life satisfaction among China's capitalists will be positively related to their level of regime support.

As seen in Table 5.3, most respondents in our survey were either satisfied or very satisfied with their material lives (81 percent) and social status (64 percent). If life satisfaction causes an attitudinal tendency to support the status quo regardless of whether the regime is democratic or authoritarian, we expect to find that those who are currently satisfied with their material and social lives will have stronger support for the current regime and therefore be less likely to support political change.

Evaluation of Government's Policy Performance. Several recent studies of policy evaluation in China suggest that citizens' evaluation of government policy performance is significantly and positively associated with their support for the current regime.[26] From this finding, we can infer that those private entrepreneurs who rate the government's policy performance highly are more likely to have favorable views toward the current regime. In other words, we expect to find a positive relationship between the capitalists' assessment of the government's policy performance and their support for the incumbent regime.

Table 5.3   Life Satisfaction among China's Capitalists

	Very satisfied	Satisfied	Not sure	Dissatisfied	Very dissatisfied	Total
Are you satisfied with your material life at present?	7.9	73.0	11.5	6.8	0.9	100 (2,060)
Are you satisfied with your current social status?	3.1	61.2	25.4	9.4	0.9	100 (2,052)

Note: Numbers without parentheses are percentages, while those within parentheses are the total numbers of observations.

As we presented in Chapter 4, private entrepreneurs were in general quite positive about the government's policy performance. This general finding contrasts with those from an earlier survey study utilizing similar survey items and measurement scale, which shows that ordinary people gave mediocre "grades" (below the "so so" level) for most government policies.[27] Such a contrast apparently reinforces a common observation that private entrepreneurs have benefited more from policies of the current party-state and hence tend to have more favorable views about the government's policies than do ordinary people.

In summary, we expect that respondents' subjective values will have contrasting effects: satisfaction with their material and social lives and the government's policy performance will enhance their support for the regime, but stronger democratic values and dissatisfaction with official corruption will weaken it.

Sociodemographic Attributes and Socioeconomic Contextual Factors: Control Variables

Do private entrepreneurs' political embeddedness and subjective orientations, as specified above, influence their attitudes toward the regime independently of some key demographic and contextual factors? To answer this question, we examine the potential impact of two sets of control variables. One set includes sociodemographic variables, such as gender, age, education, and firm characteristics, and the other concerns the local economic context.

A large body of literature on democratic societies has found that sociodemographic variables may affect people's political attitudes.[28] This is mainly because, in both democratic and nondemocratic societies, sociodemographic attributes may affect people's political socialization processes, which in turn have a strong and lasting impact on their attitudes toward political regimes. We therefore control for the age, gender, and level of education of the capitalists in our sample. In addition, we include three other variables regarding the respondents' firms that may also be related to their support for the regime. The first is the size of the firm, measured by its fixed assets, which previous research in China has found to be a significant factor influencing the political behavior and attitudes of their owners.[29] This is largely because the corporate issues that firms face (e.g., corporate tax, market expansion, relationship with the governments, and employment responsibility) and the capacities that they have to deal with these issues vary with the size of firms. This variation in turn may have an impact on firm owners' views about important political issues, including support for the current political system.[30] The second firm characteristic we consider is the percentage of sales from exports. Higher levels of exports integrate capitalists into the global economy, making them more dependent on contracts with foreign customers than on the Chinese state. If they are less dependent on the state for their success in business, they should exhibit less regime support. The third firm characteristic is whether it was originally part of an SOE. This indicates its close connection to the state and should enhance regime support.[31] In our sample, 30 percent of the firms were former SOEs; among these firms, 30 percent of their owners were former SOE managers and half of their owners were CCP members.[32]

The local economic context was measured in two separate ways: per capita GDP and the provincial setting. The central argument of modernization theory is that political values are directly related to level of economic development: as societies become more prosperous (and relatedly, more urban and better educated), people in these societies are less willing to accept an authoritarian regime and more likely to support democratic change.[33] Following this argument, we expect that the local level of economic development should influence private entrepreneurs' attitudes toward the status quo, with those in more developed regions being less likely to support the regime. We also include dummy variables for four of the five provinces in our study (using Shandong as the reference point) to capture local contextual factors not captured by GDP alone.

Results of the Multivariate Analysis

Table 5.4 presents multiple regression (OLS) models to capture the impact of the independent variables specified above on private entrepreneurs' attitudes toward the current regime. Model 1 shows the results when measures of political embeddedness alone are considered. As expected, CCP members and those who have applied to join have significantly higher levels of regime support than do capitalists who are not CCP members and are not interested in joining. Among red capitalists, the group with the biggest impact (as seen by its standardized beta coefficient) is former cadres. Red capitalists who were formerly SOE managers and those who were regular party members also have higher regime support than do non–CCP members, although the difference is not as large as for former cadres.[34] Ironically, those who have applied to join the CCP but have not yet become members have a significantly higher level of regime support than the capitalists who are outside the CCP: even the aspiration to be embedded is correlated with regime support.

Table 5.4 Predictors of Regime Support among China's Capitalists

	Model 1			Model 2			Model 3		
	b	SE	β	b	SE	β	b	SE	β
Political embeddedness									
CCP member, former official	1.686***	0.429	0.092	0.918*	0.316	0.050	0.776*	0.356	0.043
CCP member, former SOE manager	1.142**	0.387	0.070	0.657*	0.321	0.041	−0.309	0.344	−0.019
CCP, other	1.063***	0.297	0.086	0.254	0.247	0.021	−0.307	0.250	−0.025
Applied to join CCP	1.759***	0.420	0.098	0.777*	0.344	0.044	0.023	0.339	0.001
ACFIC	0.757**	0.242	0.072	0.076	0.202	0.007	0.268	0.214	0.026
Subjective values									
Life satisfaction				0.579***	0.078	0.149	0.601***	0.079	0.152
Government's policy performance				0.212***	0.016	0.285	0.126***	0.017	0.168
Democratic values				−0.425***	0.029	−0.298	−0.436***	0.029	−0.303
Corruption				−0.625***	0.092	−0.142	−0.711***	0.093	−0.162
Individual and firm characteristics									
Age							−0.011	0.014	−0.016
Gender							−0.106	0.306	−0.007
Education							−0.158	0.142	−0.023
Fixed assets							0.035	0.063	0.012
Exports (as % of total sales)							−0.010***	0.003	−0.070
Ex-SOE							0.278	0.215	0.026
Local economic and political context									
Level of development (per capita GDP)							0.004	0.007	0.010
Location[a]									
Jiangsu							−1.259***	0.306	−0.109
Zhejiang							−2.923***	0.308	−0.244
Fujian							−4.190***	0.387	−0.256
Guangdong							−3.568***	0.334	−0.293
Constant	31.390***	0.206		28.326***	1.029		34.766***	1.300	
No. of observations	1,888			1,777			1,588		
R^2	.031			.369			.461		
Adjusted R^2	.028			.366			.455		

[a] Shandong is used as the base category for comparison; each of the other provinces is a dummy variable.

*$p < .05$ **$p < .01$ ***$p < .001$

Membership in the ACFIC, the official business association, is also positively correlated with regime support. However, the amount of explained variance (adjusted R^2) is rather small: these measures of political embeddedness account for less than 3 percent of the variation in regime support. There is a statistically significant relationship between these indicators of political embeddedness, but they explain very little of the variation in levels of regime support among our survey respondents.

Model 2 shows the results when subjective values are added in. The results show that all the subjective values have large and statistically significant impacts. Altogether, these subjective orientations increased the amount of explained variance in regime support by a large magnitude of 33.8 percent. Those with higher levels of life satisfaction were more likely to support the regime. This is consistent with the findings of Inglehart and of Finifter and Mickiewicz in other contexts, namely, that life satisfaction correlates with regime support regardless of regime type. Similarly, those who give a positive evaluation of the government's performance in specific policy areas are also more likely to support the regime. Conversely, those who feel that corruption is widespread and getting worse are less likely to support the regime. This reinforces the CCP's concern with the plague of corruption: even when other variables are held constant, dissatisfaction with corruption undermines support for the regime. Most important, democratic values also reduce regime support: the higher the respondents' level of democratic values, all else being equal, the less likely they are to support the regime. The impact of this one variable is the largest among all subjective values: it has the largest standardized coefficient. In short, to the extent that the regime's pro-growth strategy has made capitalists satisfied with their overall life situation and the government's policy performance, it has also generated increased regime support; but those who supported democratic principles and who perceived severe and rampant corruption were more likely to have diminished support for this regime.

In contrast, when political embeddedness and political values are considered together, the impact of political embeddedness is reduced, as can be seen from the smaller standardized coefficients. Moreover, rank-and-file CCP members are no longer significantly different from non-CCP capitalists in terms of regime support, and ACFIC members are also not significantly different from nonmembers. These results suggest that the effect of these indicators of embeddedness is muted by the overwhelming impact of subjective values. In other words, the subjective orientations are likely to play a more decisive role than embeddedness in shaping capitalists' attitudes toward the current CCP regime.

Model 3 shows the results when political embeddedness, subjective values, and control variables are all combined together. The addition of the control variables increases the amount of explained variation in regime support by another 8.3 percent, and the combined model explains almost half of the overall variation. Among the measures of political embeddedness, only one—party members who used to be cadres—continues to have a significant but weak effect on regime support. This group of red capitalists was most embedded in the party-state before going into the private sector, and its previous relationship with the state continues to pay big dividends in generating regime support. In contrast, the other measures of embeddedness do not have any significant impact when other variables are controlled for. However, all the subjective values remain significant predictors of regime support even when all else is constant: life satisfaction and approval of the regime's policy performance enhance regime support, while democratic values and discontent with corruption undermine it. Democratic values again stand out as the most important explanatory variable among the subjective values: even in the combined model, it has the largest standardized coefficient. In short, whereas the introduction of control variables watered down the impact of political embeddedness, subjective values remain robust predictors of regime support, with democratic values having the most important—and negative—effect.

Among the control variables, the individual and firm characteristics are not significant in the full model, with one exception: the more a firm relies on exports, the less its owner supports the regime. This supports our hypothesis that the more entrepreneurs are linked to foreign markets, the less dependent they are on the Chinese state and consequently the less they need to support the regime in order to be successful in business. But local context has a dramatic effect on regime support: compared with Shandong, capitalists in other provinces in our survey exhibited lower levels of regime support. The farther south a province is—in other words, the farther it is away from Beijing—the lower the level of regime support, with the respondents in Guangdong having the lowest levels. We suspect, however, that the proper interpretation of the strong and significant impact of the local context is not simply about geography. Alan Liu has argued that the political culture in north China is more traditionalist and more supportive of the state, whereas in south China the political culture is more modern, more oriented toward the outside world, and therefore less attached to the state.[35] An alternative explanation may be the level of foreign investment and foreign trade in Fujian and Guangdong, which makes the firms less dependent on the state for needed capital and access to markets and by extension may make them less beholden to the regime as a whole. Our data cannot directly address this question,[36] and further research will be necessary to determine why provincial characteristics have such a dramatic effect on regime support. Finally, among the contextual variables, the level of local economic development does not have an independent effect on regime support and falls just short of statistical significance even when the provincial dummies are omitted.

In sum, it is private entrepreneurs' subjective orientations that play the most critical role in determining their support for the regime. If the CCP can continue to generate high levels of life satisfaction and support for its policy performance, it will enhance the capitalists' support for the regime. But if they become less satisfied with their own social and material lives and the ability of the government to deliver public goods, if discontent with the prevalence and severity of corruption deepens, and especially if democratic values become more commonplace, support for the regime among capitalists is likely to decline. How well the CCP balances these countervailing trends will help determine the level of regime support in the future and will by extension help determine whether China's capitalists remain supporters of the status quo or whether the potential is raised for them to support proponents of change. When subjective orientations and control variables are held constant, being a former cadre has a significant yet weak impact on the level of regime support, while other embeddedness variables fail to do so. This suggests that the party's strategy of co-opting capitalists and encouraging its members to go into the private sector has been only marginally successful in generating political loyalty among capitalists. Subjective values and the local context are much more important in generating and undermining regime support among China's capitalists.

Are levels of regime support among China's capitalists—and the underlying factors that determine regime support—changing? Because our survey was taken at one point in time, there is no way to determine whether regime support and its determinants are rising, falling, or staying the same. As noted earlier in the book, even though our findings are consistent in principle with previous studies, those studies do not provide a benchmark for systematic comparison because they used indirect ways of measuring political values and did not inquire into the causes of regime support. We hope that our study will provide a point of reference for determining whether support for the regime and the causes of that support are undergoing change in the future.

Implications and Conclusion

The results presented in this chapter and in Chapter 4 together address two critical and much debated questions among scholars. First of all, are China's capitalists, the major beneficiaries of economic reform, likely to support changes in the political system or even serve as agents of political change? Our survey data are consistent with most previous empirical work on the topic and make us pessimistic about this outcome. On one hand, the capitalists surveyed in this project showed a high level of regime support. On the other hand, they registered low levels of support for most measures of democratic values and institutions examined in this study. Although strong majorities favored multicandidate elections of government leaders, they apparently prefer such elections to be confined within the current one-party system; most respondents did not support a multiparty competition or expanding political participation to nonstate actors. It is quite obvious that elections without other supporting institutions, such as the opening of multiparty contests and the guarantee of individual political rights, do not constitute a democracy. Thus, it could be said that most private entrepreneurs in China want a political system similar to what Larry Diamond calls a "politically closed authoritarian" regime, which resembles the current CCP regime.[37] In this type of nondemocratic system, elections may exist at various levels but are firmly controlled by the single ruling party. In short, China's private entrepreneurs support the current regime and hence are less likely to support any fundamental political change toward democracy.

The other main question we have addressed in this chapter concerns what factors influence these capitalists' orientation toward the incumbent regime. The more the capitalists are satisfied with the government's policy performance and their material and social lives, the more likely they are to support the status quo. This is the wager the CCP is making: improved governance and living standards are designed to enhance popular support and as a result dampen demands for more fundamental political reform. However, as corruption continues to plague China, resentment—even among the capitalists who help fuel the problem—may undermine support for the regime. Above all, it is the strength of support for democratic norms and institutions that predicts the level of regime support. As these views become more prevalent, support for the CCP and its regime is likely to diminish. More important, it is the individuals' subjective values far more than their CCP membership and relationship to the state that determines whether they are regime supporters. Only red capitalists who are former cadres are likely to be reliable supporters of the regime when subjective values are also considered.

Finally, the findings about the impact of the control variables also provide some useful insights. We have found that none of the sociodemographic attributes, including gender, age, and education, were significant factors when subjective orientations were taken into account. This finding suggests that, at least among this privileged subgroup of Chinese society, socioeconomic variables were nowhere near as influential as attitudinal factors in shaping capitalists' attitudes toward the regime. Similarly, the size of their firms and the local level of economic development were not significant predictors of regime support when other explanatory variables were controlled for. But the local political and economic context did matter: regime support fell as the distance from Beijing grew. We have suggested that this may be due to differences in the overall political culture in the provinces in our sample or to the presence of foreign capital, but more research will be necessary to determine why such a strong relationship exists between provinces and the level of regime support.

Absent a fundamental change in their political values—particularly their level of democratic values—and a sharp deterioration in the government's policy performance, China's capitalists do not seem prepared to support political change. Rather than present a challenge to the CCP's continued domination of the political system, China's capitalists may prove to be a key source of political support. But the conditions under which their support for the regime could waver are also clear: a decline in the capitalists' overall life satisfaction, poorer evaluations of the government's policy performance, increasing concerns over the severity and prevalence of official corruption, and above all an increase in their support for democratic values and institutions. Whether capitalists continue to be allies of the CCP in promoting continued economic development or transfer their support to new challengers, or even be agents of change themselves, will be a key element in the survival of the current regime.

CHAPTER SIX

Political Activities of Private Entrepreneurs in China

A S MENTIONED in the previous chapters, the development of China's private sector has led to speculation that China's private entrepreneurs may prove to be agents of political change. Such speculation assumes that these private entrepreneurs hold prodemocratic beliefs and that these beliefs will translate into political action among entrepreneurs. To assess the validity of these assumptions, this chapter will analyze the link between political embeddedness and political beliefs of China's private entrepreneurs, on the one hand, and the range of political activities they engage in, on the other. These activities include voting in local PC elections, contacting officials, supporting academic activities, and petitioning.

Whereas previous research has examined the political embeddedness and political beliefs of China's entrepreneurs and different aspects of their political activities, these studies have not provided a systematic look at the link between their embeddedness and beliefs and their behavior.[1] In this chapter, we are interested in two key questions: How do private entrepreneurs' links with official political and business organizations influence the extent of their political participation? To what extent do their attitudes toward democracy affect the types of political participation they engage in? Drawing on our original survey data, we will analyze how institutional ties, individual values, and contextual factors influence the political activities of China's private entrepreneurs.

The Forms and Intensity of Political Activities

In order to assess the causes of private entrepreneurs' political behavior, we need first to have a good understanding of the major forms and extent of political participation in which entrepreneurs typically engage. Since the outset of post-Mao economic and political reforms in the late 1970s, more and more citizens have been participating in public affairs and politics in both urban and rural areas of China,[2] even though China's political system has never been democratic—especially by Western standards. In our survey, we asked eleven questions regarding political activities in which private entrepreneurs were likely to engage. Rather than arbitrarily group them into separate categories, we conducted an exploratory factor analysis with these eleven questions in order to detect naturally occurring clusters among them. The results of the factor analysis indicate that there are four distinct factors or clusters among these questions (see Table 6.1). These four factors deal with four types of social and political activities: direct action (contacting officials and engaging in collective action), indirect action (contacting the media and submitting petitions), supporting academic activities, and voting in local PC elections. These four factors together explain about half (47.98 percent) of the variance among the eleven questions. While the cluster of direct action with four questions accounts for 18 percent of the variance, the clusters of voting in local PC elections, direct action, supporting academic activities, and indirect action explain 11 percent, 10 percent, and 8 percent of the variance, respectively.

These four clusters of political activities by no means exhaust all possible types of activities—especially those deemed "illegal" or "radical" by the government—in which private entrepreneurs engage. Nonetheless, they can serve as representative and reliable indicators of political activities among private entrepreneurs. First of all, according to our field observations and earlier studies of political participation in China, these four clusters have proven to be the most common political acts that have been engaged in by citizens in post-Mao China.[3] Thus, the acts in these clusters represent the current trends of political participation in China. Second, these clusters of acts are considered legitimate in China, at least in theory, though not totally risk-free. Thus, the respondents in our survey were less likely to give untruthful answers to the questions about these acts in order to avoid negative political repercussions. Thus, we believe that these four clusters can provide a valid indication of the intensity of political participation by the private entrepreneurs and consequently offer a reliable test of the hypothesized relationship between kinds of participation and their potential causes.

Table 6.1 Factor Analysis of Political Activities

Item	Direct action	Indirect action	Academic support	Voting
Contact party or government official	.774			
Contact deputies to people's congress	.701			
Joined with other firms to lobby the government	.689			
Joined with others to try to solve some of the community's problems	.577			
Sent a collective petition		.781		
Sent an individual petition		.777		
Wrote to media		.477		
Gave financial support to social consulting organizations and scholars carrying out policy research			.691	
Participated in academic activities			.674	
Supported the publication and distribution of newspapers, magazines, and academic journals			.634	
Voted in the most recent district or county election for people's congress				.660

Note: Figures in this table are factor loadings of .25 of larger from the varimax-rotated matrix for all factors with eigenvalues greater than 1.0.

In the sections below, we will describe the nature of each of the four clusters of acts, presented in order of most common to least common. We then explain how political values, key institutional ties, socioeconomic characteristics, and contextual factors affect these forms of behavior among China's capitalists.

Voting Behavior

In this study, voting behavior refers to participation in a local PC election. Of all four major forms of mass political participation examined here, voting has been the most common political act engaged in by ordinary citizens as well as by private entrepreneurs. In contrast to the central role of elections in democratic political systems, however, elections in China have different characteristics, and voting behavior has different connotations. The PRC constitution stipulates that the local PCs should represent citizens' interests and supervise governments and their officials in their respective areas.[4] But in effect, the congresses and their deputies have not met such constitutional expectations. The CCP has imposed strict political and ideological constraints on the elections for local PCs. In order to prevent any organized or individual opposition from challenging its position of absolute rule, the CCP directly or indirectly controls virtually the entire process of local PC elections: from the nomination of candidates, to the deliberation of the electorate, and finally to the determination of final candidates on the ballot. Such political control has been done mainly through the party-dominated local election committees.[5] As Andrew Nathan points out, therefore, these elections are still "not open to all contenders but are controlled by the Chinese Communist Party."[6] To ensure the political dependability of PC delegates, 60–80 percent of them at all levels are typically CCP members.[7]

The second constraint imposed by the CCP in these elections is an ideological one. First of all, the party prohibits any large-scale or "publicized" electoral campaign that is considered part of "bourgeois democracy" (as opposed to "socialist democracy"), and it requires that all electoral activities and deliberations be carried out within a limited scope (e.g., work unit, or *danwei*) under firm control by the party-dominated election committee.[8] By doing so, the CCP essentially eliminates any effective channels for potential dissidents to articulate their opinions in local elections.

In short, the net outcomes of these elections have been very much in accordance with the CCP's expectations. Politically, most of the winning candidates are party members, none of them are part of an organized opposition, and very few of them are independent candidates who operate without the party's support or approval. Ideologically, very few of the winning candidates advocate political views different from the party line, although some of them make "constructive suggestions" on some specific local policy issues.

This assessment of the election of local PC deputies helps us understand the subjective motivation for voting. Through various institutional mechanisms and political controls, the CCP prevents the local PCs and their deputies from playing a true representative and legislative role. Voters therefore have little expectation that PC delegates will represent their interests and do not see voting in these elections as a form of democratic participation. Instead, voting in the local PC elections is less about promoting democratic values and more about showing support for the existing political system.

As seen in Table 6.2, in our survey 61.8 percent of the respondents in the sample voted in the most recent PC election (i.e., the one before the time of the survey). As a rough comparison, the 2002 Asian Barometer Survey found that only 41.2 percent of the general population had voted in the previous election. As will be shown below, however, although the absolute level of voting among private entrepreneurs may be higher than in the general population, the variables that explain voting behavior are quite similar.

Voters were also much more satisfied with the outcome of the elections than were nonvoters: 73.3 percent of voters expressed satisfaction with the elections' results compared with just 24.3 percent of nonvoters. A remarkable 67.7 percent of nonvoters said they were "not clear" whether they were satisfied with the results; this "not clear" response often implies a negative answer and is used when the respondent does not want to give an explicitly negative answer. Familiarity is also an advantage: people who were familiar with the candidates were not only more likely to vote but also more likely to be satisfied with the outcome.

Direct Action

What we label as "direct action" includes a variety of informal and unofficial activities. Specifically, we look at four types of behavior: directly contacting party or government officials, directly contacting delegates of local PCs, lobbying the government in conjunction with other firms, and engaging in collective action to solve local problems. In contrast to voting,

Table 6.2   Voting Behavior among China's Private Entrepreneurs

Did you vote in the most recent district or county election for people's congress?		
	Frequency	%
Yes	1,275	61.8
No	644	31.2
Don't remember	145	7.0
Total	2,064	100.0
Were you satisfied with the outcome of the election?		
Very satisfied	144	7.1
Fairly satisfied	960	47.3
Not clear	770	38.0
Not too satisfied	115	5.7
Very unsatisfied	40	2.0
Total	2,029	100.0

these activities are initiated by the respondents and are not the result of state mobilization. As such, they entail less explicit government control than voting. Nevertheless, they are still aimed at eliciting approvals and favors that are controlled by state officials. Specifically, this category of political acts can be regarded as "particularistic" political activities in China.[9] By engaging in such acts, private entrepreneurs express their concerns about and interests in concrete personal or business-related issues. The issues dealt with in this category, therefore, do not directly relate to fundamental norms—such as democratic values—and formal structures of the political system.[10] As a result, the government usually does not consider such acts as a political threat to the regime (unless this kind of act turns out to be an organized movement). In most cases, therefore, the party not only allows but encourages citizens to participate in these direct personalized activities of contacting various leaders and officials as this improves the party's image among the people.[11]

Most respondents in our survey engaged in at least one form of direct action, and many engaged in more than one form (see Table 6.3). The most common form of direct action was contacting party and government officials: a slight majority of respondents had contacted officials during the year prior to the survey. Slightly fewer respondents reported that they had engaged in lobbying and other types of collective action. Contacting PC delegates was a less common form of direct action. This is not surprising: local PCs are not seen as influential actors, and consequently they are not seen as an effective means of problem solving. Moreover, local residents are often unsure of whom their delegate is and how the delegate is supposed to represent their interests.[12] As a result, contacting delegates is a less common form of political activity: almost twice as many respondents contacted officials as contacted PC deputies.

The respondents in our survey also reported very high levels of satisfaction concerning the outcome of direct action. Approximately three-quarters or more of the respondents who engaged in a given form of direct action were satisfied with the results. This is roughly comparable to the 73 percent of voters who were satisfied with the outcome of the election, as reported above. For both voting and direct action, the odds of being satisfied are quite high for those who engage in the activity.

Supporting Academic Activities

Entrepreneurs' support for academic activities is another form of political activity. This category of political participation includes engaging in academic activities, sponsoring publication of academic and media materials,

Table 6.3   Direct Action by China's Private Entrepreneurs

	Frequency	%	% of which satisfied with outcome
Contacted officials	1,108	50.9	74.8
Engaged in lobbying	824	42.9	74.0
Engaged in collective action	713	37.9	83.1
Contacted PC deputies	513	26.9	75.9
Index of direct action (how many types of activities)			
0	599	33.2	
1	387	21.4	
2	364	20.0	
3	274	15.2	
4	185	10.2	
Total	1,806		

and providing financial support for private think tanks. In sharp contrast to voting and direct action, support for academic activities has a more overtly political motivation: support for many types of academic activities is motivated by desire to promote development of civil society, rule of law, and in some cases even more ambitious forms of political reform. Not all support for academic research is politically motivated, of course. Some companies fund feasibility studies, research and development, marketing techniques, and related industry issues that do not have direct political implications. But support for research is one of the few safe avenues for private entrepreneurs in China to promote politically oriented issues.

Academic support by entrepreneurs was particularly common in the late 1980s and early 1990s in the wake of the 1989 demonstrations.[13] Recently graduated students would make quick money, and because of their support for the goals of the 1989 demonstrations, they would fund projects on reform-related topics. Over time, this became less common as memories of the demonstrations began to fade and the potential for influencing the political system seemed remote. Among the respondents in our survey, members of the "1989 generation" were not more inclined to political change than older or younger entrepreneurs. This is found in a multivariate analysis (not shown here) using the same model for regime support used in Chapter 5 but replacing the age of the respondents with a dummy variable for those who were 18–30 years old in 1989. The coefficient for this dummy variable was positive and statistically significant ($p < .05$), indicating that this group had a higher level of regime support than did the older and younger cohorts.[14] In other words, being a member of the 1989 generation may incline some to political activity, but on the whole this subgroup has a higher level of regime support than did others in the survey.

At least some entrepreneurs have been interested in the development of civil society and even democratization, but their financial support has mostly been ad hoc and personal. There are no private institutions or foundations that scholars can apply to for funding; instead scholars get funding for their projects by getting to know generous entrepreneurs and gaining their support. According to Chinese scholars, it is fairly common for academics and research institutions to receive such support for conferences, book projects, and other publications. For example, the NGO Research Center at Tsinghua University and the China Center for Economic Research at Peking University both get substantial contributions from private firms, and the journal of the NGO Research Center, the *China Nonprofit Review (Zhongguo Feiyingli Pinglun)*, first published in 2007, was created with support from the private sector. More prominently, the Association of China's Private Economy Studies (ACPES), the most authoritative research organization in private-economy studies in China, has been financially supported by the contributions from private entrepreneurs since its establishment in 1993. This research association has organized the Forum of China's Private Economy since 2000, which has become the most influential forum for scholars and private entrepreneurs alike to advocate and defend private enterprises in China.[15]

Because this form of political activity is often motivated by an interest in political reform, it is a less common activity than either voting or direct action. Most studies of China's private entrepreneurs have concluded they are by and large not interested in political affairs, much less democracy,[16] and most entrepreneurs in our survey did not support academic activities. However, a significant minority—one-quarter—did support at least one type of academic activity in different ways, either by their personal participation or financial support for research and publication (see Table 6.4).

Indirect Action

The fourth category of political activity included in our study we label "indirect action" and includes contacting the media and submitting both

Table 6.4   Academic Support by China's Private Entrepreneurs

	Frequency	%
Participated in academic activities	373	18.6
Supported the publication and distribution of newspapers, magazines, and academic journals	309	15.4
Gave financial support to social consulting organizations and scholars conducting policy research	162	8.1
Index of academic support (how many types of activities)		
0	1,355	67.6
1	495	24.7
2	113	5.6
3	41	2.1
Total	2,004	

individual and collective petitions. Firms seek favorable media coverage in order to enhance their image, but more relevant to our study are examples of firms using the media to put pressure on the government. For example, when the Henan provincial government tried to close down privately owned cement companies in 2006, a group of these companies convened a meeting in Beijing to bring attention to their plight. They invited a number of nationally renowned economists and legal experts, who claimed that Henan could not use administrative rationale to close legitimate firms. More than a dozen media later picked up the story, revealing the illegal measures being used by the Henan government. Similarly, a group of owners of private petrol firms waged a two-year battle with the Shaanxi provincial government to protect their "legal rights" *(hefa quanyi),* culminating in a series of meetings in Beijing. These meetings were attended by economists and lawyers, who questioned the behavior of the Shaanxi government. The story was covered by domestic and international media, which of course was the goal of the firms involved. Media coverage of heavy-handed government action not only arouses public sympathy but more importantly aims to get the attention of higher level officials in the hope that they will intervene on behalf of the victims of improper actions by lower-level officials.[17]

Petitioning includes both writing letters to and visiting upper-level government officials (up to the central level). The main goals of these political acts include protecting private property and business interests, seeking equal access to markets and bank loans, and fighting official corruption. For example, since 1998, the president of Longqing Petrochemical Corporation in Harbin, Heilongjiang Province, has continuously led presidents of several other small and medium firms in that industrial sector to petition the National Development and Reform Commission in Beijing for equal access to petroleum markets and to bank loans for small and medium firms.[18] These acts are generally seen as the last hope for people with few other resources. Many private entrepreneurs have the political, economic, and social status that allows them to rely on other forms of behavior to assert their interests. Nevertheless, petitioning is an officially recognized and permitted method of addressing grievances to the state.

In general, these political acts have two important characteristics that distinguish themselves particularly from direct action and voting. First of all, they are more "demanding" than voting and direct action through normal or conventional channels. Because they are more difficult and require more initiative for participants, the frequencies of these acts tend to be lower than the other acts. Second, the act of petitioning officials is more "purposive, and autonomous."[19] Due to this characteristic, these activities are engaged in by participants who tend to be more independent in thinking and more critical of the utility of conventional participatory channels; they are also more likely have a clear set of goals to achieve.

Indirect action is an especially rare political activity among entrepreneurs: only 7.5 percent contacted the media, and just over 3 percent had submitted either individual or collective petitions in the year prior to the survey (see Table 6.5). According to our field observations and other studies, most of these acts are engaged in by entrepreneurs of small and medium firms, who have fewer personal resources and less effective access to upper-level government agencies or officials than do those of large firms and who have tried but failed to pursue their goals through more conventional channels (e.g., by directly contacting the relevant government agencies and officials).

Given the relative infrequency of these types of political activities, especially petitioning, it is remarkable that those who choose these activities report such high levels of satisfaction with the results. Over half of the respondents who contacted the media and submitted collective petitions reported that they were satisfied with the outcome, and for individual petitioners almost 70 percent were satisfied. This is remarkable because the petition system is generally seen as ineffective and inefficient.

Table 6.5   Indirect Action among China's Private Entrepreneurs

	Frequency	%	% of which satisfied with outcome
Contacted media	139	7.5	54.4
Individual petition	60	3.3	68.3
Collective petition	58	3.2	57.4
Index of indirect action (how many types of activities)			
0	1,626	90.0	
1	140	7.8	
2	32	1.8	
3	8	0.4	
Total	1,806		

Research by Yu Jianrong found that less than 1 percent of petitions were granted. Yu recommended abolishing the "letters and visits" system because it is so dysfunctional that it dramatically undermines support for the central government.[20] Similarly, Li Lianjiang's study of petitioning by Chinese farmers found that the farmers' overwhelming degree of dissatisfaction with the outcome of their petitions serves to undermine their trust and confidence in the central government's commitment to improving their welfare.[21] The results from our study stand in sharp contrast to the usual conception of petitioning. Although rare, it seems to be an effective means of political action, at least among China's capitalists. Of course, they may get preferential treatment from the officials who receive their petitions because of their privileged status.

Analysis

Why do private entrepreneurs in an authoritarian, one-party-ruled political system such as China's engage in these types of political activities? Are they simply mobilized by the government? If not, how do entrepreneurs' political ties and subjective values, such as their orientation toward democracy, affect each type of political acts? As mentioned at the beginning of this chapter, previous research has not systematically studied how private entrepreneurs' political embeddedness and political beliefs influence their political behavior. As a result, our theoretical starting point for the exploration of these two critical questions will be based mainly on the previous studies of mass political participation in China as well as in other nondemocratic settings, especially former communist societies.

To the first question of whether political acts in a one-party state are all mobilized and controlled by the state, at least two contending approaches can be found in the literature. One is the so-called mobilization model, which describes participation in communist societies as "almost entirely a product of regime-directed mobilization" and little individual motivation.[22] The other is the motivation model, which sees mass participation in those societies more as a result of individual subjective motivations, even though the leadership still suppresses any opposition that could threaten its one-party rule.[23] The mobilization approach seems to be more applicable to mass participation in pre-reform, orthodox communist societies such as the Stalinist-era Soviet Union and the Maoist-era People's Republic of China. This is because, in these systems, as Bahry and Silver point out, "not only were . . . political institutions authoritarian, but society itself seemed inhospitable to democratic values."[24] The motivation approach appears to be more suitable for political participation in reform, nonorthodox communist societies such as post-Mao China. In these societies, not only do more legitimate channels and opportunities become available for mass participation, but also the public itself becomes more open-minded and critical about public policies and politics in general. In particular, some recent empirical studies based on field interviews have found that many private entrepreneurs are motivated by their business interests or/and "higher political goals," such as "promoting system change," to engage in different types of political acts.[25]

More important, although there is a consensus among the motivation analysts themselves that individual subjective orientations significantly influence political participation especially during the reform period, the question of which kinds of subjective orientations influence what types of political acts has by no means been settled. Nonetheless, the common ground among these analysts is that different kinds of subjective values and contextual factors may variably affect citizens' political behavior. As Bahry and Silver noted in their study of the Soviet Union under reform, it is "not only that individual attitudes ought to matter in determining how much people participated but also that a different combination of them would come into play for each type of activism."[26] From different perspectives, therefore, studies by motivation analysts provide some theoretical and empirical baselines for our inquiry into the correlates of private entrepreneurs' political behavior in contemporary China. In this study, we focus on the private entrepreneurs' political embeddedness and subjective orientations—such as democratic support, evaluation of government's policy performance, and interest in public affairs. In addition, we also introduce some key individual characteristics and local contextual factors as control variables.

Independent Variables

Political embeddedness.   We measure political embeddedness by membership in the CCP, the local chapter of the ACFIC (an officially sponsored business association), and such political institutions as local PCs and PPCCs. As detailed in Chapter 3, China's capitalists are well integrated into China's political system: 37 percent of our respondents were CCP members, 31.8 percent were PC/PPCC deputies, and 64.5 percent were members of the ACFIC. We expect that these measures of political embeddedness will be positively correlated with political activities that involve high levels of state control (e.g., voting and direct action) but will be negatively related to those involving less state control (e.g., supporting academic activities and indirect action).

In addition, we include membership in self-organized business associations (who may also belong to the CCP and the ACFIC). We believe that the willingness to form or join these unofficial associations indicates that these individuals are more proactive and assertive and therefore more likely to support academic activities and engage in indirect political action, such as contacting the media and submitting petitions.

Subjective Values.   We assess three types of political values in our analysis of political activity: support for democratic values, evaluation of the government's policy performance, and interest in current affairs. We will explain each of these key variables below.

First, to assess support for democratic values among China's private entrepreneurs, we use the same index as described in Chapter 4. This index measures support for a multiparty system as opposed to the current one-party regime and the importance of individual liberties relative to political order. Both of these conceptual dimensions of beliefs are essential for democratic governance.[27]

In terms of the impacts of attitudinal support for democracy and democratization on voting, there are at least two distinct views. One argues that people's attitudes toward so-called high-politics issues, such as democratization and regime legitimacy, have a significant positive effect on voting in local PC elections in post-Mao China.[28] That is, those who support democratic values and institutions tend to engage in formal and conventional activities. This view suggests that the current "semidemocratic" (vs. "totalitarian" or "nondemocratic") electoral system has provided citizens with limited yet genuine opportunities to express their opinions and exert their influence.

In contrast, the other view contends that such a high-politics orientation as support for democracy has either a negative impact or no impact on formal and conventional forms of participation, such as voting and direct action.[29] This is because, according to this view, all these formal and conventional channels of participation have been firmly controlled by the party, and such a tight control has in turn alienated democratic supporters. As a result, those who support democratic values and principles tend to see the formal and conventional channels as a formality, which "serves only the function of legitimizing the non-democratic, one-Party rule."[30] As such, democratic supporters either ignore these channels or boycott them in protest of the one-party rule.

In addition, because direct action (contacting officials and engaging in collective action) is largely concerned with the pursuit of private interests rather than public welfare, we expect that the democratic beliefs of the respondents will not be correlated with their likelihood of engaging in direct action. In contrast, supporting academic activities and engaging in indirect action (e.g., contacting the media and submitting petitions) indicate a desire to bring about change, and we therefore expect democratic values to have a positive influence on these activities.

Second, we explore the impact of capitalists' evaluation of government policy performance on their political behavior. In Chapter 5, we showed that private entrepreneurs' evaluation of government policy performance is significantly and positively associated with their support for the current regime. This finding is consistent with several recent studies of Chinese citizens as a whole, which also showed how "specific" support for the government's policy performance created "diffuse" support for the regime as a whole.[31] From this finding, we can infer that those private entrepreneurs who rate highly the government's policy performance are more likely to have favorable views toward the current regime. Consequently, those respondents who are satisfied with the government's policy performance tend to vote in local PC elections, since such elections, as mentioned earlier, are controlled by the party and are considered a channel of expressing support for the regime. Conversely, these respondents may not be actively participating in the other activities (i.e., contacting officials, supporting academic activities, and submitting petitions), since these activities are engaged in to make demands on the regime.

Third, we expect that interest in current affairs will be positively correlated with capitalists' inclination to participate in the types of political activities examined in this chapter. Drawing on indicators for political interest used in early studies of Chinese and non-Chinese settings,[32] we measured interest in political and public affairs among our respondents by asking three questions. These questions concerned their interest in major issues at three major levels: local, national, and international. As shown in Table 6.6, the respondents in our survey expressed high levels of interest in local, national, and international affairs. We combine the responses to these three questions to form an additive index to measure the extent of interest in current affairs.

Control Variables

In addition to the explanatory variables described above, we use two types of control variables: individual characteristics and the local socioeconomic context. A large body of literature on political behavior has found that sociodemographic variables have a consistent and predictable impact. For most forms of political participation, older and better educated people are more likely to participate than others, and we expect that relationship to hold true here as well. As is true in most countries, China's political system is predominated by men, and China's capitalists are also predominated by men, so we expect that men will be more likely than women to be politically active.

In addition, we control for the size of the firm, measured by fixed assets. We expect that owners of larger firms, all else being equal, will be more likely to vote, engage in direct action, and support academic activities, but owners of smaller firms are more likely to engage in indirect action (i.e., contacting the media and submitting petitions) for the reasons described above.

The local economic context is measured in two separate ways: per capita GDP and the provincial setting. The central argument of modernization

Table 6.6   Interest in Current Affairs

	Very interested	A little interested	Not much interested	Not interested at all
Local issues	45.9	47.1	6.8	0.2
National issues	38.4	52.5	8.3	0.8
International issues	27.6	49.7	19.1	3.6

theory is that political values are directly related to the level of economic development: as societies become more prosperous (and relatedly, more urban and better educated), people in these societies become less willing to accept an authoritarian regime and are more likely to support democratic change.[33] Following this argument, we expect that the local level of economic development should influence private entrepreneurs' political activities, with those in more developed regions being more likely to be active. We also include dummy variables for the five provinces in our study to capture local contextual factors not captured by GDP alone.

Multivariate Analyses

To test the hypotheses regarding the impact of the independent variables specified above, we ran a multivariate regression for each of the four types of political participation (i.e., voting in local PC elections, direct action, supporting academic activities, and indirect action). In general, the results of the regressions support our hypotheses.

Voting.   The findings presented in Table 6.7 reveal several key points. First, the importance of party membership in voting behavior is huge: 77.69 percent of CCP members voted, compared with only 52.95 percent of nonmembers; in other words, CCP members are about 50 percent more likely to vote. This reflects the CCP's ability to mobilize its members for political participation. ACFIC members were also more likely to vote; because the ACFIC is under the jurisdiction of the CCP's United Front Department, it may similarly mobilize its members to vote. Those who are PC/PPCC deputies are also more likely to vote and for the same reason: they will be expected to vote in local elections to show their involvement in and support for the political system. Membership in self-organized business associations, in contrast, has a negative coefficient, as expected, but is not statistically significant. These organizations are not created to support the state and do not mobilize their members to vote. The importance of political embeddedness as a determinant of voting reinforces the hypothesis that voting is not motivated by democratic support; instead, it is a means of expressing regime support.

Both the respondents' evaluation of the government's policy performance and their interest in current affairs are positively correlated with voting, but democratic values are not. This may seem surprising, because voting is seen as the sine qua non of a democratic political system. However, in nondemocratic systems, voting often takes on a different meaning.

Table 6.7   Determinants of Voting among China's Private Entrepreneurs

	b	*SE*	β
Political embeddedness			
CCP member	0.147***	0.026	0.144
PC/PPCC deputy	0.205***	0.028	0.194
ACFIC member	0.084**	0.026	0.085
Self-organized business association member	−0.035	0.025	−0.035
Subjective values			
Democratic values	0.000	0.003	0.001
Government's policy performance	0.006**	0.002	0.076
Interest in current affairs	0.023***	0.007	0.082
Individual and firm characteristics			
Age	0.006***	0.002	0.097
Gender	0.003	0.036	0.002
Education	−0.046**	0.017	−0.069
Firm size (fixed assets)	−0.011	0.008	−0.041
Local economic and political context[a]			
Level of development (per capita GDP)	0.004***	0.001	0.125
Jiangsu	−0.012	0.037	−0.011
Zhejiang	0.252***	0.037	0.206
Fujian	0.034	0.042	0.024
Guangdong	−0.007	0.039	−0.006
Constant	−0.129	0.122	
No. of observations	1,553		
R^2	0.194		
Adjusted R^2	0.186		

[a] Shandong is used as the base category for comparison; each of the other provinces is a dummy variable.
**$p < .01$ ***$p < .001$

As mentioned above, studies in China and other nondemocratic countries have found that democratic values are not correlated with voting and in some cases are even negatively correlated. In short, the finding from our survey is consistent with previous research.

Among the individual characteristics used as control variables, our survey provides mixed results for our predictions. As expected, age is positively correlated with voting—older people are more likely to vote, all else being equal. However, men were not more likely to vote than women. More surprising, the level of education was significantly but negatively correlated with voting: those with high levels of education were less likely vote to than other respondents.[34] This suggests that (when other variables are held constant) those who are better educated recognize the limited effectiveness of voting as a form of political activity and therefore choose not to do so. The size of the firm was not statistically significant.

Contextual factors made a notable difference. Consistent with the expectations of modernization theory, capitalists in the more prosperous areas were most likely to vote. This is a curious finding because it seems to contradict our earlier argument that democratic supporters tend either to ignore or to boycott elections. The basic logic of modernization theory is that economic development leads to democratic support among people. Accordingly, those who are from more economically developed areas should have higher support for democracy and therefore be less likely to vote in nondemocratic elections, such as those in China. But here we find that the level of development does influence the likelihood of voting, even though democratic values do not (democratic values are not statistically significant even when the level of development and provincial dummies are left out of the model). In addition, capitalists in Zhejiang were much more likely to have voted in the previous election than were capitalists in the other four provinces included in our survey (coefficients for Zhejiang and the other three provinces listed in the model are relative to the fifth province in our survey, Shandong). In fact, being from Zhejiang was the single largest determinant of voting, as seen by the beta coefficient. More research will be needed to find out why voting is so common among Zhejiang's capitalists.

However, when we examine the respondents' satisfaction with outcome of the election, a different story emerges. Most explanatory variables have the same impact on both voting and satisfaction with results, but the impact of democratic values is distinctive. Although democratic values are not a motive for the act of voting, they are strongly and negatively correlated with the degree of satisfaction with results (see Table 6.8). As expected in a nondemocratic setting, those with more democratic values are less likely to be satisfied with the results of these semicompetitive elections. Ironically, this is true regardless of whether the respondent voted: in either case, democratic values were negatively correlated with satisfaction with results. This is a crucial finding, for it suggests that those with democratic values are not satisfied with the results of these local elections. Rather than seeing voting as a legitimate and meaningful form of political participation, capitalists with democratic values may become cynical with the experience of local elections and may even be more inclined to engage in other types of political activities in order to act on their beliefs.

The large, negative, and statistically significant coefficient for Guangdong is also noteworthy: capitalists in Guangdong were not only the least

Table 6.8   Satisfaction with Outcome of Most Recent Election

	b	SE	β
Political embeddedness			
CCP member	0.154***	0.040	0.095
PC/PPCC deputy	0.223***	0.044	0.133
ACFIC member	0.115**	0.041	0.073
Self-organized business association member	−0.042	0.038	−0.026
Subjective values			
Democratic values	−0.027***	0.005	−0.123
Government's policy performance·	0.031***	0.003	0.246
Interest in current affairs	0.060***	0.011	0.134
Individual and firm characteristics			
Age	0.001	0.003	0.011
Gender	−0.179	0.056	−0.007
Education	−0.022	0.027	−0.021
Firm size (fixed assets)	−0.029*	0.012	−0.066
Local economic and political context[a]			
Level of development (per capita GDP)	0.002	0.001	0.030
Jiangsu	−0.016	0.058	−0.009
Zhejiang	−0.029	0.058	−0.015
Fujian	0.003	0.067	0.001
Guangdong	−0.217***	0.061	−0.116
Constant	1.529***	0.191	
No. of observations	1,526		
R^2	0.235		
Adjusted R^2	0.227		

[a] Shandong is used as the base category for comparison; each of the other provinces is a dummy variable.

$*p < .05$ $**p < .01$ $***p < .001$

likely to vote (44 percent compared with 66 percent in other provinces) but also the least likely to be satisfied with the results (29 percent compared with 61 percent). Given Guangdong's reputation for political apathy, the low level of voting comes as no surprise, but the strong negative evaluation of the outcome indicates a large degree of dissatisfaction rather than indifference.

Direct Action.   As noted above, direct action is similar to voting in that both involve relatively high levels of state control. As a result, the explanatory variables have a similar impact on direct action as they do on voting (see Table 6.9). The most important variables are measures of political embeddedness. The coefficients for CCP members, ACFIC members,

Table 6.9   Determinants of Direct Action

	b	SE	β
Political embeddedness			
CCP member	0.301***	0.074	0.106
PC/PPCC deputy	0.780***	0.081	0.262
ACFIC member	0.335***	0.073	0.122
Self-organized business association member	0.032	0.070	0.011
Subjective values			
Democratic values	−0.002	0.010	−0.005
Government's policy performance	−0.016*	0.006	−0.063
Interest in current affairs	0.081***	0.020	0.104
Individual and firm characteristics			
Age	0.001	0.005	0.004
Gender	0.158	0.102	0.038
Education	−0.078	0.050	−0.042
Firm size (fixed assets)	0.076***	0.022	0.096
Local economic and political context[a]			
Level of development (per capita GDP)	0.003	0.002	0.028
Jiangsu	−0.322**	0.105	−0.101
Zhejiang	0.292**	0.107	0.085
Fujian	0.437***	0.121	0.110
Guangdong	0.008	0.110	0.002
Constant	−0.112	0.347	
No. of observations	1,442		
R^2	0.211		
Adjusted R^2	0.208		

[a] Shandong is used as the base category for comparison; each of the other provinces is a dummy variable.

*$p < .05$ **$p < .01$ ***$p < .001$

and PC/PPCC deputies are all positive and statistically significant.[35] In a stepwise regression (not shown here), three-quarters of the explained variance is accounted for by political embeddedness. Membership in self-organized business associations is not correlated with direct action when other variables are controlled for, just as it was not a significant predictor of voting.

Among subjective values, our prediction that democratic values would not be correlated with direct action is borne out by the data. This result also reinforces our hypothesis that these types of political activities are not motivated by democratic support; instead, they provide those who are embedded with a channel to address political as well as nonpolitical issues. Evaluation of the government's policy performance is negatively correlated with direct action, as would be expected: if the government was doing its job, the capitalists in the survey would not have had to contact government officials or PC delegates, lobby the government, or take it upon themselves to solve local problems collectively.

Among the control variables, firm size was positively correlated with direct action; that is, larger firms have both the means and incentive to engage in either individual or collective action. The local context is also a significant factor: although the level of development per se is not a predictor of direct action, there is great variation among the five provinces in our study, with direct action being more likely in Zhejiang and Fujian than in Shandong (the reference point for the provincial dummy variables), less likely in Jiangsu, and about equally likely in Guangdong.

Just as democratic values were not correlated with the act of voting but were negatively correlated with satisfaction with the outcome, so too did they have the same impact on direct action. As noted above, democratic values were not a significant factor in predicting who would engage in direct action, but these values are correlated with whether people were satisfied with the outcome of the action. In separate regressions for each of the four types of contacting behavior (contacting government officials, contacting delegates, lobbying, and engaging in collective action), the coefficient is negative, meaning that those with democratic values are more likely to be dissatisfied.[36] For three types of contacting (contacting officials, contacting PC/PPCC deputies, and lobbying), the coefficient is both negative and statistically significant.

Not surprisingly, the strongest predictor of satisfaction is whether a respondent holds a post in the PC and/or PPCC. For all four types of direct action, the coefficient for "PC/PPCC deputy" is always positive and always statistically significant. A main motivation for becoming a deputy in the first place is that it gives individuals regular access to other officials and makes them more likely to be successful in their contacting and lobbying activities. According to our survey data, this strategy is generally successful: being a PC/PPCC deputy is the single most important predictor of who engages in direct action and also explains who is most satisfied with the outcome.

Support for Academic Activities.   Because support for academic activities is a more politically motivated action than either voting or direct action, and because it is initiated by the capitalists themselves and not controlled by the government, the determinants of academic support are also quite different. The key measures of political embeddedness—being a CCP member and/or PC/PPCC deputy—are not statistically significant.

Instead, membership in business associations, both the officially sponsored ACFIC and self-organized associations, has a positive and statistically significant impact (see Table 6.10). It is little surprise that members of self-organized associations are more likely to support academic activities, since these associations are created to fill voids not addressed by the state or official business associations. However, it is noteworthy that members of the ACFIC are also more likely than nonmembers to support academic activities, since the ACFIC is a state-organized business association, even though membership is voluntary.[37] Support for academic activities by ACFIC members is not totally surprising, however. ACFIC members are typically more prosperous than other entrepreneurs and can therefore afford to offer such support. Moreover, ACFIC membership

Table 6.10 Determinants of Academic Support

	b	SE	β
Political embeddedness			
CCP member	0.045	0.038	0.032
PC/PPCC deputy	0.068	0.041	0.047
ACFIC member	0.109**	0.038	0.079
Self-organized business association member	0.102**	0.036	0.074
Subjective values			
Democratic values	0.017***	0.005	0.090
Government's policy performance	−0.001	0.003	−0.007
Interest in current affairs	0.053***	0.010	0.135
Individual and firm characteristics			
Age	0.002	0.002	0.023
Gender	−0.006	0.053	−0.003
Education	0.116***	0.026	0.127
Firm size (fixed assets)	0.01	0.011	0.026
Local economic and political context[a]			
Level of development (per capita GDP)	0.002	0.001	0.034
Jiangsu	0.037	0.055	0.023
Zhejiang	0.044	0.055	0.026
Fujian	0.016	0.063	0.008
Guangdong	0.031	0.058	0.019
Constant	−0.811***	0.182	
No. of observations	1,499		
R^2	0.105		
Adjusted R^2	0.096		

[a] Shandong is used as the base category for comparison; each of the other provinces is a dummy variable.

** $p < .01$ *** $p < .001$

is also used as a stepping stone for membership in PCs and PPCCs, as described in Chapter 5. Providing support for academic activities may be an effort to show their public spiritedness.

Whereas democratic values were not predictors of voting or direct action, they are for academic support. This fits our prediction: because academic support is more politically motivated and less controlled by the state, it is more likely to be influenced by individuals with stronger democratic values. Interest in current affairs is also a strong predictor of academic support. Among the control variables, only education is a significant factor: the higher a person's education, the more likely he or she was to support academic activities. Those with a college education were almost twice as likely to provide academic support as capitalists with lower levels of education. This is consistent with the anecdotal observation above that capitalists who support academic activities are themselves relatively well educated.

In our survey, we did not ask whether respondents were satisfied with the outcome of the academic activities they supported, so cannot analyze this question the same way we did for satisfaction with voting and direct action. This is not too much of a missed opportunity, though. Support for academic activities is of necessity a long-term project, and expecting immediate returns is unrealistic. But as a way of identifying potential "agents of change" among China's private entrepreneurs, support for academic activities may be a useful indicator.

Indirect Action.   Because of the small number of respondents who have contacted the media or submitted petitions, we use a more restricted regression model, dropping the less theoretically interesting explanatory and control variables. Given the rarity of engaging in indirect action, our findings are tentative but nonetheless intriguing. First of all, party membership is not a significant factor in predicting who will choose to engage in indirect action, but membership in self-organized business associations is (see Table 6.11). Indirect action involves less state control than does voting and direct action, where party membership and other indicators of political embeddedness were positive and significant factors. Membership in self-organized business associations, in contrast, is a significant factor for political activities that involve less state control: academic support and indirect action.

Similarly, democratic values were not a significant predictor of who participates in the activities that are highly state controlled (i.e., voting and direct action), but they are a positive and significant factor for predicting indirect action, just as they were for predicting academic support.

Table 6.11   Determinants of Indirect Action

	b	SE	β
Political embeddedness			
CCP member	0.019	0.023	0.022
Self-organized business association member	0.093***	0.022	0.110
Subjective values			
Democratic values	0.006*	0.003	0.053
Individual and firm characteristics			
Age	−0.002	0.001	−0.037
Gender	−0.047	0.032	−0.036
Education	−0.002	0.016	−0.003
Firm size (fixed assets)	−0.017*	0.007	−0.069
Local economic and political context [a]			
Level of development (per capita GDP)	0.003***	0.001	0.092
Constant	0.217**	0.082	
No. of observations	1,569		
R^2	0.029		
Adjusted R^2	0.024		

[a] Shandong is used as the base category for comparison; each of the other provinces is a dummy variable.

*$p<.05$ **$p<.01$ ***$p<.001$

Both of these kinds of activities are less controlled by the state and therefore more influenced by individual initiative and political beliefs.

Among the control variables, only the size of the firm is a significant factor, in this case a negative one: all else being equal, smaller firms are more likely to engage in indirect action than large ones. This is consistent with the general wisdom on petitioning: it is the last resort for those with few other resources. Larger firms have more economic resources at their disposal, provide more tax revenue, and supply more jobs; therefore, they are more likely to have other means of asserting their interests and are less likely to rely on indirect action. The local level of development is positive and significant: indirect action is more common in relatively prosperous communities.

We cannot analyze satisfaction with the results of indirect action the way we did with voting and direct action, again because the small numbers make for inconclusive results. Using difference of means as a minimal test, we find that those who were satisfied with the results of contacting the media and submitting individual and collective petitions have lower scores on the democratic values index, but the difference is statistically significant only for contacting the media ($p < .001$). This is generally consistent with other political activities: those with higher democratic values are less likely to be satisfied with the outcome of their political actions, regardless of whether it involves voting, direct action, or indirect action.

Implications and Conclusion

For democrats among China's capitalists, opportunities for engaging the state are consistently frustrating. The experience of capitalists unsuccessfully working through formal channels may lead to what Mary Gallagher refers to as "informed disenchantment": the creation of people knowledgeable about how the formal channels are supposed to work but disenchanted by their inadequacy in practice.[38] This personal experience in the inadequacy of China's formal political institutions may produce more cynicism and an inclination to adopt other informal and unconventional means to pursue their interests.

Democratic values are not a significant factor influencing the most common forms of political behavior (i.e., voting and direct action) among China's capitalists. These forms of behavior are not seen as adequate or effective channels to promote democracy and democratization in China's political context. As a result, prodemocratic values do not influence these forms of activities. Instead, they are primarily determined by types of political embeddedness, especially being a CCP member and a PC/PPCC deputy. However, democratic values do influence people's assessment of (i.e., their satisfaction or dissatisfaction with) the results of these activities. We cannot separate cause and effect on this question. It may be that dissatisfaction with the results of voting and direct action creates democratic values among these disappointed individuals. It may also be that democratic values predispose people to be dissatisfied with these nondemocratic activities. Regardless of the causality, one of the clear and consistent findings of our study is that the capitalists with democratic orientations are less likely to be satisfied with the results of their political activities than are others.

Democratic values do influence other forms of political activity—support for academic activities and indirect action—that do not directly engage the state but may be more oriented toward political change. For example, financial support for research, publications, and conferences takes on a political significance in China's nondemocratic political environment that is not found in other settings. The motives behind this form of political activity are also different from those underlying voting and direct action, as examined in this chapter. Here, democratic values have a positive and statistically significant influence on this somewhat unconventional and indirect form of political behavior. In addition, democratic values also influence indirect political action—contacting the media and petitioning the state. These are much less common forms of behavior, but capitalists with democratic values are not only more likely to undertake indirect action but also more likely to be dissatisfied with the results of their action.

In short, our findings suggest that China's capitalists are politically active in a variety of ways but that the most common forms of political activities are not motivated by democratic ideals, are not designed to pursue political change, and are most likely to favor those with strong political connections. The types of activities that are motivated by democratic norms are less common, less directly engage the state, and—at least for academic support—have long-term goals rather than immediate expectations of success. This is the dilemma faced by many in China: those who most directly engage the state are not inclined to seek political change, and those who seek political change do not directly engage the state. Under these circumstances, finding capitalists who are inclined to be agents of political change remains a daunting challenge.

CHAPTER SEVEN

Conclusion: Findings and Implications

THROUGHOUT THIS BOOK, we have focused our analysis on three critical questions regarding the role of China's capitalists in political change and democratization: Do capitalists support fundamental political change toward democracy in China? Why do or do they not support such a change? And how do their political attitudes—such as those toward the party-state and toward democracy—and their institutional connections with the party-state influence their political activities? These questions are crucial for understanding the potential for political change in China. Our answers to these important questions have been developed based on our analysis of the unique set of data collected from a representative-sample survey of private entrepreneurs in five provinces that have the most developed private economy and over 70 percent of the country's private entrepreneurs. In this last chapter, we highlight the major findings from our analysis and then elucidate the key theoretical and political implications of these findings.

Political Connections, Attitudes, and Behavior

Degrees of Political Embeddedness

In studying the impact of private entrepreneurs on China's political system, our starting assumption has been that the party-state in China plays a critical role in influencing private entrepreneurs' attitudinal and behavioral orientations toward democracy, and the state plays this role often through its strong connections with entrepreneurs. Given this emphasis on the role of the state, our analysis of the data collected from the five-province survey was first focused on capitalists' institutional ties with the state. In this book, we explored two dimensions of the institutional connections between the party-state and capitalists. One dimension deals with the internal institutional inclusion of private entrepreneurs into the party-state, which is reflected in entrepreneurs' memberships within the party and governmental institutions at various levels. We have found that among all respondents in our survey, nearly 38 percent were "red capitalists," meaning that they were CCP members; about 10 percent of these party members were recruited after Jiang Zemin's "July 1 Speech" of 2001, which formally endorsed the CCP's inclusion of private entrepreneurs into the party, ending a formal ban that had been in place since the end of the popular protests of 1989. In terms of private entrepreneurs' memberships in various governmental institutions, 18 percent of them were deputies to either the NPC or PCs at subnational levels, while about 21 percent of private entrepreneurs in our sample were members of either the CPPCC or its subnational branches. These figures represent one key dimension of the party-state's efforts to integrate itself with the private sector and to incorporate private entrepreneurs into China's formal political institutions.

The other institutional connection between the party-state and the private sector concerns external institutional links, which are mainly manifested as memberships in two types of business organizations: government-sanctioned organizations and self-organized organizations. The two main official business associations are the All-China Federation of Industry and Commerce (ACFIC) and the Private Enterprises Association (PEA). Both of them are national umbrella organizations with local chapters throughout the country. These official associations get their budgets and main personnel from the CCP or the government and are designed to serve as bridges between the state and business. They incorporate most capitalists, at least in terms of formal membership. Among the capitalists in our survey, about 78 percent belonged to the ACFIC and/or PEA. In contrast, a much smaller share of our respondents—only about 39 percent—belonged to some kind of self-organized organization.[1] These organizations are normally industry specific and limited to one locality or another, rather than having vertical or horizontal ties with other similar organizations, as do the ACFIC and the PEA. Although they are self-organized, they are not completely autonomous. Many of them also have affiliations with the local state, and most of their members also belong to the official business associations. Only 19 percent of the capitalists in our survey were outside the reach of the state, in that they did not belong to any business association, whether officially sponsored or self-organized. Just as China's party-state actively incorporated capitalists into the political system, so too has it created a range of external institutions to link itself to the private sector.

Our analysis of political embeddedness showed that membership in the CCP and official business associations closely reflected the party-state's strategy for integrating itself with the private sector. First of all, the growth in the percentage of red capitalists increased steadily in the 1990s, as did the CCP's support for the private sector as a whole. Second, red capitalists tend to operate the largest firms. This is similar to the CCP's "grasp the large, release the small" *(zhuada, fangxiao)* strategy toward SOE reform: the CCP targets the largest firms because they have the most workers and contribute the most toward economic growth rates and tax revenues. To some extent, targeting these kinds of firms is a more efficient means of integrating the CCP and the private sector. Third, the CCP favors capitalists who have previous connections with the party-state—for instance, former party and government officials and SOE managers. These previous ties not only are assets in business; they also suggest that the private sector in China is not likely to be a source of political change because so many of the leading beneficiaries of economic reform came out of the state sector. Fourth, the different indicators of political embeddedness overlap to a remarkable degree. They are nested and cumulative rather than discrete and independent indicators. For capitalists who aspire to government posts, joining the CCP and the official business associations is an important precondition. In short, the CCP has devised a coherent strategy for integrating capitalists into the political elite. The increased presence of capitalists in China's formal political institutions is not simply driven by capitalists' desire for representation; more important, it is the consequence of the CCP's initiatives. Rather than seeing political embeddedness as an indicator of democratization, we believe it more accurate to regard it as an indicator of the CCP's strategy of selective inclusion.

The Level and Determinants of Democratic Support

Second, we have explored entrepreneurs' attitudes toward democratic values and institutions. We have found that while most private entrepreneurs are in favor of multicandidate elections under the current one-party system, they are not eager to support and participate in fundamental political change toward a democratic system characterized by multiparty competition and political liberties (e.g., the right to demonstrate and to form nongovernmental organizations). These findings, as mentioned earlier, confirm some earlier studies by both U.S.-based scholars[2] and China-based scholars,[3] suggesting that China's capitalists tend to be more conservative and status quo oriented and hence are less likely to serve as agents of democratization in China. Although our conclusions are similar, we believe that our measurements for democratic support are more valid and more reliable. This is because (1) these measurements directly gauge different dimensions of democracy rather than rely on indirect inferences, (2) they rely on multiple measures of each dimension of democratic support instead of abstract and thin indicators of the concept, and (3) they rely on theoretical frameworks developed in earlier studies of democratic support in various sociopolitical settings.

In terms of the main determinants of democratic support among private entrepreneurs, we have found that the private entrepreneurs' financial and value connections with the state and their evaluation of government policy significantly influence their attitudinal orientation toward democracy. Specifically, our study found that private entrepreneurs were less supportive of democracy if they received loans from state-controlled banks, strongly believed in the state's leadership role in economic and political reforms, highly evaluated the government's policy performance, or perceived the pace of political reform to be appropriate (or too fast). All these findings support one of the central hypotheses we established in Chapter 1—that is, the closer the affinity between capitalists and the state, the less enthusiastic they will be about democracy and democratization. However, we also found a surprising result: the direct institutional ties between the party-state and the private entrepreneurs had little if any impact on their level of democratic support. Furthermore, it should be noted that among all four types of relationships analyzed in this study (i.e., financial, institutional, value, and policy evaluation), the value connections between the state and private entrepreneurs (measured by entrepreneurs' support for the state's leading role in initiating reforms, their approval of the pace of political reform, and their satisfaction with government's policy performance) exerted the most influential impact on capitalists' attitudes toward democracy.

Variation in Levels of Regime Support

Third, closely related to private entrepreneurs' support for democracy, we have also examined their attitudinal orientation directly toward the CCP regime. Our findings revealed that a clear majority of our respondents strongly supported the current political regime. Specifically, they supported the fundamental values and key political institutions of the CCP regime. These findings in general are consistent with those from a variety of empirical studies that suggest that most of China's private entrepreneurs tend to be supportive of the party-state and in favor of the status quo.[4] However, our findings offer a more systematic and detailed account of the factors that determine the level of regime support among China's private entrepreneurs. We have found that several subjective values are the most important factors influencing such support—that is, life satisfaction and approval of governmental policy performance enhance regime support, while support for democratic values/institutions and discontent with corruption undermine it. Moreover, among these subjective values, support for democratic values/institutions serves as the most powerful variable explaining capitalists' support for the CCP regime. In other words, our findings suggest that most of China's new capitalists support the CCP regime mainly because they do not believe that democracy is the political system they prefer or need.

One of the key findings of our study has not been appreciated by previous studies: most indicators of political embeddedness do not produce significantly higher levels of regime support when other variables are held constant. This finding is particularly surprising given the CCP's determined efforts to integrate capitalists into the political system and link the party and the private sector with institutional ties. But only one group of red capitalists had a significantly higher level of regime support when other variables were held constant: those who formerly had worked as party and government officials. We would expect these ties to generate increased regime support, and they do. What is surprising, however, is that the other types of red capitalists, namely, former SOE managers and rank-and-file party members, do not have significantly higher levels of regime support compared with non–party members. Other indicators of political embeddedness, such as membership in the official business associations and acting as deputies in local PCs and PPCCs, also do not produce higher levels of regime support when other variables are held constant. Instead, it is the political beliefs of capitalists that are the strongest determinates of regime support.

Another novel finding from our study concerns the regional variation in regime support. Part of the folk wisdom of Chinese politics is that political support is highest in Beijing and tapers off in regions farther away from the capital. We found more specific evidence for this view when we measured the level of regime support among the capitalists in our survey. Regime support was highest in Shandong, the northernmost province in our study, and declined steadily farther south. From our available data, we could not determine whether the cause of this variation was cultural (for instance, if different provinces had distinct political cultures that influenced levels of regime support), structural (for instance, if greater interaction with the international economy reduced dependence on the state and therefore lowered regime support among private entrepreneurs), or due to some other factor. The importance of regional variation on levels of regime support demonstrates the importance of the multisite research design we employed in our study and improves upon findings that are based on single-location and potentially idiosyncratic case studies. Further research will be necessary to answer why this pattern exists.

Political Activities of China's Capitalists: Motives and Reactions

Finally, in this study, we have explored various forms of private entrepreneurs' political participation and the impact of both their political embeddedness and democratic support on these participatory forms. Whereas previous studies of China's capitalists have explored lobbying activities, participation within formal institutions, and strategies for coping with and avoiding the state,[5] we focused on a wider variety of available avenues for interacting with the state and offered a more systematic explanation of the motivations and results of capitalists' political activities. We have identified four distinct clusters of political activities in which China's private entrepreneurs engage. These four clusters include (1) voting in local PC elections, (2) direct action (contacting officials and engaging in collective action), (3) indirect action (contacting the media and submitting petitions), and (4) supporting academic activities. In the current context of the Chinese political system, the first two clusters of participation (i.e., voting in local elections and direct action) have been more tightly controlled by the party-state, and hence they have not been deemed by citizens (including private entrepreneurs) as channels to promote democracy. Instead, their purpose is to demonstrate support for the status quo by voting for officially approved candidates in local elections and by seeking cooperation with incumbent officials. Accordingly, these are the most common forms of political activities among China's capitalists. In contrast, the other two clusters (i.e., indirect action and supporting academic activities) are less scrutinized by the state, and hence these channels provide citizens with some limited opportunities to express democratic views.

Due to this variation in the state's control over various forms of popular participation, levels of democratic support among China's capitalists have variable impact on these forms. Democratic support does not significantly affect which capitalists vote in local PC elections, contact officials, or engage in collective action. The capitalists in our study did not consider these channels as suitable participatory forms to facilitate democracy because they are so heavily controlled by the state. In contrast, democratic values do have a significant influence on political activities that are not as strongly controlled by the state. Democratic supporters among private entrepreneurs are more likely to express and promote their democratic views by contacting the media, submitting petitions, and supporting academic activities. Whether or not attitudes toward democracy have a significant effect on whether a person engages in a type of political activity, democratic values do influence satisfaction with the participation. For all types of political activities, democratic supporters were less satisfied with the results of their action than were capitalists with weaker democratic values.

In sum, the findings of our study strongly and consistently suggest that China's capitalists *as a whole* do not support democracy, but instead they strongly support the current CCP regime. More important, our findings illuminate the individual factors that influence levels of both democratic support and regime support. Thus, the capitalists are not likely to support a fundamental political change toward democracy in China, at least not in the near future. In order for China's capitalists to become agents of change, their orientation toward the party-state and their core political values would have to undergo substantial change. What political and theoretical implications do these findings have? This important question will be addressed in the next section.

Theoretical and Political Implications

The literature on the role of economic change in democratization falls into two broad categories. The first is based on modernization theory and suggests that more prosperous countries are more likely to be democratic.[6] Economic modernization is said to have both endogenous and exogenous effects on democracy. On the one hand, the conventional wisdom is that as countries become prosperous, they will also become democratic. This is the perspective that has had the largest influence on U.S. foreign policy toward developing countries and has also led some to predict that China will become democratic at a point in the not-too-distant future.[7] This endogenous theory of democratization has been empirically challenged for the post–World War II time period, even though it does seem to have greater explanatory power for the first and second waves of democracy.[8] On the other hand, the second aspect of modernization theory is exogenous: countries may become democratic at any level of development, but prosperous countries will be more likely to remain democratic. This aspect of modernization theory seems to apply to all three waves of democratization, although it has had less influence than the endogenous version on the thinking of scholars and policy makers.

Our study cannot determine whether China's experience is consistent with either variant of modernization theory for the simple reason that it is not yet democratic, but our study does shed light on some of the causal mechanisms behind the endogenous variant. We have shown that democratic values are not correlated with the level of economic development in the areas covered by our survey, nor are they correlated with individual levels of education. These are two of the important components of modernization, but in the case of China's capitalists they do not have the predicted effects. The level of development does influence the likelihood of voting, but as we noted in Chapter 6 and above, voting is not seen as a prodemocratic form of behavior in China's political system. In short, our findings do not support the endogenous dimension of modernization theory.

The second category of research on development and democracy concerns social classes. Much of this literature has focused on the impact of capitalists as promoters of or obstacles to democracy. Barrington Moore's seminal work was the source of one of the most well-known hypotheses in the social sciences: "no bourgeois, no democracy." More recent research, however, has shown that capitalists are not inherently or inevitably prodemocratic but more often cooperate with nondemocratic rulers. As Bellin argues, capitalists may come to be champions of democracy but for contingent reasons and not by universal dictum.[9] Whether they support the perpetuation of authoritarian rule or shift to the side of other prodemocratic actors is contingent on their relationships with the state and with other social classes—particularly labor—and their fear of political instability. The particular conditions of late development—especially the strong role of the state in leading economic development—may dampen capitalists' enthusiasm for democratization, but there is also the possibility of democratic enthusiasm as conditions in late-developing countries change.

Instead of viewing Chinese capitalists in terms of their class interests, we find that it is more useful to weigh their relations with the state. The Chinese case is different from most other cases of privatization in communist and postcommunist countries. The Chinese government is more embedded in the private sector because so many capitalists came out of the state. Although many of Russia's richest businessmen also came out of the state sector, they were few in number and hence acquired the nick-name "oligarchs." The distinctive feature of China's case is how wide-spread this practice was. Unlike the Russian case, there was no concentra-tion of wealth in the hands of just a few early winners in the privatization process; instead, the beneficiaries of reform in China have been remark-ably numerous.[10] As we showed in Chapter 2, most of China's capitalists previously worked for the party-state, some as SOE managers or work-ers, others as party and government officials. Moreover, the CCP has ac-tively encouraged its members to go into business and has strategically co-opted new members from among the successful capitalists. This social and professional background of China's capitalists dampens their sup-port for democracy for multiple reasons. First, their membership in the CCP provides tangible benefits in business but brings their political ac-tivities under greater scrutiny. Second and relatedly, membership in the CCP (and to a lesser extent the official business associations) involves some degree of secondary socialization as they are required to engage in political study and attend party meetings. They may not fully internalize these messages, but they nevertheless are understandably reluctant to publicly display viewpoints and behaviors that are inconsistent with the party line. Third, their self-interest may lead them to identify with and support the current regime. To the extent that their business success is dependent on good relations with and easy access to local officials, they will be less inclined to see the benefits of regime change. It is hard to speak of class conflict of the kind Moore saw where there is so much overlap between the state and capitalists in China.

While our general finding and that of other scholars is that most of China's capitalists are not strong proponents of democracy, it is also true that some of them clearly do have prodemocratic values and that their political activities are influenced by those values. This was first evi-denced in the 1989 demonstrations, when Wan Runnan and a variety of *getihu* supported the demonstrators with money, food, and materials. More recently, capitalists have provided financing for academic research, conferences, and publications in order to foster public discussion of sociopolitical issues, ranging from the relatively innocuous (such as the examination system) to the potentially transformational (such as consti-tutional governance). Future research will be needed to better understand their interest in politically salient topics and to assess the impact of these activities.

Further research will also be necessary to answer two other important questions for which we lack adequate data. First, are current levels of (low) democratic support and (high) regime support among China's capitalists rising, falling, or stable? Second, are their political views and behaviors distinctive from other social groups? Both of these questions are essential for determining the ultimate political impact of privatization in China. Unfortunately, we have no way of providing definitive answers at present, since our data are based on a cross-sectional survey at one point in time and limited to private entrepreneurs (rather than both private entrepreneurs and other social classes).

Although earlier studies have looked at the political attitudes of private entrepreneurs in China, we cannot compare our findings with these prior results to determine trends over time. Other studies used different and indirect questions, often inferring respondents' beliefs rather than measuring and analyzing them directly. However, in different ways, the many studies of China's capitalists all indicate that they are supportive of the status quo and not inclined to challenge or change the political system that has allowed them to prosper. But knowing whether their support is waxing or waning may help us better understand the prospects for political change in China. If anything, we hope that our study can provide a benchmark for future work in this area.

How much would democratic values have to rise and regime support fall before the survival of the regime is jeopardized? In other words, is there a tipping point for political support among China's capitalists? There is no way of determining *ex ante* what level of democratic support or decline in regime support would tip the scale in favor of political change. At best, we can only put this relationship in probabilistic terms—that is, an increase in democratic values would make it more likely that regime support will decline. But what level of regime support is necessary for regime survival? There is no way to know for sure, either for us or the CCP. That is why the issue merits continued research by interested scholars and constant monitoring by the ruling party.

Another obstacle to measuring change over time is the issue of "preference falsification," in which people deny their true preferences in public.[11] For our study, the very issue of measuring political support for both the political institutions and current policies in China (what Easton called "diffuse" and "specific" support, respectively) merits special attention. If respondents are not truthful, for instance, if they give what they believe are the "correct" answers instead of their actual beliefs, then the analysis of their responses can be suspect. Asking questions about political issues in an authoritarian regime can be quite sensitive, and we tried to devise questions that would accurately measure democratic and regime support, on the one hand, and also yield a high response rate, on the other. To address this problem, we utilized multiple questions to measure each of these core concepts. While the cumulative responses indicated low support for democracy and high support for the regime, they were not uniformly so. The variation in responses made it possible for us to find patterns in the relationship between variables but leaves open the question of whether they accurately measured the underlying values of our respondents. This is an inherent problem in survey research, particularly in authoritarian countries. We leave it to the reader to determine how well we have addressed the problem.

The second question that remains unanswered in our study is how well the views of China's capitalists compare with the population at large or specific social groups. Are they more conservative or more liberal than others? Although we cannot directly compare our findings regarding China's capitalists with research on the general population or other groups, our findings are similar. According to both our present study and other previous studies, support for the regime is generally high, and support for a democratic alternative is generally low.[12] We focused on private entrepreneurs not because we expected their views to be distinctive but because comparative research indicated they could be particularly influential in the course of political change. At a minimum, they could be "harbingers of democratization" (to paraphrase Margaret Pearson):[13] they may not be the instigators of democratization, but they could help determine the outcome, depending on whether they remain loyal to the regime or shift support to potential challengers. That is why studying their political attitudes and activities is so important: not just whether they directly engage the state but also whether they support the politically oriented activities of others. As we showed in Chapter 6, this is already happening, but it remains small scale and ad hoc. If these activities become more prevalent, more public, and more organized, they will become worthy of more attention.

China's Capitalists as Potential Agents of Change

The main conclusion of our study is that China's capitalists are unlikely to be agents of change because their support for the current regime is stronger than their support for an alternative democratic political system. This is not a novel finding, as most other scholars have reached the same conclusion. However, as noted above, we have added additional details and uncovered new patterns that had not been identified previously. We have also identified a variety of developments that could cause the current levels of democratic support and regime support among China's capitalists to change.

The level of regime support among China's capitalists is currently quite strong, but are there factors that would cause this to change? Our study found several factors that could have an impact. First, capitalists' regime support is highly influenced by their assessment of the government's policy performance, so a decline in that performance would also negatively impact their support for the regime. This includes not only economic factors where the government gets high marks, such as promoting the growth of private enterprises, controlling inflation, and protecting entrepreneurs' legal rights, but also broader social issues where the capitalists give more middling scores, such as medical care, welfare for the needy, and housing conditions. To the extent that regime support is contingent on the quality of the government's policy performance, then deterioration in that performance would lead to a decline in the capitalists' support.

A second factor that would diminish regime support is corruption. Among the list of twelve policy areas used to evaluate the government, capitalists rate the fight against corruption the lowest. Given this low evaluation of the government's efforts to address official corruption, it is somewhat surprising that most capitalists see the problem of corruption in their communities as getting better. Nevertheless, the acute perceptions about the prevalence and severity of corruption and the negative evaluation of the government's efforts to address the problem could also undermine regime support. Relatedly, a change in social norms regarding acceptability of corruption as a part of business, or regarding what constitutes an acceptable level of corruption, would adversely affect capitalists' support for their regime. This is a sensitive and explosive issue, since at least some capitalists are complicit in corrupt exchanges, but remains an area of concern.

Third, changes in the level of democratic support could also change regime support. We found a very strong negative relationship between democratic values and regime support, and we expect the direction of that relationship to remain stable: so long as the regime remains as it is, democrats will continue to have lower levels of regime support. However, the level of democratic support may very well fluctuate in the future, which would have a direct impact on regime support. The experience of capitalists' political activities could be one of the factors that change levels of democratic support. As we showed in Chapter 6, capitalists with stronger democratic values were less likely to be satisfied with the outcome of their political activities, regardless of whether that involved voting in local legislative elections, contacting officials or the media, or submitting petitions. If this level of dissatisfaction leads to more support for democracy, then continued political activity may reduce regime support. Tracing the kinds of political activities capitalists engage in and, more importantly, whether they are satisfied with the results of their actions may therefore give us one indicator of their potential to be agents of political change.

Finally, another precursor of a decline in regime support would involve increased political activism among capitalists in south China. We found significant regional differences in key variables such as political embeddedness, regime support, and political activities. Moreover, we found similar variation in the degree of satisfaction with political activities: for example, capitalists in Guangdong are not only less likely to vote but also less likely to be satisfied with the results of the election. Increased political activity among these disaffected capitalists may also indicate a decline of their support for the regime.

The converse of what could diminish regime support is what the CCP can do to generate regime support. In a general sense, the CCP has intended economic modernization to be a main source of legitimacy, hoping that as incomes and standards of living rise, so will popular support for the regime. This has by and large proven to be a successful strategy. Previous research has found very high levels of political support among China's urban population.[14] The 2008 Pew Global Attitudes Survey found that over 80 percent of Chinese respondents believed that the country was on the right track, and in particular that economic conditions were good, compared with only 20 percent in the United States in 2008.[15] Beyond simply maintaining high rates of growth, what else can the CCP do to maintain popular support?

One of the surprising findings of our study is that the CCP's strategy for integrating itself with the private sector has not by itself produced increased regime support among China's capitalists. Although it has co-opted successful entrepreneurs into the party, encouraged party members to go into business, and established corporatist-style business associations to provide institutional links with the private sector, these efforts have not produced an independent significant impact on regime support. Various indicators of political embeddedness, including membership in the CCP and the ACFIC, and previous ties to the state sector do not produce more regime support; the only exception to this rule was for capitalists who were former party or government officials, and even there the effect was relatively weak. The CCP will undoubtedly continue its policies of co-optation and corporatism, but doing so may have little direct impact on capitalists' support for the regime.

More important for generating regime support are subjective values. First, to maintain support, the CCP must continue to generate high levels of life satisfaction and policy support. People who are generally satisfied with their material and social status are more likely to support their regime, whether that regime is democratic or nondemocratic.[16] China's capitalists generally are highly satisfied in this regard, and the consequence is high support for the regime. Similarly, the quality of governance is strongly and positively correlated with regime support. As noted above, capitalists are generally well satisfied with the performance of the government in most policy areas. Both life satisfaction and policy evaluation are to a large extent within the CCP's ability to control. Conversely, in the long run, improved levels of life satisfaction may serve to undermine regime legitimacy as people come to expect more.[17] But the long run may be too far away to worry about. The CCP needs support now, and life satisfaction and policy evaluation are both strong sources of it.

In order to maintain support, the CCP also must limit the scale and scope of corruption. As noted above, corruption is seen by many as a necessary part of doing business, but when it becomes excessive or even predatory in nature, it will serve to undermine support for the regime and especially incumbent leaders. Corruption—and perhaps more importantly, perceptions of corruption—serve to delegitimize the party's agenda of market reforms.[18] Even among capitalists, attitudes toward corruption strongly affect regime support. This has been an issue that has concerned party leaders from the beginning of the reform era to the present, and our study offers clear and tangible evidence for why this is such a concern.

The most important subjective value for undermining regime support is its corollary: democratic support. In our multivariate analysis of regime support, democratic values had the largest impact, serving to undermine regime support. From the CCP's perspective, it can maintain the support of capitalists if it limits support for democracy among them. This could be done in several ways: continuing to provide preferential access to capitalists so that they do not seek greater transparency and accountability in the political system; maintaining pro-business, pro-growth policies that capitalists support; and defending private property rights and other business interests. Given the recent political and economic environments in China, these seem quite plausible developments.

In order to maintain the support of China's capitalists, the CCP may also be compelled to limit the shift toward populism that has been so apparent under the leadership of Hu Jintao and Wen Jiabao.[19] If this populist shift were to target in particular the capitalists, for instance by rolling back market-oriented reforms and privatization, rather than simply the unintended and illegal consequences of reform, capitalists' support for the regime would undoubtedly diminish.[20] At the same time, the CCP may choose to limit the ability of big business to organize and mobilize itself. Throughout the reform era, shifts in favor of the private sector have created not only ideological resistance within the party but also resentment among the general population. The privileged access of capitalists into the political system, the very cozy and often corrupt relationships between individual capitalists and party and government officials, and the emphasis on growth over equity and social welfare throughout the Jiang Zemin era created an eventual backlash. If capitalists were able to organize more effectively and attempt to influence the policy process more openly, the perception that interests of capital controlled the CCP would become more pronounced. Limiting the ability of business to organize and coordinate action against the state will not improve regime support among capitalists but is necessary for the CCP's image among the larger society. It also limits the capitalists' autonomy and keeps their business success to some degree dependent on the state, which in turn keeps capitalists supporting the regime and prevents support for democratic reforms. In short, the CCP must strike a balance between the pro-growth policies that favor business and the populist policies that serve those who have yet to enjoy the benefits of the reform and opening policies.

Conclusion

China's dramatic economic growth over the past three decades, driven largely by the formation and expansion of the private sector, has piqued the curiosity of many observers. While some have attempted to explain the decision-making process and the political struggle among central elites regarding the pace and direction of reform, and others have offered explanations about the economic results of the reform and opening policies, still others have concentrated on the political implications of privatization in China. Is the formation of a private sector creating new pressures for political change, a role that capitalists have played in previous cases of democratization? Can an authoritarian political system coexist with a free-market economy? The findings of our study indicate that China's capitalists are unlikely to be agents of political change; instead, they are closely tied to the regime and strongly support it. This conclusion is consistent with most previous studies of China's private entrepreneurs, whether based on single-location case studies or multiregional surveys. By relying upon a research design that captured key sources of variation, such as level of development, firm size, and industrial or commercial sector, we have been able to provide a more nuanced and also more robust analysis of the capitalists' behavioral and attitudinal relationships with the state. This approach not only established the key factors in these relationships; it also indicated contingencies that could lead to a decline in regime support and conversely a rise in support for democracy. Were that to happen, the prospects for political change in China would increase. While neither imminent nor inevitable, signs of shifting support deserve continued attention and analysis.

The relationship between the CCP and the private sector has evolved considerably throughout the reform era and will continue to do so. This relationship consists of institutional links, financial ties, personal connections, and a wide range of formal and informal political activities. The result has been an increasingly integrated, mutually reinforcing, and symbiotic relationship that has allowed the capitalists to prosper and the CCP to remain in power. As long as both sides of this relationship continue to find advantage in the other, China's capitalists are unlikely to initiate or support efforts to bring about democratic change. But our study also has found a variety of areas where the relationship could weaken and encourage capitalists to reassess their support for the current regime. As our analysis shows, attitudinal factors outweigh institutional ties in determining support for both democracy and the current regime. China's capitalists may be important allies of the state at present, but their loyalty cannot be guaranteed in the long run. Understanding the changes in this relationship will provide an important indicator of the survival of the regime as a whole and will continue to merit further study.

Research Design and Data Analysis

Survey Design

The original data presented in this book come from a survey of private entrepreneurs from five coastal provinces: Shandong, Jiangsu, Zhejiang, Fujian, and Guangdong. The survey was conducted in late 2006 and early 2007. It was funded by a grant from the National Science Foundation (SES-05550444/0550518).

The sample was designed to capture firms of different sizes and types of operations, and in areas of different levels of development. Respondents were selected with a multistage random sampling technique. In the first stage, all county-level units (counties, county-level cities, and urban districts, hereafter referred to collectively as "counties") within each province were stratified into three levels—high, medium, and low—according to their levels of economic development (measured by per capita GDP). Counties were randomly selected from each level of economic development in each province, using the probability proportional to size (PPS) technique, in which the probability of selection is proportionate to the number of private enterprises in the county. In this sampling stage, a total of forty counties were selected: fourteen, twelve, and fourteen counties, respectively, from high, medium, and low levels of economic development. In the second stage, the registered private enterprises within each selected county were grouped into industrial/commercial sectors (e.g., manufacturing, transportation, retail, and food service),[1] and then enterprises were randomly chosen from each sector, again with the probability of selection proportional to the size of the sector. A total of 2,300 enterprises were selected from the second sampling stage. At the final stage, one representative of each selected enterprise was selected. This representative had to be either the owner or one of the major investors of a selected enterprise. In this survey, a total of 2,071 questionnaires were completed, with a response rate of 90 percent (out of 2,300). In sum, these sampling procedures facilitated the selection of our sample of private entrepreneurs within the five coastal provinces, who were presumably representative of various economic development levels, diverse industrial/economic sectors, and different sized firms.

The survey questionnaire was originally designed by the coauthors in the United States. To minimize linguistic misinterpretations and unnecessary political sensitivity, the wording and content of the original questionnaire were then reviewed and modified based on consultations with our Chinese research partners, Li Lulu and Dai Jianzhong. As experts in survey research on private entrepreneurs, they had previously conducted several national and regional surveys of private entrepreneurs concerning socioeconomic and sociopolitical issues before the implementation of this survey. Subsequently, the modified questionnaire was assessed in a small pretest among private entrepreneurs of different sizes and kinds of firms. Given the results from the test, we further revised the wording and content of the questionnaire. In this round of revisions, we focused particularly on the questions that were essential to this study yet are often considered politically sensitive in China's sociopolitical environment, such as attitudes toward democracy and the current regime. On the basis of the feedback from private entrepreneurs in the pretest, we adjusted the wording of those questions so that our respondents would be more likely to offer truthful responses. We also took several steps to guarantee the validity of the revised questions, such as checking and rechecking the actual meaning of each revised question with our Chinese research partners and with individual private entrepreneurs who had participated in the pretest. As a result, the final version of the questionnaire was not only adapted to China's current political environment but also remained consistent with the theoretical issues that informed our study.

The actual survey was conducted by our research partners, Li and Dai, in cooperation with local chapters of the All-China Federation of Industry and Commerce. The involvement of the ACFIC, a government-affiliated business association, might raise concerns about the representativeness of the sample and the willingness of respondents to provide valid responses to our questions. However, the ACFIC was not involved in the selection of the sample, which was done by Li and Dai, using the sampling strategy we had agreed upon. Moreover, for a survey of this size, there is no alternative but to obtain the cooperation of local officials. For a survey of private entrepreneurs, this meant the local chapter of the AFCIC.

Before the survey, all interviewers were trained by Li and Dai, who were also in charge of the overall implementation of the survey. During the actual survey, respondents were assured of unconditional confidentiality and encouraged to provide answers that best captured their true feelings. To encourage honest and complete answers, the respondents were promised anonymity; no identifying information was recorded about any of the respondents. In general, circumstantial evidence provided by interviewers suggested that our final questionnaire, which went through several revisions as mentioned above, did not cause major concerns over political sensitivity among respondents, and therefore they felt free to express their views about issues tackled in the survey, including those related to their attitudes toward democracy and the regime.

Selected Survey Questions

In this section, we present the English and Chinese wording of the key questions in our study.

Democratic Values

Elections to governmental positions at all levels should be conducted in such a way that there is more than one candidate for each post.
各级政府的主要领导人应以差额选举的方式选出。

Elections for local government at the village level could be expanded to townships/towns and districts/counties.
农村基层政权选举可以由村扩展到乡镇和区县。

A one-party system promotes economic, social, and political development in China and is most suitable to China's current circumstances.
党政一元化领导有利于我国经济、社会、政治的发展，最适合中国的国情。

If a country has multiple parties, it can lead to political chaos.
一个国家如果有好几个政党，会导致政治混乱。

Public demonstrations can easily turn into social disturbances and impact social stability, and should be forbidden.
集会游行容易造成社会混乱和影响社会稳定，应该受到禁止。

Social harmony will be damaged if people form nongovernmental organizations.
成立各种非政府组织容易破坏社会和谐。

Government leaders are like the head of a family; we should all follow their decisions.
政府领导人就像一家之长，应该服从他们的决定。

State's Leadership Role in Economic and Political Reform

Measures to further promote political reform should be initiated by the party and government, not by society.
进一步推动政治体制改革主要是党和政府的责任，而不是老百姓。

Measures to further promote economic reform should be initiated by party and government leaders, not by society.
进一步推动经济体制改革主要是党和政府的责任，而不是老百姓。

Evaluation of the Government's Policy Performance

Controlling inflation	控制通货膨胀
Providing job security	提供就业保证
Narrowing the gap between rich and poor	缩小贫富差距
Improving housing conditions	改善住房条件
Maintaining social order	维护社会秩序
Providing adequate medical care	提供医疗保障
Tax policy	税收政策
Providing welfare to the needy	提供社会救济
Combating pollution	治理环境污染
Combating official corruption	打击贪污腐败
Protecting legal rights of private enterprises	保护私企合法权利
Policies to promote enterprise development	促进企业发展的政策

Regime Support

I believe that the Communist Party represents my interests.
我相信，共产党是代表我的利益的。

I believe that the National People's Congress represents and articulates the interests of the majority of the population.
我相信，全国人民代表大会是代表和为绝大多数人民利益服务的.

I believe that the military is capable of defending the country.
我相信，解放军能够保卫我们的祖国。

I trust that the police are able to enforce laws impartially.
我相信，我国公安机关能够公正执法。

I believe that the courts are impartial.
我相信，我国司法机关能够公正司法。

I support my country's political institutions.
我拥护我国的政治制度。

I feel that my personal values are the same as those advocated by the government.
我的观点与政府倡导的价值观是很一致的。

Corruption

Compared with the past, is corruption in your county or city

   (1) getting better
   (2) about the same
   (3) getting worse

与过去相比，腐败状况在您当地发生了怎样的变化？

   (1) 得到治理，有所改善
   (2) 与以前相比，没有什么变化
   (3) 愈演愈烈，更为糟糕

How widespread do you think corruption and bribe taking are in your county or municipal government? Would you say

(1) Very few officials are corrupt
(2) Some officials are corrupt
(3) Most officials are corrupt

您认为腐败和受贿行为在当今社会很普遍吗?

(1) 很少有干部涉及腐败和受贿行为
(2) 有一些干部涉及了腐败
(3) 大多数干部涉及了腐败

Life Satisfaction

Are you satisfied with your material life at present?
您对自己现在的物质生活满意吗?

Are you satisfied with your current social status?
您对自己现在的社会地位满意吗?

Voting Behavior

Did you vote in the most recent election for the local People's Congress?
在近一次地方人民代表的选举中,您是否参加了投票?

Were you satisfied with the outcome of the election?
您对最近一次地方人大代表选举是否满意?

Direct Action

In the past year, did you take part in the following kinds of activities? If so, were you satisfied with the results?
在过去一年里,您有下列经历吗? 如有过,结果怎样(满 意不满意)?

Contact party or government official
曾经向党和政府反映过意见。

Contact deputies to People's Congress
曾经向人大代表反映过意见。

Joined with others to try to solve some of the community's problems
和其他人一起解决社区存在的共同问题。

Joined with other firms to lobby the government
与其他企业一起向政府有关部门提出意见。

Academic Support

In recent years, which of the following activities have you engaged in?
近年来,您参加过下列活动吗?

Participate in academic activities
参加学术活动

Support the publication and distribution of newspapers, magazines, and academic journals
帮助报纸杂志、学术刊物的出版发行

Give financial support to social consulting organizations and scholars carrying out policy research
资助民间咨询机构和学者进行政策研究

Indirect Action

In the past year, did you take part in the following kinds of activities?
在过去一年里，您有下列经历吗？

(1) Sent an individual petition
个人上访。

(2) Sent a collective petition
参与群体上访。

(3) Wrote to media
给新闻媒体写过信，反映过意见。

Data Analysis

In the previous chapters, we have used ordinary least-squares (OLS) regressions to test our major theoretical hypotheses against the data from our sample survey of private entrepreneurs conducted in the five coastal provinces. Specifically, these OLS regressions have been employed to estimate the effects of the various demographic, socioeconomic, and sociopolitical variables—as independent variables—on private entrepreneurs' democratic support (see Table 4.14), regime support (see Table 5.4), and different forms of political participation (see Tables 6.7–11) as the dependent variables. Since the OLS regression statistical technique is critical for investigating these key causal relationships, it is worth shedding some light on the potential bias and actual suitability of this statistical technique for this analysis.

According to its inherent assumption, the OLS regression does not account for the potential "feedback effect"[2] of the hypothesized independent variable on the hypothesized dependent variable. As a result, estimates made with OLS regression will be biased, if the feedback effect or endogenous relationship between the hypothesized dependent and independent variables is assumed by the researcher to exist. In this case, the two-stage least-squares (2SLS) regression should be used, because it provides estimates of the effects of endogenous variables (and instrumental variables) on the dependent variable,[3] and hence it is suitable for a test of the endogenous relationship.

Theoretically, however, we do not assume in this study that there are endogenous relationships among the major dependent variables—democratic support (see Chapter 4), regime support (see Chapter 5), and political participation (see Chapter 6)—and a range of independent variables specified to explain variation in each of the dependent variables. Instead, on the basis of our theoretical assumptions as explained in the previous chapters, we have expected that each of the key independent variables independently (as opposed to endogenously) influences each of the dependent variables. In addition, since our data were collected from a cross-sectional survey conducted at one point in time, we do not have different time periods that could be used to facilitate "lagged value" of any variable,[4] the value that is typically used in a 2SLS regression to explore endogenous effects. Consequently, our data would not support an exploration of endogenous relationships among variables. All in all, given our theoretical expectations explained in the previous chapters and given the nature of our data, we believe that OLS regressions are the straightforward statistical models that are most suitable for the study presented in this book.

Notes

1. Introduction

1. Liu Jie and Tong Hao, "Private Companies Playing a Bigger Role," *China Daily*, January 29, 2008; "More Chinese Find Jobs in Private Sectors," *Xinhua*, October 6, 2007. Estimates of the size of China's private sector vary for at least two reasons. First, the Chinese government does not provide accurate and complete data on firm ownership. Second, and as a result of the first reason, different analysts use different definitions of private, sometimes a strict definition that includes only firms formally registered as private, in other cases a broader definition that includes most non-state-owned (or non-public) enterprises. For our purposes, the exact size of the private sector is less important than its political implications.

2. Jonathan Unger, "'Bridges': Private Business, the Chinese Government and the Rise of New Associations," *China Quarterly*, no. 147 (September 1996): 795–819; Christopher Earle Nevitt, "Private Business Associations in China: Evidence of Civil Society or Local State Power," *China Journal*, no. 36 (July 1996): 25–45; Margaret M. Pearson, *China's New Business Elite: The Political Consequences of Economic Reform* (Berkeley: University of California Press, 1997); David L. Wank, *Commodifying Communism: Business, Trust, and Politics in a Chinese City* (New York: Cambridge University Press, 1999); David S. G. Goodman, "The New Middle Class," in Merle Goldman and Roderick MacFarquhar, eds., *The Paradox of China's Post-Mao Reforms* (Cambridge, Mass.: Harvard University Press, 1999); Bruce J. Dickson, *Red Capitalists in China: The Party, Private Entrepreneurs, and Prospects for Political Change* (New York: Cambridge University Press, 2003); Kellee S. Tsai, *Capitalism without Democracy: The Private Sector in Contemporary China* (Ithaca, N.Y.: Cornell University Press, 2007); Bruce J. Dickson, *Wealth into Power: The Communist Party's Embrace of China's Private Sector* (New York: Cambridge University Press, 2008).

3. Seymour Martin Lipset, "Some Social Requisites of Democracy: Economic Development and Political Legitimacy," *American Political Science Review* 53, no. 1 (March 1959): 69–105; Gabriel Almond and Sidney Verba, *Civic Culture: Political Attitudes and Democracy in Five Nations* (Princeton, N.J.: Princeton University Press, 1963); Ronald Inglehart, *Modernization and Postmodernization: Cultural, Economic, and Political Change in 43 Societies* (Princeton, N.J.: Princeton University Press, 1997); Larry Diamond, *Developing Democracy: Toward Consolidation* (Baltimore: Johns Hopkins University Press, 1999).

4. Adam Przeworski and Fernando Limongi, "Modernization: Theories and Facts," *World Politics* 49, no. 2 (January 1997): 155–183; Adam Przeworski, Michael E. Alvarez, Jose Antonio Cheibub, and Fernando Limongi, *Democracy and Development: Political Institutions and Well-Being in the World, 1950–1990* (Cambridge: Cambridge University Press, 2000). See also Ross E. Burkhart and Michael A. Lewis-Beck, "Comparative Democracy: The Economic Development Thesis," *American Political Science Review* 88, no. 4 (December 1994): 903–910. Boix and Stokes present a spirited rebuttal, but their study is based mostly on first wave democracies, whereas Przeworski and Limongi focus on the period between 1950 and 1990. See Carles Boix and Susan C. Stokes, "Endogenous Democratization," *World Politics* 55, no. 4 (July 2003): 517–549.

5. Barrington Moore, Jr., *Social Origins of Dictatorship and Democracy: Lord and Peasant in the Making of the Modern World* (Boston: Beacon Press, 1996), 418.

6. Samuel P. Huntington, "Social and Institutional Dynamics of One-Party Systems," in Samuel P. Huntington and Clement H. Moore, eds., *Authoritarian Politics in Modern Society: The Dynamics of Established One-Party Systems* (New York: Basic Books, 1970), 20.

7. Eva Bellin, "Contingent Democrats: Industrialists, Labor, and Democratization in Late-Developing Countries," *World Politics*, 52, no. 2 (January 2000): 175–205.

8. Samuel P. Huntington, *The Third Wave: Democratization in the Late Twentieth Century* (Norman: Oklahoma University Press, 1991); Sylvia Maxwell and Ben Ross Schneider, eds., *Business and the State in Developing Countries* (Ithaca, N.Y.: Cornell University Press, 1997); Bellin, "Contingent Democrats"; Edmund Terence Gomez, *Political Business in East Asia* (London: Routledge, 2002).

9. See especially Bruce Gilley, *China's Democratic Future: How It Will Happen and Where It Will Lead* (New York: Columbia University Press, 2004).

10. Henry S. Rowen, "The Short March: China's Road to Democracy," *National Interest*, no. 45 (Fall 1996): 61–70; "When Will the Chinese People Be Free?" *Journal of Democracy* 18, no. 3 (July 2007): 38–62; see also the replies by Minxin Pei and Dali L. Yang in the same issue.

11. Shaohua Hu, *Explaining Chinese Democratization* (Westport, CT: Praeger, 2000).

12. Kristen Parris, "Local Initiative and National Reform: The Wenzhou Model of Development," *China Quarterly*, no. 134 (June 1993): 242–263; Gordon

White, "Democratization and Economic Reform in China," *Australian Journal of Chinese Affairs*, 31 (1994): 73–92; Gordon White, Jude Howell, and Shang Xiaoyuan, *In Search of Civil Society: Market Reform and Social Change in Contemporary China* (Oxford: Oxford University Press, 1996); Baogang He, *The Democratic Implications of Civil Society in China* (New York: St. Martin's Press, 1997).

13. Margaret Pearson, "The Janus Face of Business Associations in China: Socialist Corporatism in Foreign Enterprises," *Australian Journal of Chinese Affairs*, no. 31 (January 1994): 25–46.

14. Kellee S. Tsai, "Adaptive Informal Institutions and Endogenous Institutional Change in China," *World Politics* 59 (2006): 116–141.

15. Dickson, *Red Capitalists in China* and *Wealth into Power*.

16. For examples of criticisms, see Timothy Mitchell, "The Limits of the State: Beyond Statist Approaches and Their Critics," *American Political Science Review* 85 (1991): 77–96; Joel S. Migdal, *State in Society: Studying How Sates and Societies Transform and Constitute One Another* (New York: Cambridge University Press, 2001); Robert Bates, *When Things Fell Apart: State Failure in Late-Century Africa* (New York: Cambridge University Press, 2008).

17. See Robert Wade, *Governing the Market: Economic Theory and the Role of Government in East Asian Industrialization* (Princeton, N.J.: Princeton University Press, 1990); Meredith Woo-Cumings, ed., *The Developmental State* (Ithaca, N.Y.: Cornell University Press, 1999); Jean C. Oi, *Rural China Takes Off: Institutional Foundations of Economic Reform* (Berkeley: University of California Press, 1999); T. J. Pempel, "The Developmental Regime in a Changing World Economy," in Meredith Woo-Cumings, ed., *The Developmental State* (Ithaca, N.Y.: Cornell University Press, 1999); Bellin, "Contingent Democrats"; Atul Kohli, *State-Directed Development: Political Power and Industrialization in the Global Periphery* (Princeton, N.J.: Princeton University Press, 2004); Vivek Chibber, *Locked in Place: State Building and Late Industrialization in India* (Princeton, N.J.: Princeton University Press, 2003); Xueguang Zhou, *The State and Life Chances in Urban China* (Cambridge: Cambridge University Press, 2004).

18. Alexander Gerschenkron, *Economic Backwardness in Historical Perspective: A Book of Essays* (Cambridge, Mass.: Belknap Press of Harvard University Press, 1962).

19. Albert Hirschman, "The Political Economy of Import Substituting Industrialization in Latin America," *Quarterly Journal of Economics* 82 (1968): 2–32.

20. Kohli, *State-Directed Development*, 8.

21. Gerschenkron, *Economic Backwardness in Historical Perspective*, 6–7.

22. According to Packenham, these international economic conditions include the terms of trade that tend to move systematically against late developers, and the keener international competition they face that is more intense than that faced by earlier industrializers. See Robert Packenham, *The Dependency Movement: Scholarship and Politics in Development Studies* (Cambridge, Mass.: Harvard University Press, 1992), 16–17.

23. Theda Skocpol, "Bringing the State Back In: Strategies of Analysis in Current Research," in Peter Evans, Dietrich Rueschemeyer, and Theda Skocpol, eds., *Bringing the State Back In* (New York: Cambridge University Press, 1985), 9.

24. Ibid.

25. For examples, see Dietrich Rueschemeyer, Evelyne Huber Stephens, and John D. Stephens, *Capitalist Development and Democracy* (Chicago: University of Chicago Press, 1992); Peter Evans, *Embedded Autonomy: States and Industrial Transformation* (Princeton, N.J.: Princeton University Press, 1995).

26. Skocpol, "Bringing the State Back In," 17.

27. Ibid., 21.

28. Dietrich Rueschemeyer and Peter Evans, "The State and Economic Transformation: Toward an Analysis of the Conditions Underlying Effective Intervention," in Evans, Rueschemeyer, and Skocpol, eds., *Bringing the State Back In*.

29. Chibber, *Locked in Place*, 7.

30. See Evans, *Embedded Autonomy*.

31. Alice H. Amsden, *Asia's Next Giant: South Korea and Late Industrialization* (New York: Oxford University Press, 1989).

32. See Rueschemeyer and Evans, "The State and Economic Transformation," 59.

33. Daniel Kelliher, *Peasant Power in China: The Era of Rural Reform, 1979–1989* (New Haven, Conn.: Yale University Press, 1992); Kate Xiao Zhou, *How the Farmers Changed China: Power of the People* (Boulder, Colo.: Westview, 1996).

34. Joseph Fewsmith, *Dilemmas of Reform in China: Political Conflict and Economic Debate* (Armonk, N.Y.: M. E. Sharpe, 1994), 19; see also the reflection of Zhao Ziyang in *Prisoner of the State: The Secret Journal of Premier Zhao Ziyang* (New York: Simon and Schuster, 2009), especially 138–144.

35. See Kellee Tsai's discussion of "adaptive informal institutions" in *Capitalism without Democracy*.

36. See Margaret Pearson, *China's New Business Elite: The Political Consequences of Economic Reform* (Berkeley: University of California Press, 1997); Daniel Bell, "After the Tsunami: Will Economic Crisis Bring Democracy to Asia," *New Republic* 218, no. 10 (March 9, 1998): 22–25; David Martin Jones, "Democratization, Civil Society, and Illiberal Middle Class Culture in Pacific Asia," *Comparative Politics* 30, no. 2 (1998): 147–169; Eui Hang Shin, "Social Change, Political Elections, and the Middle Class in Korea," *East Asia: An International Quarterly* 17, no. 3 (1999): 28–60; Bellin, "Contingent Democrats"; Eva Bellin, *Stalled Democracy: Capital, Labor, and the Paradox of State-Sponsored Development* (Ithaca, N.Y.: Cornell University Press, 2002); Chibber, *Locked in Place*; Dickson, *Red Capitalists in China*; Kellee S. Tsai, "Capitalists without a Class: Political Diversity among Private Entrepreneurs in China," *Comparative Political Studies* 38, no. 9 (2005): 1130–1158; Xueguang Zhou, *The State and Life Chances in Urban China* (Cambridge: Cambridge University Press, 2004).

37. See Chibber, *Locked in Place*.

38. Wade, *Governing the Market*; Thomas Gold, *State and Society in the Taiwan Miracle* (Armonk, N.Y.: M. E. Sharpe, 1986).

39. See Evans et al., *Bringing the State Back In*, 253.
40. See, for example, Bell, "After the Tsunami"; Jones, "Democratization, Civil Society, and Illiberal Middle Class Culture in Pacific Asia"; Shin, "Social Change, Political Elections, and the Middle Class in Korea"; Bellin, "Contingent Democrats"; and Bellin, *Stalled Democracy*. On the role of uncertainty in episodes of democratization, see Adam Przeworski, "Some Problems in the Transition to Democracy," in Guillermo O'Donnell, Philippe C. Schmitter, and Laurence Whitehead, eds., *Transitions from Authoritarian Rule, vol. 3: Comparative Perspectives* (Baltimore: Johns Hopkins University Press, 1986).
41. See Bellin, "Contingent Democrats."
42. Unger, "'Bridges'"; Wank, *Commodifying Communism*; David S. G. Goodman, "The Interdependence of State and Society: The Political Sociology of Local Leadership," in Chien-min Chao and Bruce J. Dickson, eds., *Remaking the Chinese State: Strategies, Society, and Security* (London: Routledge, 2001); An Chen, "Capitalist Development, Entrepreneurial Class, and Democratization in China," *Political Science Quarterly* 117 (2002): 401–422; He Li, "Middle Class: Friends or Foes to Chinese Leadership?" *Journal of Chinese Political Science* 8 (Fall 2003): 87–100; Tsai, *Capitalism without Democracy*; Dickson, *Wealth into Power*.
43. For detailed discussion on the distinction between these two kinds of survey results, see, for example, Melanie Manion, "Survey Research in the Study of Contemporary China: Learning from Local Samples," *China Quarterly* 139 (1994): 741–765.
44. For more detailed discussion on the generalizability of findings about relationships between variables from single- and multiple-location samples in the study of contemporary China, see, for example, works by Manion, "Survey Research"; and Andrew Walder, "Zouping in Perspective," in Andrew G. Walder, ed., *Zouping in Transition: The Process of Reform in Rural North China* (Cambridge, Mass.: Harvard University Press, 1998).
45. Melanie Manion, "The Electoral Connection in the Chinese Countryside," *American Political Science Review* 90 (December 1996): 736–748; Kent Jennings, "Political Participation in the Chinese Countryside," *American Political Science Review* 91 (1997): 361–372; M. Kent Jennings, "Gender and Political Participation in the Chinese Countryside," *Journal of Politics* 60 (1998): 954–973.
46. Wenfang Tang, *Public Opinion and Political Change in China* (Stanford, Calif.: Stanford University Press, 2005), chap. 3; Jie Chen, *Popular Political Support in Urban China* (Stanford, Calif.: Stanford University Press, 2004).
47. Manion, "Survey Research," 747.

2. The Evolution of the Private Sector in China

1. Kellee S. Tsai, *Capitalism without Democracy: The Private Sector in Contemporary China* (Ithaca, N.Y.: Cornell University Press, 2007), especially chap. 5.
2. Kathleen Thelen, "How Institutions Evolve: Insights from Comparative Historical Analysis," in James Mahoney and Dietrich Rueschemeyer, eds.,

Comparative Historical Analysis in the Social Sciences (New York: Cambridge University Press, 2003), 208–240.

3. Tianjian Shi has made this argument regarding the formulation and implementation of policy toward village-level elections. See Tianjian Shi, "Village Committee Elections in China: Institutional Tactics for Democracy," *World Politics* 51, no. 3 (April 1999): 385–412.

4. Barry Naughton, *Growing Out of the Plan: Chinese Economic Reform, 1978–1993* (New York: Cambridge University Press, 1995).

5. Tony Smith, *Thinking Like a Communist: State and Legitimacy in the Soviet Union, China, and Cuba* (New York: Norton, 1987).

6. Zhao Ziyang, *Prisoner of the State: The Secret Journal of Premier Zhao Ziyang* (New York: Simon and Schuster, 2009), 120.

7. Wu Jinglian, *Understanding and Interpreting Chinese Economic Reform* (Singapore: Thomson/South-Western, 2005), 65n44, 182.

8. Keming Yang, *Entrepreneurship in China* (Aldershot, England: Ashgate, 2007).

9. Tsai, *Capitalism without Democracy*, 15.

10. Kristen Parris, "Local Initiative and National Reform: The Wenzhou Model of Development," *China Quarterly*, no. 134 (June 1993): 242–263. In his revisionist look at Chinese-style capitalism, Yasheng Huang argues that this portrayal of TVE privatization is overstated. He claims that "as early as 1985, more than 10 million of 12 million TVEs were private"; see *Capitalism with Chinese Characteristics: Entrepreneurship and the State* (New York: Cambridge University Press, 2008), 129. According to Huang, this is exclusive of red-hat enterprises. The discrepancy in these estimates is largely due to terminology: whereas most scholars refer to larger TVEs controlled by township and village governments, Huang focuses on the small-scale firms owned by individual entrepreneurs, most of whom resided in villages.

11. Jonathan Unger, "'Bridges': Private Business, the Chinese Government and the Rise of New Associations," *China Quarterly*, no. 147 (September 1996): 795–819; Christopher Earle Nevitt, "Private Business Associations in China: Evidence of Civil Society or Local State Power," *China Journal*, no. 36 (July 1996): 25–45.

12. According to Kellee Tsai, local chapters of the SELA were created as early as 1980 and local chapters of the PEA in 1988. See *Capitalism without Democracy*, 61.

13. Richard Baum, "The Road to Tiananmen: Chinese Politics in the 1980s," in Roderick MacFarquhar, ed., *The Politics of China*, 2nd ed. (Cambridge: Cambridge University Press, 1997), 375–376.

14. Scott Kennedy, "The Stone Group: State Client or Market Pathbreaker?" *China Quarterly*, no. 152 (December 1997): 746–777.

15. Joseph Fewsmith, *China since Tiananmen: The Politics of Transition* (New York: Cambridge University Press, 2001).

16. Deng Xiaoping, "June 9 Speech to Martial Law Units," in Michel Oksenberg, Lawrence R. Sullivan, and Marc Lambert, eds., *Beijing Spring, 1989: Confrontation and Conflict: The Basic Documents* (Armonk, N.Y.: M. E. Sharpe, 1990), 377.

17. "Full Text of Gists of Deng Xiaoping's Speech to Members of New Politburo Standing Committee," in Oksenberg, Sullivan, and Lambert, eds., *Beijing Spring, 1989*, 385.

18. "State Council Decision Regarding Vigorously Strengthening Tax Collection Work in Urban and Rural Individual Industries and Commercial Enterprises and Private Enterprises," State Council Document #60, *State Council Bulletin*, no. 16 (September 20, 1989): 626–629, cited in Susan Whiting, *Power and Wealth in Rural China: The Political Economy of Institutional Change* (New York: Cambridge University Press, 2001), 137n31.

19. Fewsmith, *China since Tiananmen*, 55–60.

20. Zhang Houyi, "Kuaisu chengzhang de Zhongguo siying qiyezhu jieceng" [The rapid growth of China's private entrepreneurs], in *2005 Nian: Zhongguo shehui xingshi fenxi yu yuce* [Blue book of China's society 2005: Analysis and forecast of China's social development] (Beijing: Shehui kexue wenxian chubanshe, 2005), 329.

21. Edward S. Steinfeld, *Forging Reform in China: The Fate of State-Owned Industry* (New York: Cambridge University Press, 1998).

22. Shahid Yusuf, Kaoru Nabeshima, and Dwight Perkins, *Under New Ownership: Privatizing China's State-Owned Enterprises* (Palo Alto, Calif., and Washington, D.C.: Stanford University Press and the World Bank, 2006), 16; Stephen Green and Guy S. Liu, eds., *Exit the Dragon? Privatization and State Control in China* (London: Blackwell, 2005), 4.

23. Jiang Zemin, "Hold High the Great Banner of Deng Xiaoping Theory for an All-Round Advancement of the Cause of Building Socialism with Chinese Characteristics into the 21st Century: Report Delivered at the 15th National Congress of the Communist Party of China on September 12, 1997," *Beijing Review* 40, no. 40 (October 6–12, 1997): 19.

24. This new policy was announced in the communiqué of the Fifth Plenum of the 15th Central Committee of the CCP; see Xinhua, press release, October 11, 2000.

25. Elizabeth J. Perry, "Chinese Conceptions of 'Rights': From Mencius to Mao—and Now," *Perspectives on Politics* 6, no. 1 (March 2008): 41–42.

26. Barry Naughton, *The Chinese Economy: Transitions and Growth* (Cambridge, Mass.: MIT Press, 2007): 454–460.

27. Kellee S. Tsai, *Back-Alley Banking, Private Entrepreneurs in China* (Ithaca, N.Y.: Cornell University Press, 2002).

28. Scott Kennedy, "China's Emerging Credit Rating Industry: The Official Foundations of Private Authority," *China Quarterly*, no. 193 (March 2008): 65–83.

29. Huang, *Capitalism with Chinese Characteristics*, 1–10.

30. Joseph Kahn, "A Chinese Robin Hood Runs Afoul of Beijing," *New York Times*, August 24, 2003, http://www.nytimes.com/2003/08/24/world/a-chinese-robin-hood-runs-afoul-of-beijing.html; "Entrepreneur Sun Dawu Gets Three Year Sentence," *China Daily*, November 1, 2003, http://www.chinadaily.com.cn/en/doc/2003–11/01/content_277524.htm, both accessed June 3, 2009.

31. Joseph Kahn, "China Sentences Flower Tycoon to 18 Years for Fraud and Bribery," *New York Times*, July 15, 2003, http://www.nytimes.com/2003/07/15/world/china-sentences-flower-tycoon-to-18-years-for-fraud-and-bribery.html, accessed June 3, 2009.

32. He Qing, "Behind the Arrest of Gong," *China Business Feature*, March 8, 2007, http://www.cbfeature.com/chinese_company/news/behind_the_arrest_of_gong, accessed June 3, 2009.

33. Tania Branigan, "Chinese Tycoon 'Held' in Share Trading Mystery," *Guardian*, November 24, 2008, http://www.guardian.co.uk/business/2008/nov/24/huang-guangyu-china-share-violations, accessed June 3, 2009.

34. Edward S. Steinfeld, *Forging Reform in China: The Fate of State-Owned Industry* (New York: Cambridge University Press, 1998); Yusuf, Nabeshima, and Perkins, *Under New Ownership*.

35. X. L. Ding, "The Illicit Asset Stripping of Chinese State Firms," *China Journal*, no. 43 (January 2000): 1–28.

36. Ting Gong, "Jumping into the Sea: Cadre Entrepreneurs in China," *Problems of Post-Communism* 43, no. 4 (July–August 1996): 26–34.

37. Sun Yan, *Corruption and Market in Contemporary China* (Ithaca, N.Y.: Cornell University Press, 2004); Minxin Pei, *China's Trapped Transition: The Limits of Developmental Autocracy* (Cambridge, Mass.: Harvard University Press, 2006), chap. 4; Bruce J. Dickson, *Wealth into Power: The Communist Party's Embrace of China's Private Sector* (New York: Cambridge University Press, 2008), 200–217.

38. These percentages for previous occupations do not sum to 100 because some respondents had more than one type of previous job.

3. Political Embeddedness among China's Capitalists

1. Ken Jowitt, *New World Disorder: The Leninist Extinction* (Berkeley: University of California Press, 1992), 90–91.

2. For more details, see Bruce J. Dickson, *Wealth into Power: The Communist Party's Embrace of China's Private Sector* (New York: Cambridge University Press, 2008), chap. 3.

3. On the questionnaire, we asked respondents whether they were already in the party before becoming entrepreneurs: 77.8 percent replied that they were, and only 22.2 percent joined after they were in private business. However, due to unclear wording on the questionnaire, one-third of the red capitalists did not answer the question. We know that the large number of nonresponses was due to unclear wording, not the sensitivity of the question, because most non–party members also answered the question even though they were not supposed to.

4. Dickson, *Wealth into Power*, 97–98.

5. This is roughly comparable to the 2006 ACFIC survey, which found that just under 30 percent of surveyed firms had party cells. See "2006 nian Zhongguo diqici siying qiye chouyang diaocha shuju fenxi zonghe baogao (jiexuan)," at http://www.chinapec.com.cn/websites/news/newscontent.asp?id=1922.

6. Philippe C. Schmitter, "Still the Century of Corporatism?" in Philippe C. Schmitter and Gerhard Lehmbruch, eds., *Trends toward Corporatist Intermediation* (Beverly Hills, Calif.: Sage, 1979), 13.

7. For example, corporatism as an analytical model has been criticized for too narrowly focusing on state relations within authoritarian countries and for excluding a variety of state relations in nonauthoritarian systems. See Paul S. Adams, "Corporatism and Comparative Politics: Is There a New Century of Corporatism?" in Howard J. Wiarda, ed., *New Directions in Comparative Politics* (Boulder, Colo.: Westview Press, 2002), 20.

8. For examples of studies based on corporatism in East Asia, see Robert Wade, *Governing the Market: Economic Theory and the Role of Government in East Asian Industrialization* (Princeton, N.J.: Princeton University Press, 1990); Jonathan Unger and Anita Chan, "China, Corporatism, and the East Asian Model," *Australian Journal of Chinese Affairs*, no. 33 (1995): 29–53. For examples in Europe, see Samuel H. Beer, *British Politics in the Collectivist Age* (New York: Knopf, 1965); Stein Rokkan, "Norway: Numerical Democracy and Corporate Pluralism," in Robert Dahl, ed., *Political Oppositions in Western Democracies* (New Haven, Conn.: Yale University Press, 1965); Martin O. Heisler, *Politics in Europe: Structures and Processes in Some Postindustrial Democracies* (New York: McKay, 1973).For examples in Latin America, see Philippe C. Schmitter, *Interest Conflict and Political Change in Brazil* (Stanford, Calif.: Stanford University Press, 1971); Howard J. Wiarda, *Corporatism and National Development in Latin America* (Boulder, Colo.: Westview Press, 1981); Richard Morse, "Claims of Political Tradition," in Howard J. Wiarda ed., *Politics and Social Change in Latin America: Still a Distinct Tradition* (Boulder, Colo.: Westview Press, 1992).

9. Pluralism contends that an infinite number of societal groups may exist "with minimal or no government direction or control"; see Adams, "Corporatism and Comparative Politics," 20. In a pluralist system, the role of the state is to "umpire and referee the group struggle but not try to control it"; see Howard J. Wiarda, *Corporatism and Comparative Politics: The Other Great "Ism"* (Armonk, N.Y.: M. E. Sharpe, 1997), 68.

10. Adams, "Corporatism and Comparative Politics," 20.

11. Wiarda, *Corporatism and Comparative Politics*, 68.

12. Adams, "Corporatism and Comparative Politics," 28.

13. See, for example, Schmitter, *Interest Conflict and Political Change in Brazil*; Philippe C. Schmitter, *Corporatism and Public Policy in Authoritarian Portugal* (London: Sage, 1975); Wiarda, *Corporatism and National Development in Latin America*; Wade, *Governing the Market*.

14. See, for example, Gerhard Lehmbruch, "Liberal Corporatism and Party Government," *Comparative Political Studies* 10 (1977): 91–126; Leo Panitch, "Recent Theorizations of Corporatism: Reflections on a Growth Industry," *British Journal of Sociology* 31 (1980): 159–187; Peter Katzenstein, "Small Nations in an Open International Economy: The Converging Balance of State and Society in Switzerland and Austria," in Peter Evans, Dietrich Rueschemeyer,

and Theda Skocpol, eds., *Bringing the State Back In* (New York: Cambridge University Press, 1985).

15. See, for example, Unger and Chan, "China, Corporatism, and the East Asian Model"; Jonathan Unger, "'Bridges': Private Business, the Chinese Government and the Rise of New Associations," *China Quarterly* no. 147 (September 1996): 795–819; Thomas B. Gold, "Urban Private Business and Social Change," in Deborah Davis and Ezra Vogel, eds., *Chinese Society on the Eve of Tiananmen: The Impact of Reform* (Cambridge, Mass.: Council on East Asian Studies, Harvard University, 1990); Ronald M. Glassman, *China in Transition: Communism, Capitalism, and Democracy* (New York: Praeger, 1991); Benjamin L. Read, "Democratizing the Neighborhood? New Private Housing and Home-Owner Self-Organization in Urban China," *China Journal*, no. 49 (2003): 31–60; Joseph Fewsmith, "The New Shape of Elite Politics," *China Journal*, no. 45 (2001): 83–93.

16. Jonathan Unger and Anita Chan, "Corporatism in China: A Developmental State in an East Asian Context," in Barrett L. McCormick and Jonathan Unger, eds., *China after Socialism: In the Footsteps of Eastern Europe or East Asia?* (Armonk, N.Y.: M. E. Sharpe, 1996), 48.

17. Fewsmith, "The New Shape of Elite Politics," 85.

18. See, for example, Christopher Earle Nevitt, "Private Business Associations in China: Evidence of Civil Society or Local State Power," *China Journal*, no. 36 (July 1996): 25–45; Margaret M. Pearson, *China's New Business Elite: The Political Consequences of Economic Reform* (Berkeley: University of California Press, 1997); Jean C. Oi, *Rural China Takes Off: Institutional Foundations of Economic Reform* (Berkeley: University of California Press, 1999); Kenneth W. Foster, "Embedded within State Agencies: Business Associations in Yantai," *China Journal*, no. 47. (January 2002): 41–65; Bruce J. Dickson, *Red Capitalists in China: The Party, Private Entrepreneurs, and Prospects for Political Change* (New York: Cambridge University Press, 2003).

19. Pearson, *China's New Business Elite*, 38.

20. Foster, "Embedded within State Agencies," 42.

21. Tony Saich, "Negotiating the State: The Development of Social Organizations in China," *China Quarterly*, no. 161 (March 2000): 124–141.

22. For an extended discussion of the CCP's united front strategy, see Gerry Groot, *Managing Transitions: The Chinese Communist Party, United Front Work, Corporatism, and Hegemony* (New York: Routledge, 2004).

23. Foster, "Embedded within State Agencies"; Scott Kennedy, *The Business of Lobbying in China* (Cambridge, Mass.: Harvard University Press, 2005).

24. Alfred C. Stepan, *The State and Society: Peru in Comparative Perspective* (Princeton, N.J.: Princeton University Press, 1978).

25. Joseph Fewsmith, "Chambers of Commerce in Wenzhou Show Potential and Limits of 'Civil Society' in China," *China Leadership Monitor*, no. 16 (Fall 2005) (http://www.hoover.org/publications/clm/issues/2898951.html).

26. Ao Daiya, "Siying qiyezhu zhengzhi canyu yanjiu baogao" [Research report on private entrepreneurs' political participation], in Zhang Houyi et al., eds.,

Zhongguo siying qiye fazhan baogao [A report on the development of China's private enterprises] (Beijing: Social Sciences Academic Press, 2005).

27. Li Xueqing, "Siying qiyezhu zhengzhi canyu fenxi" [Analysis of political participation by private entrepreneurs], *Jiangsu sheng shehui zhuyi xueyuan xuebao* [Journal of the Jiangsu Socialism Institute], 2 (February 2007): 54–57; Ao Daiya, "Siying qiyezhu zhengzhi canyu yanjiu baogao."

28. Jiang Nanyang, "Lun Gongshanglian de tongzhanxing, jingjixing yu minjianxing" [on the Federation of Industry and Commerce's united-front, economic, and public functions], in Zhang Houyi et al., *Zhongguo siying qiye fazhan baogao*, 343–346.

29. Melanie Manion, "When Communist Party Candidates Can Lose, Who Wins? Assessing the Role of Local People's Congresses in the Selection of Leaders in China," *China Quarterly*, no. 195 (September 2008): 607–630.

30. Kevin J. O'Brien, *Reform without Liberalization: China's National People's Congress and the Politics of Institutional Change* (New York: Cambridge University Press, 1990); Murray Scot Tanner, *The Politics of Lawmaking in Post-Mao China: Institutions, Processes, and Democratic Prospects* (New York: Oxford University Press, 1999); Young Nam Cho, *Local People's Congresses in China: Development and Transition* (New York: Cambridge University Press, 2008).

31. "More Private Entrepreneurs Enter China's Top Advisory Body," *Xinhua News Agency*, March 2, 2003 (http://china.org.cn/english/features/57139.htm).

32. Zhang Houyi, "Jinru xin shiqi de Zhongguo siying qiyezhu jiceng" [Chinese private entrepreneurs enter a new era], in *2004 nian: Zhongguo shehui xingshi fenxi yu yuce* [Blue book of China's society 2004: Analysis and forecast of China's social development) (Beijing: Shehui kexue wenxian chubanshe, 2004), 318.

33. This figure is similar to the results from two national surveys of private entrepreneurs conducted in 2002 (17.4 percent) and 2004 (18 percent). Summaries of the findings of these surveys are available at http://finance.sina.com.cn/g/20030330/1651312771.shtm (for the 2002 survey) and http://www.southcn.com/finance/gdmqgc/gdmqyyrl/200502030218.htm (for the 2004 survey); the raw data are available from the Universities Service Centre of Chinese University of Hong Kong. However, these numbers are higher than in several previous studies. Dickson found that only 10.5 percent belonged to local PCs and approximately 5 percent to PPCCs; Tsai found only 5.6 percent and 6.5 percent, respectively; and Ao's study of political participation by entrepreneurs in Wenzhou and Guangzhou found only 4.35 percent were PPCC members. Dickson, *Wealth into Power*, 183; Tsai, *Capitalism without Democracy*, 125; Ao, "Siying qiyezhu zhengzhi canyu yanjiu baogao," 69.

34. "Private Firm Bosses Take to Politics," *China Daily*, July 2, 2003; "Private Entrepreneurs Sparkle in Political Stage," *China Daily*, December 3, 2003; "Yin Mingshan: First Private Entrepreneur to Enter Municipal Leadership," http://www.china.org.cn/english/NM-e/54414.htm.

35. The Hurun Report is produced by Rupert Hoogerwerf, who originally produced annual lists of China's wealthiest individuals for Forbes magazine. After

Forbes severed its ties with him, Hoogerwerf continued ranking the wealthiest and the most charitable Chinese, among other lists (see http://www.hurun.net/indexen.aspx).

36. See http://www.hurun.net/detailen72,people2.aspx.
37. See http://english.cri.cn/4406/2007/05/16/47@227651.htm, http://www.chinadaily.com.cn/china/2006–10/20/content_713250.htm.
38. See http://en.chinaelections.org/NewsInfo.asp?NewsID=16233
39. See http://www.china.org.cn/china/opinion/2008–03/17/content_12844712.htm.
40. See http://www.chinadaily.com.cn/bizchina/2006–03/27/content_553392.htm.
41. See http://www.caijing.com.cn/English/Others/2008–03–11/51888.shtml.
42. See http://www.womenofchina.cn/Profiles/Businesswomen/9801.jsp.
43. See http://news.xinhuanet.com/english/2006–03/08/content_4275968.htm; http://news.xinhuanet.com/english/2006–03/08/content_4276798.htm.
44. See http://www.china.org.cn/government/NPC_CPPCC_sessions2008/2008–03/10/content_12137568.htm.
45. See http://www.chinadaily.com.cn/cndy/2008–03/15/content_6538512.htm.
46. See http://english.cri.cn/4026/2008/04/02/1361@340775.htm.
47. See http://english.cri.cn/2946/2008/03/15/191@334170.htm.
48. See http://www.china.org.cn/government/NPC_CPPCC_sessions2008/2008–03/10/content_12137568.htm.
49. See http://news.xinhuanet.com/english/2005–11/21/content_3814907.htm; http://news.xinhuanet.com/english/2006–05/30/content_4622657.htm.
50. See http://www.chinadaily.com.cn/chinagate/doc/2006–03/06/content_527199.htm.
51. See http://english.cri.cn/2946/2007/03/11/168@204174.htm.
52. See http://www.jyet.gov.cn/news/26/2004101220438.htm.
53. See http://english.cri.cn/4406/2007/05/21/47@229478.htm.
54. See http://english.cri.cn/2946/2008/03/05/195@330152.htm.
55. See http://www.chinadaily.com.cn/china/2008npc/2008–03/07/content_6516420.htm.
56. See http://www.chinadaily.com.cn/china/2007–03/15/content_828183.htm.
57. See http://news.xinhuanet.com/english/2004–02/11/content_1332748.htm; http://news.xinhuanet.com/english/2004–02/24/content_1332831.htm.
58. See http://english.cri.cn/2946/2008/03/10/168@332306.htm.
59. See http://www.china.org.cn/archive/2007–03/15/content_1203077.htm.
60. Kevin J. O'Brien, "Agents and Remonstrators: Role Accumulation by Chinese People's Congress Deputies," *China Quarterly*, no. 138 (June 1994): 359–380; Manion, "When Communist Party Candidates Can Lose, Who Wins?"; Young Nam Cho, *Local People's Congresses in China: Development and Transition* (New York: Cambridge University Press, 2009).
61. See http://www.cppcc.gov.cn/English/brf_intro/.
62. See http://news.xinhuanet.com/ziliao/2003–03/10/content_768951_1.htm.
63. Beta is a standardized regression coefficient that allows us to see the impact of each independent variable relative to the others. The size of the beta coefficient indicates the change in the mean value of the dependent variable, mea-

sured in standard deviations, for each standard deviation change in the independent variable.

64. We use fixed assets as a measure of firm size because it is less variable year to year than the other measures of size (number of workers and sales volume). Moreover, we use only one measure of firm size because they are so highly correlated that they are not truly independent variables. Including all of them in a regression model turns them all into insignificant variables.

4. The Level and Sources of Capitalists' Democratic Support

1. Guillermo O'Donnell and Philippe C. Schmitter, *Transitions from Authoritarian Rule: Tentative Conclusions about Uncertain Democracies* (Baltimore: Johns Hopkins University Press, 1986); Robert Wade, *Governing the Market: Economic Theory and the Role of Government in East Asian Industrialization* (Princeton, N.J.: Princeton University Press, 1990); Guillermo O'Donnell, "Substantive or Procedural Consensus? Notes on the Latin American Bourgeoisie," in Douglas Chalmers, Maria de Souza, and Akko A. Boron, eds., *The Right and Democracy in Latin America* (New York: Praeger, 1992); Eva Bellin, *Stalled Democracy: Capital, Labor, and the Paradox of State-Sponsored Development* (Ithaca, N.Y.: Cornell University Press, 2002; Vivek Chibber, *Locked in Place: State Building and Late Industrialization in India* (Princeton, N.J.: Princeton University Press, 2003).

2. Eva Bellin, "Contingent Democrats: Industrialists, Labor, and Democratization in Late-Developing Countries," *World Politics* 52, no. 2 (January 2000): 175–205.

3. Ibid.

4. Peter H. Smith, *Democracy in Latin America: Political Change in Comparative Perspective* (New York: Oxford University Press, 2005).

5. For detailed arguments of modernization theory, see, for example, Seymour Martin Lipset, "Some Social Requisites of Democracy: Economic Development and Political Legitimacy," *American Political Science Review* 53, no. 1 (March 1959): 69–105; Gabriel Almond and Sidney Verba, *Civic Culture: Political Attitudes and Democracy in Five Nations* (Princeton, N.J.: Princeton University Press, 1963); Ronald Inglehart, *Modernization and Postmodernization: Cultural, Economic, and Political Change in 43 Societies* (Princeton, N.J.: Princeton University Press, 1997); Walt W. Rostow, *Stages of Economic Growth: A Non-Communist Manifesto*, 3rd ed. (Cambridge: Cambridge University Press, 1991).

6. See, for example, Ronald M. Glassman, *China in Transition: Communism, Capitalism, and Democracy* (New York: Praeger, 1991); Kristen Parris, "Local Initiative and National Reform: The Wenzhou Model of Development," *China Quarterly*, no. 134 (June 1993): 242–263; Gordon White, "Democratization and Economic Reform in China," *Australian Journal of Chinese Affairs*, no. 31 (1994): 73–92; Gordon White, Jude Howell, and Shang Xiaoyuan, *In Search of Civil Society: Market Reform and Social Change in Contemporary China* (Oxford: Oxford University Press, 1996); Baogang

He, *The Democratic Implications of Civil Society in China* (New York: St. Martin's Press, 1997); Yongnian Zheng, *Will China Become Democratic? Elite, Class, and Regime Transition* (Singapore: Eastern Universities Press, 2004).

7. Glassman, *China in Transition*, 103.

8. Zheng, *Will China Become Democratic?* 255.

9. See, for example, Margaret Pearson, *China's New Business Elite: The Political Consequences of Economic Reform* (Berkeley: University of California Press, 1997); Pearson, "China's Emerging Business Class: Democracy's Harbinger," *Current History* 97, no. 620 (September 1998): 268–272; An Chen, "Capitalist Development, Entrepreneurial Class, and Democratization in China," *Political Science Quarterly* 117(2002): 401–422; Bruce J. Dickson, *Red Capitalists in China: The Party, Private Entrepreneurs, and Prospects for Political Change* (New York: Cambridge University Press, 2003); Dickson, *Wealth into Power: The Communist Party's Embrace of China's Private Sector* (New York: Cambridge University Press, 2008); Ao Daiya, "Siying qiyezhu zhengzhi canyu yanjiu baogao" [Research report on private entrepreneurs' political participation], in Zhang Houyi et al., eds., *Zhongguo siying qiye fazhan baogao* [A report on the development of China's private enterprises] (Beijing: Social Sciences Academic Press, 2005).

10. Margaret Pearson, "The Janus Face of Business Associations in China: Socialist Corporatism in Foreign Enterprises," *Australian Journal of Chinese Affairs*, no. 31 (January 1994): 25–46; see also Pearson, "China's Emerging Business Class."

11. Dickson, *Red Capitalists* and *Wealth into Power*.

12. Kellee Tsai, *Capitalism without Democracy: The Private Sector in Contemporary China* (Ithaca, N.Y.: Cornell University Press, 2007).

13. Ao, "Siying qiyezhu zhengzhi canyu yanjiu baogao," 79–83.

14. Chunmin Zhang, "Zhongchan jieceng de zhengzhi canyu" [Political participation of the middle class], in Zhou Xiaohong, ed., *Zhongguo zhongchan jieceng diaocha* [Survey of the Chinese middle class] (Beijing: Social Sciences Academic Press, 2005), 304–305.

15. For example, to infer support for democracy, Pearson used interview questions about support for economic reform, private ownership, and political liberalization, and Dickson asked whether the government should have the leading role in initiating reform or if society should also play a part. See Pearson, *China's New Business Elite*; Dickson, *Red Capitalists*; Dickson, *Wealth into Power*.

16. For example, to measure support for the democratic political system among private entrepreneurs, Tsai used the question, "how would you appraise the different types of political systems in the world?" with "democracy" listed as one of the choices. See Tsai, *Capitalism without Democracy*, 94. Despite finding that her survey respondents evaluated democracy as superior to political dictatorship, technocracy, and military dictatorship, Tsai warned readers that "it would not be appropriate to conclude that China's private entrepreneurs therefore hope that China will undergo a democratic transition," because the

wording of the question and the sensitivity of the issue made the findings suspect; see Tsai, *Capitalism without Democracy*, 93–96.

17. James L. Gibson, "'A Mile Wide but an Inch Deep' (?): The Structure of Democratic Commitments in the Former USSR," *American Journal of Political Science* 40, no. 2 (May 1996): 396–420; James L. Gibson and Raymond M. Duch, "Emerging Democratic Values in Soviet Political Culture," in Arthur H. Miller, William M. Reisinger, and Vicki L. Hesli, eds., *Public Opinion and Regime Change* (Boulder, Colo.: Westview Press, 1993): 69–94; James L. Gibson, Raymond M. Duch, and Kent L. Tedin, "Democratic Values and the Transformation of the Soviet Union," *Journal of Politics* 54, no. 2 (1992): 329–371.

18. Almond and Verba, *Civic Culture*; Robert A. Dahl, *Polyarchy: Participation and Opposition* (New Haven, Conn.: Yale University Press, 1971); Ronald Inglehart, *Cultural Shift in Advanced Industrial Society* (Princeton, N.J.: Princeton University Press, 1990).

19. For application of this conceptualization, see studies by Gibson and Duch, "Emerging Democratic Values"; Gibson et al., "Democratic Values and the Transformation." For application in China, see Jie Chen and Yang Zhong, "Defining the Political System of Post-Deng China: Emerging Public Support for a Democratic Political System," *Problems of Post-Communism* 45, no. 1 (1998): 30–42; Chen and Zhong, "Valuation of Individual Liberty vs. Social Order among Democratic Supporters: A Cross-Validation," *Political Research Quarterly* 53 (2000): 427–439; Jie Chen, *Popular Political Support in Urban China* (Stanford, Calif.: Stanford University Press and Woodrow Wilson Center Press, 2004).

20. Gibson, "A Mile Wide but an Inch Deep' (?)," 348–349. While this conceptualization is consistent with Robert Dahl's two criteria of contestation and participation, it is broader than the two criteria.

21. Joseph A. Schumpeter, *Capitalism, Socialism, and Democracy* (New York: Harper, 1947); Dahl, *Polyarchy*; Samuel P. Huntington, *The Third Wave: Democratization in the Late Twentieth Century* (Norman: Oklahoma University Press, 1991); Gibson and Duch, "Emerging Democratic Values"; Gibson et al., "Democratic Values and the Transformation."

22. Samuel P. Huntington, "Democracy's Third Wave," in Larry Diamond and Marc F. Plattner, eds., *The Global Resurgence of Democracy* (Baltimore: Johns Hopkins University Press, 1993), 7.

23. Gibson and Duch, "Emerging Democratic Values," 80–82; Gibson et al., "Democratic Values and the Transformation," 349–552; Ada Finifter and Ellen Mickiewicz, "Redefining the Political System of the USSR: Mass Support for Political Change," *American Political Science Review* 86 (1992): 857–874.

24. Samuel Huntington, *The Third Wave: Democratization in the Late Twentieth Century* (Norman: Oklahoma University Press, 1991), 9.

25. Lucian W. Pye, *The Spirit of Chinese Politics* (Cambridge, Mass.: Harvard University Press, 1992), xi; Jie Chen and Peng Deng, *China since the Cultural Revolution: From Totalitarianism to Authoritarianism* (Westport, Conn.: Praeger, 1995), 2–4.

26. Dahl, *Polyarchy;* Ian Shapiro, *Democratic Justice* (New Haven, Conn.: Yale University Press, 1999); Philip Pettit, "Democracy, Electoral and Contestatory," in Ian Shapiro and Stephen Macedo, eds., *Designing Democratic Institutions* (New York: New York University Press, 2000).

27. Technically speaking, China is a multiparty system: it has eight so-called democratic parties, leftovers from the pre-1949 period that today are intended to symbolize the CCP's united front approach. However, these parties do not function as opposition parties: they are too small to challenge the CCP, are not allowed to compete for votes in open elections, and are under the leadership of the CCP.

28. Gibson et al., "Democratic Values and the Transformation," 341.

29. See Gibson and Duch, "Emerging Democratic Values." For the application of this argument, see also James L. Gibson, "The Resilience of Mass Support for Democratic Institutions and Processes in Nascent Russian and Ukrainian Democracies," in Vladimir Tismaneanu, ed., *Political Culture and Civil Society in Russia and the New States of Eurasia* (Armonk, N.Y.: M. E. Sharpe, 1995), 53–111; Gibson et al., "Democratic Values and the Transformation."

30. Andrew Nathan, *China's Transition* (New York: Columbia University Press, 1997), 204. See also Andrew J. Nathan, *China's Crisis: Dilemma of Reform and Prospects for Democracy* (New York: Columbia University Press, 1990); Robert A. Scalapino, "Current Trends and Future Prospects," *Journal of Democracy* 9 (1998): 35–40.

31. Pye, *The Spirit of Chinese Politics,* 123.

32. Chen and Zhong, "Valuation of Individual Liberty vs. Social Order."

33. Nathan, *China's Transition,* 69–70.

34. Wm. Theodore De Bary, *Asian Values and Human Rights: A Confucian Communitarian Perspective* (Cambridge, Mass.: Harvard University Press, 1998).

35. Gongqin Xiao, "The Rise of the Technocrats," *Journal of Democracy* 14, no. 1 (2003): 62.

36. The terms, such as "multi-candidate election" *(cha'e xuanju)* and "competitive election" *(jingxuan),* are also used in various government documents to regulate elections under the one-party system.

37. Kevin J. O'Brien, "Agents and Remonstrators: Role Accumulation by Chinese People's Congress Deputies," *China Quarterly,* no. 138 (June 1994): 359–380; Roderick MacFarquhar, "Provincial People's Congresses," *China Quarterly,* no. 155 (September 1998): 656–667; Melanie Manion, "When Communist Party Candidates Can Lose, Who Wins? Assessing the Role of Local People's Congresses in the Selection of Leaders in China," *China Quarterly,* no. 195 (September 2008): 607–630.

38. Harold Lasswell, *Politics: Who Gets What, When, and How* (New York: McGraw-Hill, 1936).

39. David Easton, *The Political System* (New York: Knopf, 1953).

40. John Zysman, *Governments, Markets, and Growth: Financial Systems and the Politics of Industrial Change* (Ithaca, N.Y.: Cornell University Press, 1983), 8.

41. Theda Skocpol, "Bringing the State Back in: Strategies of Analysis in Current Research," in Peter Evans, Dietrich Rueschemeyer, and Theda Skocpol, eds., *Bringing the State Back In* (New York: Cambridge University Press, 1985), 17.

42. Alice H. Amsden, *Asia's Next Giant: South Korea and Late Industrialization* (New York: Oxford University Press, 1989); Wade, *Governing the Market;* and Chibber, *Locked in Place.*

43. Amsden, *Asia's Next Giant,* 144.

44. Wade, *Governing the Market,* 187–191.

45. Amsden, *Asia's Next Giant,* 144; Chibber, *Locked in Place,* 27.

46. For a detailed and insightful discussion on the role of the Chinese government in the allocation of financial resources, see Nicholas R. Lardy, *China's Unfinished Economic Revolution* (Washington, D.C.: Brookings Institution Press, 1998); Barry Naughton, *The Chinese Economy: Transitions and Growth* (Cambridge, Mass.: MIT Press, 2007).

47. See Naughton, *The Chinese Economy,* 460–466.

48. For a more detailed discussion regarding private entrepreneurs' difficulties getting bank credit, see Kellee S. Tsai, *Back-Alley Banking: Private Entrepreneurs in China* (Ithaca, N.Y.: Cornell University Press, 2002); Houyi Zhang, Guangming Hou, Lizhi Ming, and Chuanyun Liang, *Zhongguo de siying jingji yu siying qiyezhu* [A report on the development of China's private enterprises] (Beijing: Social Sciences Academic Press, 2005).

49. Other sources from which respondents received the funds for their businesses included personal savings, loans from friends and other individuals, commercial banks and credit cooperatives, informal financial institutions (for instance, pawn shops), foreign banks, and other non-government-related funds.

50. See Alfred C. Stepan, *The State and Society: Peru in Comparative Perspective* (Princeton, N.J.: Princeton University Press, 1978), chap. 3.

51. Dickson, *Red Capitalists,* 90.

52. See, for example, Chen Dong, "Siying qiyezhu jiecen neibu fenhua jiada" [The increasing diversification within private entrepreneurs], *Dalu Qiao* [Land Bridge Horizon] 4 (April 2005): 43–47.

53. For a more detailed discussion on the increasing assertiveness of the NPC and its members in the legislative process, see, for example, Murray Scot Tanner, *The Politics of Lawmaking in Post-Mao China: Institutions, Processes, and Democratic Prospects* (New York: Oxford University Press, 1999); Ming Xia, *The People's Congresses and Governance in China: Toward a Network Mode of Governance* (London: Routledge, 2007); Young Nam Cho, *Local People's Congresses in China: Development and Transition* (New York: Cambridge University Press, 2008).

54. Jianqun Tao and Wen Zhao, "Siying qiyezhu zou xiang zhengzhi wutai" [Private entrepreneurs' marching toward political stage] *Shidai Chao* [Tide of Times] 3, no. 1 (2003): 15–19.

55. Both interviews were reported in a study of political participation by private entrepreneurs by Tao and Wen, "Siying qiyezhu zou xiang zhengzhi wutai."

56. Dickson, *Wealth into Power,* 114.
57. Christopher Earle Nevitt, "Private Business Associations in China: Evidence of Civil Society or Local State Power," *China Journal,* no. 35 (July 1996): 26.
58. See, for example, Daniel Bell, "After the Tsunami: Will Economic Crisis Bring Democracy to Asia?" *New Republic* 218, no. 10 (March 9, 1998): 22–25; David Martin Jones, "Democratization, Civil Society, and Illiberal Middle Class Culture in Pacific Asia," *Comparative Politics* 30, no. 2 (1998): 147–169; Eui Hang Shin, "Social Change, Political Elections, and the Middle Class in Korea," *East Asia: An International Quarterly* 17, no. 3 (1999): 28–60; Bellin, "Contingent Democrats"; Eva Bellin, *Stalled Democracy: Capital, Labor and the Paradox of State-Sponsored Development* (Ithaca, N.Y.: Cornell University Press, 2002).
59. See, for example, David L. Wank, *Commodifying Communism: Business, Trust, and Politics in a Chinese City* (New York: Cambridge University Press, 1999); Dickson, *Red Capitalists* and *Wealth into Power.*
60. Dickson, *Red Capitalists,* 133; Dickson, *Wealth into Power,* 141.
61. Yang Zhong, "Legitimacy Crisis and Legitimization in China," *Journal of Contemporary Asia* 26, no. 2 (1996): 201–220; Andrew J. Nathan, "Authoritarian Resilience," *Journal of Democracy* 14, no. 1 (January 2003): 6–17; Lowell Dittmer and Guoli Liu, eds., *China's Deep Reforms: Domestic Politics in Transition* (Lanham, Md.: Rowman & Littlefield, 2006).
62. See, for example, Edward N. Muller, "Behavioral Correlates of Political Support," *American Political Science Review* 71 (1977): 454–467; Edward N. Muller and Carol J. Williams, "Dynamics of Political Support-Alienation," *Comparative Political Studies* 13 (1980): 33–59; Edward N. Muller, Thomas O. Jukam, and Mitchell A. Seligson, "Diffuse Political Support and Antisystem Political Behavior: A Comparative Analysis," *American Journal of Political Science* 26 (1982): 240–264; Mitchell A. Seligson and Edward N. Muller, "Democratic Stability and Economic Crisis: Costa Rica, 1978–1983," *International Studies Quarterly* 31 (1987): 301–326; James L. Gibson and Gregory A. Caldeira, "Blacks and the United States Supreme Court: Models of Diffuse Support," *Journal of Politics* 54 (1992): 1120–1145.
63. David Easton, "A Reassessment of the Concept of Political Support," *British Journal of Political Science* 5 (1975): 437.
64. See, for example, Wenfang Tang and William L. Parish, *Chinese Urban Life under Reform: The Changing Social Contract* (Cambridge: Cambridge University Press, 2000); Chen, *Popular Political Support.*
65. Tang and Parish, *Chinese Urban Life.*
66. Ibid., 108.
67. See, for example, Li Xueqing, "Siying qiyezhu zhengzhi canyu fenxi" [Analysis of political participation by private entrepreneurs], *Jiangsu Sheng Shehui Zhuyi Xueyuan Xuebao* [Journal of the Jiangsu Socialism Institute] 2 (February 2007): 54–57; Jiang Nanyang, "Siying qiyezhu zhengzhi canyu de guocheng: tedian yu xiaoying" [The process of political participation of private entrepreneurs: Characteristics and effects], *Zhongguo Dangzheng Ganbu Luntan* [Forum of Party and Government Cadres in China] 4 (April 2005).

68. Many field observations in China have also indicated that these three issues are of the most concern among Chinese people. For a more detailed report on people's concern about these issues, see Chen, *Popular Political Support*.

69. See, for example, Gibson et al., "Democratic Values and the Transformation"; Gibson and Duch, "Emerging Democratic Values"; Chen and Zhong, "Defining the Political System of Post-Deng China"; Chen, *Popular Political Support*.

70. David L. Wank, "The Making of China's Rentier Entrepreneur Elite: State, Clientelism, and Power Conversion," in Francoise Mengin and Jean-Louis Roca, eds., *Politics in China: Moving Frontiers* (New York: Palgrave Macmillan, 2002), 118–139.

71. Tsai, *Capitalism without Democracy*, 92–93.

72. Wank, "The Making of China's Rentier Entrepreneur Elite."

73. Tsai, *Capitalism without Democracy*, 82.

74. Dickson, *Red Capitalists*; Scott Kennedy, *The Business of Lobbying in China* (Cambridge, Mass.: Harvard University Press, 2005).

75. See, for example, Wang Xiaoyan, *Siying qiyejia de zhengzhi canyu* [The political participation of private entrepreneurs)] (Beijing: Social Science Academy Press, 2007); Chen, "Siying qiyezhu jieceng neibu fenhua jiada"; Yang Henan, "Siying qiyezhu jieceng zhengzhi canyu de tezheng ye duice fenxi" [The characteristics of private entrepreneurs' political participation and its policy implications], *Tequ Jingji* [Economy of the Special Economic Zones], 5 (May 2007): 32–35.

76. Ole Odgaard, "Entrepreneurs and Elite Formation in Rural China," *Australian Journal of Chinese Affairs*, no. 28 (1992): 89–108.

77. Lipset, "Some Social Requisites of Democracy"; Inglehart, *Modernization and Postmodernization*.

78. Tsai, *Capitalism without Democracy*, 82n6.

5. Regime Support among China's Capitalists

1. David Easton, *A Systems Analysis of Political Life* (New York: Wiley, 1965); Herman D. Lujan, "The Structure of Political Support: A Study of Guatemala," *American Journal of Political Science* 18 (1974): 23–43; T. H. Rigby, "Introduction: Political Legitimacy, Weber and Communist Mono-Organizational Systems," in T. H. Rigby and A. F. Feher, eds., *Political Legitimacy in Communist States* (New York: St. Martin's Press, 1982); Arthur H. Miller, "In Search of Regime Legitimacy," in Arthur H. Miller, William M. Reisinger, and Vicki L. Hesli, eds., *Public Opinion and Regime Change: The New Politics of Post-Soviet Societies* (Boulder, Colo.: Westview Press, 1993); Jie Chen, Yang Zhong, and Jan William Hillard, "The Level and Sources of Popular Support for China's Current Political Regime," *Communist and Post-Communist Studies* 30 (1997): 45–64; Jack Citrin and Christopher Muste, "Trust in Government," in John P. Robinson, Phillip R. Shaver, and Lawrence S. Wrightsman, eds., *Measures of Political Attitudes* (San Diego: Academic Press, 1999); Richard Rose and William Mishler, *Regime Support in*

Non-Democratic and Democratic Contexts (Glasgow: University of Strathclyde, 2000).

2. Seymour M. Lipset, "Some Social Requisites of Democracy: Economic Development and Political Legitimacy," *American Political Science Review* 53 (1959): 69–105; Seymour Martin Lipset, *Political Man: The Social Bases of Politics* (Baltimore: Johns Hopkins University Press, 1960); Mitchell A. Seligson and Edward N. Muller, "Democratic Stability and Economic Crisis: Costa Rica, 1978–1983," *International Studies Quarterly* 31 (1987): 301–326; Steven E. Finkel, Edward N. Muller, and Mitchell Seligson, "Economic Crisis, Incumbent Performance and Regime Support: A Comparison of Longitudinal Data from West Germany and Costa Rica," *British Journal of Political Science* 19 (1989): 329–351.

3. James R. Millar and Elizabeth Clayton, "Quality of Life: Subjective Measures of Relative Satisfaction," in James R. Millar, ed., *Politics, Work, and Daily Life in the USSR: A Survey of Former Soviet Citizens* (Cambridge: Cambridge University Press, 1987), 31–60.

4. See, for example, Jan Pakulski, "Legitimacy and Mass Compliance: Reflections on Max Weber and Soviet-Type Societies," *British Journal of Political Science* 16 (1986): 35–56; Stephen White, "Economic Performance and Communist Legitimacy," *World Politics* 38, no. 3 (1986): 462–482; William Avery, "Political Legitimacy and Crisis in Poland," *Political Science Quarterly* 103 (1988): 111–130; Giuseppe di Palma, "Legitimation from the Top to Civil Society: Political-Cultural Change in Eastern Europe," *World Politics* 44 (1991): 49–80.

5. Ronald Inglehart, *Modernization and Postmodernization: Cultural, Economic, and Political Change in 43 Societies* (Princeton, N.J.: Princeton University Press. 1997), 15.

6. Seymour Martin Lipset, *Political Man: The Social Bases of Politics* (Garden City, N.Y.: Doubleday, 1981).

7. Easton, *A Systems Analysis of Political Life*; Easton, "Theoretical Approaches to Political Support," *Canadian Journal of Political Science* 9 (1976): 431–448.

8. Edward N. Muller and Thomas O. Jukam, "On the Meaning of Political Support," *American Political Science Review* 77 (1977): 1566.

9. Their operationalized measure of regime legitimacy (or in Easton's phrase, "diffuse support") has been used in several cross-nation and single-nation studies of political support, including some studies of political support in China. See, for example, Muller and Jukam, "On the Meaning of Political Support"; Edward N. Muller, "Behavioral Correlates of Political Support," *American Political Science Review* 71 (1977): 454–467; Edward N. Muller, Thomas O. Jukam, and Mitchell A. Seligson, "Diffuse Political Support and Antisystem Political Behavior: A Comparative Analysis." *American Journal of Political Science* 26 (1982): 240–264; Steven E. Finkel, Edward N. Muller, and Mitchell Seligson, "Economic Crisis, Incumbent Performance and Regime Support: A Comparison of Longitudinal Data from West Germany and Costa Rica," *British Journal of Political Science* 19, no. 3 (1989): 329–351;

Jie Chen, *Popular Political Support in Urban China* (Stanford, Calif.: Stanford University Press, 2004); Wenfang Tang, *Public Opinion and Political Change in China* (Stanford, Calif.: Stanford University Press, 2005), chap. 3.

10. The mean of the interitem correlations of this set of items is .45; the reliability coefficient among these items is .83.

11. Jonathan Unger, "'Bridges': Private Business, the Chinese Government and the Rise of New Associations," *China Quarterly*, no. 147 (September 1996): 795–819; Christopher Earle Nevitt, "Private Business Associations in China: Evidence of Civil Society or Local State Power," *China Journal*, no. 36 (July 1996): 25–45; Margaret M. Pearson, *China's New Business Elite: The Political Consequences of Economic Reform* (Berkeley: University of California Press, 1997); David L. Wank, *Commodifying Communism: Business, Trust, and Politics in a Chinese City* (New York: Cambridge University Press, 1999); David S. G. Goodman, "The New Middle Class," in Merle Goldman and Roderick MacFarquhar, eds., *The Paradox of China's Post-Mao Reforms* (Cambridge, Mass.: Harvard University Press, 1999); An Chen, "Capitalist Development, Entrepreneurial Class, and Democratization in China," *Political Science Quarterly* 117 (2002): 401–422; Bruce J. Dickson, *Red Capitalists in China: The Party, Private Entrepreneurs, and Prospects for Political Change* (New York: Cambridge University Press, 2003); Dickson, *Wealth into Power: The Communist Party's Embrace of China's Private Sector* (New York: Cambridge University Press, 2008); Kellee S. Tsai, *Capitalism without Democracy: The Private Sector in Contemporary China* (Ithaca, N.Y.: Cornell University Press, 2007).

12. Another measure of political embeddedness could be access to state bank loans. Lending to the private sector has not kept pace with its expansion. The ability to receive bank loans is as much about political connections as credit worthiness and remains a sore point with many private entrepreneurs. Our questionnaire included several questions regarding bank loans (the percentage of start-up capital that came from bank loans, whether they had received bank loans to expand their businesses, and the perceived difficulty in borrowing from a bank), but none had a statistically significant impact on regime support and were therefore left out of the models presented later in the chapter.

13. Dickson, *Wealth into Power*.

14. Andrew J. Nathan, *China's Transition* (New York: Columbia University Press, 1997); Suzanne Ogden, *Inklings of Democracy in China* (Cambridge, Mass.: Harvard University Asia Center, 2002); Wenfang Tang and William L. Parish, *Chinese Urban Life under Reform: The Changing Social Contract* (New York: Cambridge University Press, 2000); Chen, *Popular Political Support in Urban China*; Merle Goldman, *From Comrade to Citizen: The Struggle for Political Rights in China* (Cambridge, Mass.: Harvard University Press, 2005).

15. Pearson, *China's New Business Elite*; Tsai, *Capitalism without Democracy*; Dickson, *Wealth into Power*.

16. See, for example, Tang, *Public Opinion and Political Change in China*; Chen, *Popular Political Support in Urban China*.

17. Andrew H. Wedeman, "The Intensification of Corruption in China," *China Quarterly*, no. 180 (December 2004): 895–921; Dali L. Yang, *Remaking the Chinese Leviathan: Market Transition and the Politics of Governance in China* (Stanford, Calif.: Stanford University Press, 2004); Melanie Manion, *Corruption by Design: Building Clean Government in Mainland China and Hong Kong* (Cambridge, Mass.: Harvard University Press, 2005); Minxin Pei, *China's Trapped Transition: The Limits of Developmental Autocracy* (Cambridge, Mass.: Harvard University Press, 2006).

18. Eva Bellin, "Contingent Democrats: Industrialists, Labor, and Democratization in Late-Developing Countries," *World Politics* 52, no. 2 (2000): 175–205; Stephan Haggard and Robert Kaufman, *The Political Economy of Democratic Transitions* (Princeton, N.J.: Princeton University Press, 1995).

19. Yan Sun, *Corruption and Market in Contemporary China* (Ithaca, N.Y.: Cornell University Press, 2004), 213.

20. Melanie Manion, "Democracy, Community, Trust: The Impact of Elections in Rural China," *Comparative Political Studies* 39 (April 2006): 305.

21. Samuel H. Barnes, Barbara G. Farah, and Felix Heunks, "Personal Dissatisfaction," in Samuel H. Barnes and Max Kaase, eds., *Political Action: Mass Participation in Five Western Democracies* (Beverly Hills, Calif.: Sage, 1979), 381; see also Jacques J. A. Thomassen, "Economic Crisis, Dissatisfaction, and Protest," in M. Kent Jennings et al., eds., *Continuities in Political Action: A Longitudinal Study of Political Orientations in Three Western Democracies* (New York: Walter de Gruyter, 1989), 103–134.

22. Ronald Inglehart, *Culture Shift in Advanced Industrial Societies* (Princeton, N.J.: Princeton University Press, 1990); Inglehart, *Modernization and Postmodernization*.

23. Jie Chen and Yang Zhong, "Defining the Political System of Post-Deng China: Emerging Public Support for a Democratic Political System," *Problems of Post-Communism* 45 (January/February 1998): 30–42.

24. Inglehart, *Modernization and Postmodernization*, 166.

25. Ada Finifter and Ellen Mickiewicz, "Redefining the Political System of the USSR: Mass Support for Political Change," *American Political Science Review* 86 (1992): 857–874.

26. Tang and Parish, *Chinese Urban Life under Reform*; Chen, *Popular Political Support in Urban China*.

27. See Chen, *Popular Political Support in Urban China*, chap. 2.

28. Chen and Zhong, "Defining the Political System of Post-Deng China"; Tang and Parish, *Chinese Urban Life under Reform*; James L. Gibson and Raymond M. Duch, "Emerging Democratic Values in Soviet Political Culture," in Arthur H. Miller, William M. Reisinger, and Vicki L. Hesli, eds., *Public Opinion and Regime Change* (Boulder, Colo.: Westview Press, 1993); James L. Gibson, Raymond M. Duch, and Kent L. Tedin, "Democratic Values and the Transformation of the Soviet Union," *Journal of Politics* 54, no. 3 (1992): 329–371; Chen, *Popular Political Support in Urban China*.

29. Scott Kennedy, *The Business of Lobbying in China* (Cambridge, Mass.: Harvard University Press, 2005); Dickson, *Wealth into Power*.

30. Chen Guangjin, "1999–2004 siying qiyezhu jieceng: yige xin shehui jieceng de chengzhang" [The class of private entrepreneurs in 1992–2004: Growth of a new social class], in Zhang Houyi et al., eds., *Zhongguo siying qiye fazhan baogao* [A report on the development of China's private enterprises] (Beijing: Social Sciences Academic Press, 2005); Wang Yuanqi. "Siying qiyezhu zhengzhi canyu de jiedu" [Understanding of private entrepreneurs' political participation], *Guangdong Shehui Zhuyi Xueyuan Xuebao* [Journal of the Guangdong Socialism Institute] 3 (July 2007): 11–18.

31. However, Tsai's research found that former SOE managers were even more demanding than other capitalists, so it may be that familiarity with the regime is counterproductive in creating support for the regime. See Tsai, *Capitalism without Democracy*, 173.

32. These figures correspond to the percentages of former SOEs among private firms and CCP members among SOE managers. According to a 2002 survey of the private sector sponsored by the ACFIC, the Chinese Academy of Social Sciences, and other groups, 25.7 percent of private firms were former SOEs, and the heads of 50.7 percent of them were party members. See http://www.acfic.org.cn/acfic/12_xw/xxzk/708_8.htm.

33. Lipset, "Some Social Requisites of Democracy"; Inglehart, *Modernization and Postmodernization*.

34. Ideally, we would want to distinguish capitalists who were in the CCP before joining the private sector from those who were co-opted into the party after being in business. Our questionnaire did include a question on this point, but because of unclear wording, one-third of party members did not answer this question. If we look only at the red capitalists who did answer this question, they were more likely to support the regime than were non–CCP members, but there is no significant difference between those who were already in the CCP before going into business and those who were co-opted; however, the large number of nonresponses may make this finding not reliable.

35. Alan Liu, "Provincial Identities and Political Cultures: Modernism, Traditionalism, Parochialism, and Separatism," in Shiping Hua, ed., *Chinese Political Culture, 1989–2000* (Armonk, N.Y.: M. E. Sharpe, 2001).

36. Provincial level statistics are available for foreign investment and foreign trade, but we were not able to collect county-level statistics on these measures for most of the counties in our survey.

37. Larry Diamond, "Thinking about Hybrid Regimes," *Journal of Democracy* 13 (2002): 21–35.

6. Political Activities of Private Entrepreneurs in China

1. Bruce J. Dickson, *Red Capitalists in China: The Party, Private Entrepreneurs, and Prospects for Political Change* (New York: Cambridge University Press, 2003); Scott Kennedy, *The Business of Lobbying in China* (Cambridge, Mass.: Harvard University Press, 2005); Kellee S. Tsai, *Capitalism without Democracy: The Private Sector in Contemporary China* (Ithaca, N.Y.: Cornell University Press, 2007); Dickson, *Wealth into Power: The Communist*

Party's Embrace of China's Private Sector (New York: Cambridge University Press, 2008).

2. Melanie Manion, "The Electoral Connection in the Chinese Countryside," *American Political Science Review* 90, no. 4 (December 1996): 736–748; Tianjian Shi, *Political Participation in Beijing* (Cambridge, Mass.: Harvard University Press, 1997); M. Kent Jennings, "Gender and Political Participation in the Chinese Countryside," *Journal of Politics* 60, no. 4 (November 1998): 954–973; Wenfang Tang and William L. Parish, *Chinese Urban Life under Reform: The Changing Social Contract* (New York: Cambridge University Press, 2000); Jie Chen, *Popular Political Support in Contemporary China* (Stanford, Calif.: Stanford University Press, 2004).

3. Shi, *Political Participation in Beijing;* Jennings, "Gender and Political Participation in the Chinese Countryside"; Chen, *Popular Political Support in Contemporary China;* Wenfang Tang, *Public Opinion and Political Change in China* (Stanford, Calif.: Stanford University Press, 2005).

4. See National People's Congress, *The Constitution of the People's Republic of China* (Beijing: China Legal Publishing House, 1999), chapter 1, General Principles.

5. Shi Weimin and Lei Jingxuan, *Zhijie xuanju: Zhidu yu chengxu* [Direct elections: System and procedure] (Beijing: Chinese Academy of Social Science Press, 1999), 21–23: Chen, *Popular Political Support in Contemporary China,* chap. 6.

6. Andrew J. Nathan, "China's Political Trajectory: What Are the Chinese Saying?" in Cheng Li, ed., *China's Changing Political Landscape: Prospects for Democracy* (Washington, D.C.: Brookings Institution Press, 2008), 27.

7. Wang Zhongtian, *Xinde bi'an: Zouxiang 21st shiji de zhongguo minzhu* [A new horizon: Marching toward the Chinese democracy in the twenty-first century] (Beijing: The Party School of the CCP's Central Committee Press, 1998), 190; Minxin Pei, *China's Trapped Transition: The Limits of Developmental Autocracy* (Cambridge, Mass.: Harvard University Press, 2006), 63–64;

8. Wang, *Xinde bi'an;* Shi and Lei, *Zhijie xuanju,* 23, 28–30.

9. Tang and Parish, *Chinese Urban Life under Reform,* 187–99.

10. Chen, *Popular Political Support in Urban China,* chap. 6.

11. Shi, *Political Participation in Beijing,* 45.

12. Kevin J. O'Brien, "Agents and Remonstrators: Role Accumulation by Chinese People's Congress Deputies," *China Quarterly,* no. 138 (June 1994): 359–380.

13. Merle Goldman, *From Comrade to Citizen: The Struggle for Political Rights in China* (Cambridge, Mass.: Harvard University Press, 2005).

14. Broader and narrow definitions of the "1989 generation" did not change the results. Whether the group was defined as being 15–30 years old in 1989, 15–25, or even 18–25 years old, the result was the same: the coefficient was always positive, indicating higher levels of regime support, and statistically significant for the 15–30 group.

15. For more information about ACPES, see http://finance.sina.com.cn/roll/20040809/1501934902.shtml (accessed July 19, 2008).

16. See especially David L. Wank, *Commodifying Communism: Business, Trust, and Politics in a Chinese City* (New York: Cambridge University Press, 1999); and Tsai, *Capitalism without Democracy.*

17. "Minqilei weiquan: Dui zhengfu yifa zhizheng ti xin kaoyan" [Rights-protection by private enterprises: New challenges to the government's rule of law], http://www.hljgh.org:8080/showArticle?id=005950 (accessed September 25, 2008).

18. See *Dalizhou qiyejia xiehui—jianbao* [Bulletin of the Entrepreneurs' Association of Dali, vol. 5], http://www.smeyndl.gov.cn/readnews.asp?newsid=1276 (accessed July 21, 2008).

19. Jennings, "Political Participation in the Chinese Countryside," 363; Jie Chen, "Subjective Motivations for Mass Political Participation in Urban China," *Social Science Quarterly* 81 (June 2000): 650.

20. Yu Jianrong, "Seeking Justice: Is China's Administrative System Broken?" talk given at the Carnegie Endowment for International Peace, April 5, 2006, transcript available from http://www.carnegieendowment.org/events/index .cfm?fa=eventDetail&id=870&&prog=zch>. A more detailed discussion of his research can be found in "Discussion with Yu Jianrong: The Confusions in the Report on the *Xinfang* System," http://www.chinaelections.org/ NewsInfo.asp?NewsID=79324, which is supposedly based on Yu's original report, entitled "Xinfang de zhiduxing queshi ji zhengzhi houguo" ["Institutional flaws of the petition system and their political consequences].

21. Lianjiang Li, "Political Trust and Petitioning in the Chinese Countryside," *Comparative Politics* 40, no. 2 (January 2008).

22. Wayne DiFranceisco and Zvi Gitelman, "Soviet Political Cultural and 'Covert Participation' in Policy Implementation," *American Political Science Review* 78 (September 1984): 603–621; Frederick C. Barghoorn and Thomas F. Remington, *Politics in the USSR* (Boston: Little, Brown, 1986); Philip G. Roeder, "Modernization and Participation in the Leninist Developmental Strategy," *American Political Science Review* 83 (September 1989): 859–884; Donna Bahry and Brian D. Silver, "Soviet Citizen Participation on the Eve of Democratization," *American Political Science Review* 48 (September 1990): 820–847, quote on p. 821.

23. Victor C. Falkenheim, "Political Participation in China," *Problems of Communism* 27 (May–June 1978): 18–32; Bahry and Silver, "Soviet Citizen Participation"; Shi, *Political Participation in Beijing*; Manion, "The Electoral Connection in the Chinese Countryside"; Jie Chen, "Subjective Motivations for Mass Political Participation in Urban China," *Social Science Quarterly* 81, no. 2 (2000): 645–662; Jie Chen and Yang Zhong, "Why Do People Vote in Semicompetitive Elections in China?" *Journal of Politics* 64, no. 1 (2002): 178–197; Li, "Political Trust and Petitioning in the Chinese Countryside."

24. Bahry and Silver, "Soviet Citizen Participation," 822.

25. Wang Xiaoyan, *Siying qiyejia de zhengzhi canyu* [The political participation of private entrepreneurs] (Beijing: Social Science Academy Press, 2007), chap. 2.

26. Bahry and Silver, "Soviet Citizen Participation," 822.

27. James L. Gibson, "'A Mile Wide but an Inch Deep' (?): The Structure of Democratic Commitments in the Former USSR," *American Journal of Political Science* 40, no. 2 (May 1996): 396–420.

28. Tianjian Shi, "Voting and Nonvoting in China: Voting Behavior in Plebiscitary and Limited-Choice Elections," *Journal of Politics* 61, no. 4 (November 1999): 1115–1139; Tianjian Shi, "Village Committee Elections in China: Institutionalist Tactics for Democracy," *World Politics* 51, no. 3 (April 1999): 385–412.

29. Chen and Zhong, "Why Do People Vote"; Yang Zhong and Jie Chen, "To Vote or Not to Vote: An Analysis of Peasants' Participation in Chinese Village Elections," *Comparative Political Studies* 35 (2002): 686–712.

30. Chen and Zhong, "Why Do People Vote," 185.

31. Tang and Parish, *Chinese Urban Life under Reform*; Chen, *Popular Political Support in Urban China*. The terms "specific" and "diffuse" are from David Easton, "A Re-Assessment of the Concept of Political Support," *British Journal of Political Science* 5, no. 4 (October 1975): 435–457.

32. See, for example, Gabriel Almond and Sidney Verba, *Civic Culture: Political Attitudes and Democracy in Five Nations* (Princeton, N.J.: Princeton University Press, 1963); Ronald Inglehart, *Modernization and Postmodernization: Cultural, Economic, and Political Change in 43 Societies* (Princeton, N.J.: Princeton University Press, 1997); Chen, *Popular Political Support in Urban China*.

33. Seymour M. Lipset, "Some Social Requisites of Democracy: Economic Development and Political Legitimacy," *American Political Science Review* 53, no. 1 (1959): 69–105; Inglehart, *Modernization and Postmodernization*.

34. This is also true if the number of years of schooling is used to measure education instead of level of education. Tests for a curvilinear relationship for both level and years of education were negative.

35. Kellee Tsai found that former SOE managers were more assertive than other capitalists she surveyed and interviewed; see Tsai, *Capitalism without Democracy*). In a bivariate analysis, our data also show that former SOE managers engaged in direct action more than did other types of capitalists in our survey, but in a multivariate analysis with other variables controlled for, it is not a significant factor.

36. The separate regressions are not shown here in order to simplify the presentation.

37. By contrast, membership in the Private Enterprises Association, which is supposedly mandatory for all registered private firms, falls short of statistical significance when added to the model.

38. Mary Gallagher, "'Hope for Protection and Hopeless Choices': Labor Legal Aid in the PRC," in Elizabeth J. Perry and Merle Goldman, eds., *Grassroots Political Reform in Contemporary China* (Cambridge, Mass.: Harvard University Press, 2007), 196–227.

7. Conclusion

1. These results are comparable to those from a 2004 national survey of private entrepreneurs. According to this national survey, about 80 percent and 40 percent of private entrepreneurs were members of FIC and/or PEA and of self-organized/managed organizations, respectively. See Li Xueqing, "Siying qiyezhu zhengzhi canyu fenxi" [Analysis of political participation by private entrepreneurs]. *Jiangsu Sheng Shehui Zhuyi Xueyuan Xuebao* [Journal of the Jiangsu Socialism Institute] 2 (February 2007): 54–57; Ao Daiya, "Siying qiyezhu zhengzhi canyu yanjiu baogao" [Research report on private entrepreneurs' political participation], in Zhang Houyi et al., eds., *Zhongguo Siying Qiye Fazhan Baogao* [A report on the development of China's private enterprises] (Beijing: Social Sciences Academic Press, 2005).

2. See, for example, Margaret Pearson, *China's New Business Elite: The Political Consequences of Economic Reform* (Berkeley: University of California Press, 1997); An Chen, "Capitalist Development, Entrepreneurial Class, and Democratization in China," *Political Science Quarterly* 117 (2002): 401–422; Bruce J. Dickson, *Red Capitalists in China: The Party, Private Entrepreneurs, and Prospects for Political Change* (New York: Cambridge University Press, 2003); Kellee S. Tsai, *Capitalism without Democracy: The Private Sector in Contemporary China* (Ithaca, N.Y.: Cornell University Press, 2007); Bruce J. Dickson, *Wealth into Power: The Communist Party's Embrace of China's Private Sector* (New York: Cambridge University Press, 2008).

3. See, for example, Ao, "Siying qiyezhu zhengzhi canyu yanjiu baogao"; Wei Zhang, *Chongtu yu bianshu: Zhongguo shehui zhongjian jieceng zhengzhi fenxi* [Conflict and uncertainty: Political analysis of the middle stratum in Chinese society] (Beijing: Shehui kexue wenxian chubanshe, 2005).

4. Jonathan Unger, "'Bridges': Private Business, the Chinese Government and the Rise of New Associations," *China Quarterly,* no. 147 (September 1996): 795–819; Christopher Earle Nevitt, "Private Business Associations in China: Evidence of Civil Society or Local State Power," *China Journal,* no. 36 (July 1996): 25–45; Pearson, *China's New Business Elite;* David L. Wank, *Commodifying Communism: Business, Trust, and Politics in a Chinese City* (New York: Cambridge University Press, 1999); David S. G. Goodman, "The New Middle Class," in Merle Goldman and Roderick MacFarquhar, eds., *The Paradox of China's Post-Mao Reforms* (Cambridge: Harvard University Press, 1999); Dickson, *Red Capitalists in China;* Dickson, *Wealth into Power;* Tsai, *Capitalism without Democracy.*

5. See especially Scott Kennedy, *The Business of Lobbying in China* (Cambridge, Mass.: Harvard University Press, 2005); Dickson, *Red Capitalists in China;* Dickson, *Wealth into Power;* Tsai, *Capitalism without Democracy.*

6. Seymour Martin Lipset, "Some Social Requisites of Democracy: Economic Development and Political Legitimacy," *American Political Science Review* 53, no. 1 (March 1959): 69–105.

7. The most confident prediction comes from Henry S. Rowen, "When Will the Chinese People Be Free?" *Journal of Democracy* 18, no. 3 (July 2007): 38–62.

James Mann offers a spirited critique of this viewpoint in his controversial book, *The China Fantasy: How Our Leaders Explain Away Chinese Repression* (New York: Viking, 2007).

8. Adam Przeworski and Fernando Limongi, "Modernization: Theories and Facts," *World Politics* 49, no. 2 (January 1997): 155–183; Carles Boix and Susan C. Stokes, "Endogenous Democratization," *World Politics* 55, no. 4 (July 2003): 517–549.

9. Eva Bellin, "Contingent Democrats: Industrialists, Labor, and Democratization in Late-Developing Countries," *World Politics* 52, no. 2 (January 2000): 175–205; see also Dietrich Rueschemeyer, Evelyne Huber Stephens, and John D. Stephens, *Capitalist Development and Democracy* (Chicago: University of Chicago Press, 1992).

10. Joel S. Hellman, "Winners Take All: The Politics of Partial Reform in Post-communist Transitions," *World Politics* 50, no. 2 (January 1998): 203–234; Dickson, *Wealth into Power.*

11. Timur Kuran, "Now out of Never: The Element of Surprise in the East European Revolution of 1989," *World Politics* 44, no. 1 (October 1991): 7–48.

12. Jie Chen, *Popular Political Support in Urban China* (Stanford, Calif.: Stanford University Press, 2004); Wenfang Tang, *Public Opinion and Political Change in China* (Stanford, Calif.: Stanford University Press, 2005); *The 2008 Pew Global Attitudes Survey in China* (Washington, D.C.: Pew Research Center, 2008); Tianjian Shi, "China: Democratic Values Supporting an Authoritarian System," in Yun-han Chu et al., eds. *How East Asians View Democracy* (New York: Columbia University Press, 2008).

13. Margaret Pearson, "China's Emerging Business Class: Democracy's Harbinger?" *Current History* 97, no. 620 (September 1998): 268–272.

14. Jie, *Popular Political Support in Urban China.*

15. "Global Economic Gloom—China and India Notable Exceptions; Some Positive Signs for U.S. Image," Pew Global Attitudes Project, http://pewglobal.org/reports/display.php?ReportID=260 (accessed October 27, 2008).

16. Ronald Inglehart, *Modernization and Postmodernization: Cultural, Economic, and Political Change in 43 Societies* (Princeton, N.J.: Princeton University Press, 1997).

17. Bruce Gilley, "Legitimacy and Institutional Change: The Case of China," *Comparative Political Studies* 41 (March 2008): 259–284.

18. Melanie Manion, *Corruption by Design: Building Clean Government in Mainland China and Hong Kong* (Cambridge, Mass.: Harvard University Press, 2004); Yan Sun, *Corruption and Market in Contemporary China* (Ithaca, N.Y.: Cornell University Press, 2004); Minxin Pei, *China's Trapped Transition: The Limits of Developmental Autocracy* (Cambridge, Mass.: Harvard University Press, 2006).

19. Cheng Li, "China's Team of Rivals," *Foreign Policy* (March/April 2009): 88–93; Li, "The New Bipartisanship within the Chinese Communist Party," *Orbis* 49, no. 3 (Summer 2005): 387–400; see also Bruce J. Dickson, "Beijing's Ambivalent Reformers," *Current History* 103, no. 674 (September 2004): 249–255.

20. According to Derek Scissors, China's leaders have already retreated from their commitment to market-oriented reforms; see "Deng Undone: The Costs of Halting Market Reform in China," *Foreign Affairs* 88, no. 3 (May/June 2009): 24–39.

Appendix

1. The information about the total number of enterprises and their sectors comes from the 2005 Statistical Yearbooks of the five surveyed provinces.
2. For a description of the "feedback effect," see, for example, Marija J. Norusis, *SPSS Professional Statistics 7.5* (Chicago: SPSS, 1997), 95.
3. For definitions of both endogenous variables and instrumental variables, see ibid., 97.
4. For the reasons for using the lagged value of the endogenous variable in the 2SLS regression, see ibid., 98.

Bibliography

Adams, Paul S. 2002. "Corporatism and Comparative Politics: Is There a New Century of Corporatism?" In Howard J. Wiarda, ed., *New Directions in Comparative Politics*. Boulder, Colo.: Westview Press.

Almond, Gabriel, and Sidney Verba. 1963. *Civic Culture: Political Attitudes and Democracy in Five Nations*. Princeton, N.J.: Princeton University Press.

Amsden, Alice H. 1985. "The State and Taiwan's Economic Development." In Peter Evans, Dietrich Rueschemeyer, and Theda Skocpol, eds., *Bringing the State Back In*. New York: Cambridge University Press.

———. 1989. *Asia's Next Giant: South Korea and Late Industrialization*. New York: Oxford University Press.

Ao, Daiya. 2005. "Siying qiyezhu zhengzhi canyu yanjiu baogao" [Research report on private entrepreneurs' political participation]. In Zhang Houyi et al., eds., *Zhongguo Siying Qiye Fazhan Baogao* [A report on the development of China's private enterprises]. Beijing: Social Sciences Academic Press.

Ao, Daiya, and Mei Weixia. 2004. "Siying qiyezhu zhengzhi canyu xianzhuang fenxi" [Analysis of the Current Forms of Private Entrepreneurs' Political Participation]. *Changbai xuekan* [Changbai Journal] 5 (May): 49–58.

Avery, William. 1988. "Political Legitimacy and Crisis in Poland." *Political Science Quarterly* 103, no. 1: 111–130.

Bahry, Donna, and Brian D. Silver. 1990. "Soviet Citizen Participation on the Eve of Democratization." *American Political Science Review* 48, no. 3: 820–847.

Barghoon, Frederick C., and Thomas F. Remington. 1986. *Politics in the USSR*. Boston: Little, Brown.

Barnes, Samuel. H., Barbara G. Farah, and Felix Heunks. 1979. "Personal Dissatisfaction." In Samuel H. Barnes, Max Kaase, and Klause R. Allerbeck, eds., *Political Action: Mass Participation in Five Western Democracies*. Beverly Hills, Calif.: Sage.

Bates, Robert. 2008. *When Things Fell Apart: State Failure in Late-Century Africa.* New York: Cambridge University Press.

Baum, Richard. 1997. "The Road to Tiananmen: Chinese Politics in the 1980s." In Roderick MacFarquhar, ed., *The Politics of China.* 2nd ed. Cambridge: Cambridge University Press.

Beer, Samuel H. 1965. *British Politics in the Collectivist Age.* New York: Knopf.

Bell, Daniel A. 1998. "After the Tsunami: Will Economic Crisis Bring Democracy to Asia?" *New Republic* 218, no. 10 (March 9): 22–25.

Bellin, Eva. 2000. "Contingent Democrats: Industrialists, Labor, and Democratization in Late-Developing Countries." *World Politics* 52, no. 2: 175–205.

———. 2002. *Stalled Democracy: Capital, Labor, and the Paradox of State-Sponsored Development.* Ithaca, N.Y.: Cornell University Press.

Boix, Carles, and Susan C. Stokes. 2003. "Endogenous Democratization." *World Politics* 55, no. 4 (July): 517–549.

Burkhart, Ross E., and Michael A. Lewis-Beck. 1994. "Comparative Democracy: The Economic Development Thesis." *American Political Science Review* 88, no. 4 (December): 903–910.

Chen, An. 2002. "Capitalist Development, Entrepreneurial Class, and Democratization in China." *Political Science Quarterly* 117: 401–422.

Chen, Dong. 2005. "Siying qiyezhu jieceng neibu fenhua jiada" [The increasing diversification within private entrepreneurs]. *Dalu qiao* [Land Bridge Horizon] 4 (April): 43–47.

Chen, Guangjin. 2005. "1992–2004 Siying qiyezhu jieceng: yige xin shehui jieceng de chengzhang" [The class of private entrepreneurs in 1992–2004: Growth of a new social class]. In Zhang Houyi et al., eds., *Zhongguo Siying Qiye Fazhan Baogao* [A report on the development of China's private enterprises]. Beijing: Social Sciences Academic Press.

Chen, Jie. 2000. "Subjective Motivations for Mass Political Participation in Urban China." *Social Science Quarterly* 81, no. 2: 645–662.

———. 2004. *Popular Political Support in Urban China.* Stanford, Calif.: Stanford University Press and Woodrow Wilson Center Press.

Chen, Jie, and Peng Deng. 1995. *China since the Cultural Revolution: From Totalitarianism to Authoritarianism.* Westport, Conn.: Praeger.

Chen, Jie, and Yang Zhong. 1998. "Defining the Political System of Post-Deng China: Emerging Public Support for a Democratic Political System." *Problems of Post-Communism* 45, no. 1: 30–42.

———. 2000. "Valuation of Individual Liberty vs. Social Order among Democratic Supporters: A Cross-Validation." *Political Research Quarterly* 53: 427–439.

———. 2002. "Why Do People Vote in Semicompetitive Elections in China?" *Journal of Politics* 64, no. 1: 178–197.

Chen, Jie, Yang Zhong, and Jan William Hillard. 1997. "The Level and Sources of Popular Support for China's Current Political Regime." *Communist and Post-Communist Studies* 30: 45–64.

Chibber, Vivek. 2003. *Locked in Place: State Building and Late Industrialization in India.* Princeton, N.J.: Princeton University Press.

Cho, Young Nam. 2008. *Local People's Congresses in China: Development and Transition*. New York: Cambridge University Press.

Citrin, Jack, and Christopher Muste. 1999. "Trust in Government." In John P. Robinson, Phillip R. Shaver, and Lawrence S. Wrightsman, eds., *Measures of Political Attitudes*, 465–532. San Diego: Academic Press.

Dahl, Robert A. 1971. *Polyarchy: Participation and Opposition*. New Haven, Conn.: Yale University Press.

———. 1989. *Democracy and Its Critics*. New Haven, Conn.: Yale University Press.

De Bary, Wm. Theodore. 1998. *Asian Values and Human Rights: A Confucian Communitarian Perspective*. Cambridge, Mass.: Harvard University Press.

Diamond, Larry. 2002. "Thinking about Hybrid Regimes." *Journal of Democracy* 13: 21–35.

Dickson, Bruce J. 2003. *Red Capitalists in China: The Party, Private Entrepreneurs, and Prospects for Political Change*. New York: Cambridge University Press.

———. 2004. "Beijing's Ambivalent Reformers." *Current History* 103, no. 674 (September): 249–255.

———. 2008. *Wealth into Power: The Communist Party's Embrace of China's Private Sector* (New York: Cambridge University Press, 2008).

DiFranceisco, Wayne, and Zvi Gitelman. 1984. "Soviet Political Cultural and 'Covert Participation' in Policy Implementation." *American Political Science Review* 78, no. 3: 603–621.

Ding, X. L. 2000. "The Illicit Asset Stripping of Chinese State Firms." *China Journal* 43 (January): 1–28.

Di Palma, Giuseppe. 1991. "Legitimation from the Top to Civil Society: Political-Cultural Change in Eastern Europe." *World Politics* 44: 49–80.

Dittmer, Lowell, and Guoli Liu, eds. 2006. *China's Deep Reforms: Domestic Politics in Transition*. Lanham, Md.: Rowman & Littlefield.

Easton, David. 1953. *The Political System*. New York: Knopf.

———. 1965. *A Systems Analysis of Political Life*. New York: Wiley.

———. 1975. "A Reassessment of the Concept of Political Support." *British Journal of Political Science* 5, no. 4 (October): 435–457.

———. 1976. "Theoretical Approaches to Political Support." *Canadian Journal of Political Science* 9, no. 3: 431–448.

Evans, Peter. 1995. *Embedded Autonomy: State and Industrial Transformation*. Princeton, N.J.: Princeton University Press.

Falkenheim, Victor C. 1978. "Political Participation in China." *Problems of Communism* 27 (May–June): 18–32.

Fewsmith, Joseph. 1994. *Dilemmas of Reform in China: Political Conflict and Economic Debate*. Armonk, N.Y.: M. E. Sharpe.

———. 2001a. *China since Tiananmen: The Politics of Transition*. New York: Cambridge University Press.

———. 2001b. "The New Shape of Elite Politics." *China Journal* 45: 83–93.

———. 2005. "Chambers of Commerce in Wenzhou Show Potential and Limits of 'Civil Society' in China." *China Leadership Monitor* 16 (Fall).

Finifter, Ada, and Ellen Mickiewicz. 1992. "Redefining the Political System of the USSR: Mass Support for Political Change." *American Political Science Review* 86, no. 4: 857–874.

Finkel, Steven E., Edward N. Muller, and Mitchell Seligson. 1989. "Economic Crisis, Incumbent Performance and Regime Support: A Comparison of Longitudinal Data from West Germany and Costa Rica." *British Journal of Political Science* 19, no. 3: 329–351.

Foster, W. Kenneth. 2002. "Embedded within State Agencies: Business Associations in Yantai." *China Journal,* no. 47 (January): 41–65.

Gallagher, Mary. 2007. "'Hope for Protection and Hopeless Choices': Labor Legal Aid in the PRC." In Elizabeth J. Perry and Merle Goldman, eds., *Grassroots Political Reform in Contemporary China,* 196–227. Cambridge, Mass.: Harvard University Press.

Gerschenkron, Alexander. 1962. *Economic Backwardness in Historical Perspective: A Book of Essays.* Cambridge, Mass.: Belknap Press of Harvard University Press.

Gibson, James L. 1995. "The Resilience of Mass Support for Democratic Institutions and Processes in Nascent Russian and Ukrainian Democracies." In Vladimir Tismaneanu, ed., *Political Culture and Civil Society in Russia and the New States of Eurasia,* 53–111. Armonk, N.Y.: M. E. Sharpe.

———. 1996. "'A Mile Wide but an Inch Deep' (?): The Structure of Democratic Commitments in the Former USSR." *American Journal of Political Science* 40, no. 2 (May): 396–420.

Gibson, James L., and Gregory A. Caldeira. 1992. "Blacks and the United States Supreme Court: Models of Diffuse Support." *Journal of Politics* 54: 1120–1145.

Gibson, James L., and Raymond M. Duch. 1993. "Emerging Democratic Values in Soviet Political Culture." In Arthur H. Miller, William M. Reisinger, and Vicki L. Hesli, eds., *Public Opinion and Regime Change,* 69–94. Boulder, Colo.: Westview Press.

Gibson, James L., Raymond M. Duch, and Kent L. Tedin. 1992. "Democratic Values and the Transformation of the Soviet Union." *Journal of Politics* 54, no. 2: 329–371.

Gilley, Bruce. 2004. *China's Democratic Future: How It Will Happen and Where It Will Lead.* New York: Columbia University Press.

———. 2008. "Legitimacy and Institutional Change: The Case of China." *Comparative Political Studies* 41 (March): 259–284.

Glassman, Ronald M. 1991. *China in Transition: Communism, Capitalism, and Democracy.* New York: Praeger.

Gold, Thomas. 1986. *State and Society in the Taiwan Miracle.* Armonk, N.Y.: M. E. Sharpe.

———. 1990. "Urban Private Business and Social Change." In Deborah Davis and Ezra Vogel, eds., *Chinese Society on the Eve of Tiananmen: The Impact of Reform.* Cambridge, Mass.: Council on East Asian Studies, Harvard University.

Goldman, Merle. 2005. *From Comrade to Citizen: The Struggle for Political Rights in China.* Cambridge, Mass.: Harvard University Press.

Gomez, Edmund Terence, ed. 2002. *Political Business in East Asia.* London: Routledge.

Gong, Ting. 1996. "Jumping into the Sea: Cadre Entrepreneurs in China." *Problems of Post-Communism* 43, no. 4 (July–August): 26–34.

Goodman, David G. 1996. "The People's Republic of China: The Party-State, Capitalist Revolution and New Entrepreneurs." In Richard Robison and David G. Goodman, eds., *The New Rich in Asia: Mobile Phones, McDonald's and Middle-Class Revolution,* 225–242. London: Routledge.

Goodman, David S. G. 1999. "The New Middle Class." In Merle Goldman and Roderick MacFarquhar, eds., *The Paradox of China's Post-Mao Reforms.* Cambridge, Mass.: Harvard University Press.

———. 2001. "The Interdependence of State and Society: The Political Sociology of Local Leadership." In Chien-min Chao and Bruce J. Dickson, eds., *Remaking the Chinese State: Strategies, Society, and Security.* London: Routledge.

Green, Stephen, and Guy S. Liu, eds. 2005. *Exit the Dragon? Privatization and State Control in China.* London: Blackwell.

Groot, Gerry. 2004. *Managing Transitions: The Chinese Communist Party, United Front Work, Corporatism, and Hegemony.* New York: Routledge.

He, Baogang. 1997. *The Democratic Implications of Civil Society in China.* New York: St. Martin's Press.

Heisler, Martin O. 1973. *Politics in Europe: Structures and Processes in Some Postindustrial Democracies.* New York: McKay.

Hellman, Joel S. 1998. "Winners Take All: The Politics of Partial Reform in Postcommunist Transitions." *World Politics* 50, no. 2 (January): 203–234.

Hirschman, Albert. 1968. "The Political Economy of Import Substituting Industrialization in Latin America." *Quarterly Journal of Economics* 82: 2–32.

Hong, Zhaohui. 2004. "Mapping the Evolution and Transformation of the New Private Entrepreneurs in China." *Journal of Chinese Political Science* 9, no. 1 (Spring): 23–42.

Hu, Shaohua. 2000. *Explaining Chinese Democratization.* Westport, Conn.: Praeger.

Huang, Keting. 2001. "Siying qiyezhu qunti xinli tanxi" [*Exploration of private enterprises' community psychology*]. *Shanghai shi shehuizhuyi xueyuan xuebao* [*Journal of the Shanghai Socialism Institute*], no. 3, 33–48.

Huang, Yasheng. 2008. *Capitalism with Chinese Characteristics: Entrepreneurship and the State.* New York: Cambridge University Press.

Huntington, Samuel P. 1970. "Social and Institutional Dynamics of One-Party Systems." In Samuel P. Huntington and Clement H. Moore, eds., *Authoritarian Politics in Modern Society: The Dynamics of Established One-Party Systems.* New York: Basic Books.

———. 1991. *The Third Wave: Democratization in the Late Twentieth Century.* Norman: University of Oklahoma Press.

———. 1992. "Democracy's Third Wave." *Journal of Democracy* 2: 12–35.

Inglehart, Ronald. 1990. *Cultural Shift in Advanced Industrial Society.* Princeton, N.J.: Princeton University Press.

———. 1997. *Modernization and Postmodernization: Cultural, Economic, and Political Change in 43 Societies.* Princeton, N.J.: Princeton University Press.

Jennings, M. Kent. 1997. "Political Participation in the Chinese Countryside." *American Political Science Review* 91: 361–372.

———. 1998. "Gender and Political Participation in the Chinese Countryside." *Journal of Politics* 60: 954–973.

Jiang Nanyang. 2003. "Lun gongshanglian de tongzhanxing, jingjixing yu minjianxing" (On the Federation of Industry and Commerce's united-front, economic, and public functions)." In Zhang Houyi et al., eds., *Zhongguo siying qiye fazhan baogao (A report on the development of China's private enterprises)*, 343–346. Beijing: Social Sciences Academic Press.

Jones, David Martin. 1998. "Democratization, Civil Society, and Illiberal Middle Class Culture in Pacific Asia." *Comparative Politics* 30, no. 2: 147–169.

Jowitt, Ken. 1992. *New World Disorder: The Leninist Extinction.* Berkeley: University of California Press.

Katzenstein, Peter. 1985. "Small Nations in an Open International Economy: The Converging Balance of State and Society in Switzerland and Austria." In Peter Evans, Dietrich Rueschemeyer, and Theda Skocpol, eds., *Bringing the State Back In.* New York: Cambridge University Press.

Kelliher, Daniel. 1992. *Peasant Power in China: The Era of Rural Reform, 1979–1989.* New Haven, Conn.: Yale University Press.

Kennedy, Scott. 1997. "The Stone Group: State Client or Market Pathbreaker?" *China Quarterly*, no. 152 (December): 746–777.

———. 2005. *The Business of Lobbying in China.* Cambridge, Mass.: Harvard University Press.

———. 2008. "China's Emerging Credit Rating Industry: The Official Foundations of Private Authority." *China Quarterly* 193 (March): 65–83.

Kohli, Atul. 2004. *State-Directed Development: Political Power and Industrialization in the Global Periphery.* Princeton, N.J.: Princeton University Press.

Kuran, Timur. 1991. "Now out of Never: The Element of Surprise in the East European Revolution of 1989." *World Politics* 44, no. 1 (October): 7–48.

Lardy, Nicholas R. 1998. *China's Unfinished Economic Revolution.* Washington, D.C.: Brookings Institution Press.

Lasswell, Harold. 1936. *Politics: Who Gets What, When, and How.* New York: McGraw-Hill.

Lehmbruch, Gerhard. 1977. "Liberal Corporatism and Party Government." *Comparative Political Studies* 10: 91–126.

Li, Cheng. 2005. "The New Bipartisanship within the Chinese Communist Party." *Orbis* 49, no. 3 (Summer): 387–400.

———. 2009. "China's Team of Rivals." *Foreign Policy* (March/April).

Li, He. 2003. "Middle Class: Friends or Foes to Chinese Leadership?" *Journal of Chinese Political Science* 8 (Fall): 87–100.

Li, Xueqing. 2007. "Siying qiyezhu zhengzhi canyu fenxi" [Analysis of political participation by private entrepreneurs]. *Jiangsu sheng shehuizhuyi xueyuan xuebao* [Journal of the Jiangsu Socialism Institute] 2 (February): 54–57.

Lianjiang Li. 2008. "Political Trust and Petitioning in the Chinese Countryside." *Comparative Politics* 40, no. 2 (January).

Lipset, Seymour M. 1959. "Some Social Requisites of Democracy: Economic Development and Political Legitimacy." *American Political Science Review* 53, no. 1: 69–105.

———. 1960. *Political Man: The Social Bases of Politics.* Baltimore: Johns Hopkins University Press.

Liu, Alan P. 2001. "Provincial Identities and Political Cultures: Modernism, Traditionalism, Parochialism, and Separatism." In Shiping Hua, ed., *Chinese Political Culture, 1989–2000.* Armonk, N.Y.: M. E. Sharpe.

Liu, Jie, and Tong Hao. 2007. "More Chinese Find Jobs in Private Sectors." *Xinhua*, October 6.

———. 2008. "Private Companies Playing a Bigger Role." *China Daily*, January 29.

Lu, Xueyi, ed. 2002. *Dangdai zhongguo shehui jieceng yanjiu baogao* [Research report on contemporary China's social classes]. Beijing: Shehui kexue wenxian chubanshe.

———, ed. 2004. *Dangdai zhongguo shehui liudong* [Social mobility in contemporary China]. Beijing: Shehui kexue wenxian chubanshe.

Lu, Ya-li. 1991. "Political Development in the Republic of China." In Thomas W. Robinson, ed., *Democracy and Development in East Asia: Taiwan, South Korea, and the Philippines*, 35–47. Washington, D.C.: AEI Press.

Lujan, Herman D. 1974. "The Structure of Political Support: A Study of Guatemala." *American Journal of Political Science* 18, no. 1: 23–43.

MacFarquhar, Roderick. 1988. "Provincial People's Congresses." *China Quarterly*, no. 155 (September).

Manion, Melanie. 1994. "Survey Research in the Study of Contemporary China: Learning from Local Samples." *China Quarterly* 139: 741–765.

———. 1996. "The Electoral Connection in the Chinese Countryside." *American Political Science Review* 90 (December): 736–748.

———. 2000. "Chinese Democratization in Perspective: Electorates and Selectorates at the Township Level." *China Quarterly*, no. 163 (September).

———. 2005. *Corruption by Design: Building Clean Government in Mainland China and Hong Kong.* Cambridge, Mass.: Harvard University Press.

———. 2006. "Democracy, Community, Trust: The Impact of Elections in Rural China." *Comparative Political Studies* 39 (April).

———. 2008. "When Communist Party Candidates Can Lose, Who Wins? Assessing the Role of Local People's Congresses in the Selection of Leaders in China." *China Quarterly*, no. 195 (September): 607–630.

Mann, James. 2007. *The China Fantasy: How Our Leaders Explain Away Chinese Repression.* New York: Viking.

Marsh, Alan, and Max Kaase. 1979. "Background of Political Action." In Samuel H. Barnes, Max Kaase, and Klause R. Allerbeck, eds., *Political Action: Mass Participation in Five Western Democracies*, 97–136. Beverley Hills, Calif.: Sage.

Maxwell, Sylvia, and Ben Ross Schneider, eds. 1997. *Business and the State in Developing Countries.* Ithaca, N.Y.: Cornell University Press.

Migdal, Joel S. 2001. *State in Society: Studying How States and Societies Transform and Constitute One Another.* New York: Cambridge University Press.

Millar, James R., and Elizabeth Clayton. 1987. "Quality of Life: Subjective Measures of Relative Satisfaction." In James R. Millar, ed., *Politics, Work, and Daily Life in the USSR: A Survey of Former Soviet Citizens,* 31–60. Cambridge: Cambridge University Press.

Miller, Arthur H. 1993. "In Search of Regime Legitimacy." In Arthur H. Miller, William M. Reiginger, and Vicki L. Hesli, eds., *Public Opinion and Regime Change: The New Politics of Post-Soviet Societies.* Boulder, Colo.: Westview Press.

Mitchell, Timothy. 1991. "The Limits of the State: Beyond Statist Approaches and Their Critics." *American Political Science Review* 85: 77–96.

Moore, Barrington. 1966. *Social Origins of Dictatorship and Democracy: Lord and Peasant in the Making of the Modern World.* Boston: Beacon Press.

Morse, Richard. 1992. "Claims of Political Tradition." In Howard J. Wiarda, ed., *Politics and Social Change in Latin America: Still a Distinct Tradition.* Boulder, Colo.: Westview Press.

Muller, Edward N. 1977. "Behavioral Correlates of Political Support." *American Political Science Review* 71: 454–467.

Muller, Edward N., and Thomas O. Jukam. 1977. "On the Meaning of Political Support." *American Political Science Review* 71, no. 4: 1561–1595.

Muller, Edward N., Thomas O. Jukam, and Mitchell A. Seligson. 1980. "Diffuse Political Support and Antisystem Political Behavior: A Comparative Analysis." *American Journal of Political Science* 26: 240–264.

Muller, Edward N., and Carol J. Williams. 1990. "Dynamics of Political Support-Alienation." *Comparative Political Studies* 13: 33–59.

Nathan, Andrew J. 1990. *China's Crisis: Dilemma of Reform and Prospects for Democracy.* New York: Columbia University Press.

———. 1997. *China's Transition.* New York: Columbia University Press.

———. 2003. "Authoritarian Resilience." *Journal of Democracy* 14, no. 1 (January): 6–17.

———. 2008. "China's Political Trajectory: What Are the Chinese Saying?" In Cheng Li, ed., *China's Changing Political Landscape: Prospects for Democracy.* Washington, D.C.: Brookings Institution Press.

Naughton, Barry. 1995. *Growing out of the Plan: Chinese Economic Reform, 1978–1993.* New York: Cambridge University Press.

———. 2007. *The Chinese Economy: Transitions and Growth.* Cambridge, Mass.: MIT Press.

Nevitt, Christopher Earle. 1996. "Private Business Associations in China: Evidence of Civil Society or Local State Power." *China Journal,* no. 36 (July): 25–45.

O'Brien, Kevin. J. 1990. *Reform without Liberalization: China's National People's Congress and the Politics of Institutional Change.* New York: Cambridge University Press.

———. 1994. "Agents and Remonstrators: Role Accumulation by Chinese People's Congress Deputies." *China Quarterly,* no. 138 (June): 359–380.

Odgaard, Ole. 1992. "Entrepreneurs and Elite Formation in Rural China." *Australian Journal of Chinese Affairs* 28: 89–108.

O'Donnell, Guillermo. 1992. "Substantive or Procedural Consensus? Notes on the Latin American Bourgeoisie." In Douglas Chalmers, Maria de Souza, and Akko A. Boron, eds., *The Right and Democracy in Latin America*. New York: Praeger.

O'Donnell, Guillermo, and Philippe C. Schmitter. 1986. *Transitions from Authoritarian Rule: Tentative Conclusions about Uncertain Democracies*. Baltimore: Johns Hopkins University Press.

Ogden, Suzanne. 2002. *Inklings of Democracy in China*. Cambridge, Mass.: Harvard University Asia Center and distributed by Harvard University Press.

Oi, C. Jean. 1995. "The Role of the Local State in China's Transitional Economy." In "China's Transitional Economy," special issue, *China Quarterly*, no. 144 (December): 1132–1149.

———. 1999. *Rural China Takes Off: Institutional Foundations of Economic Reform*. Berkeley: University of California Press.

Packenham, Robert. 1992. *The Dependency Movement: Scholarship and Politics in Development Studies*. Cambridge, Mass.: Harvard University Press.

Pakulski, Jan. 1986. "Legitimacy and Mass Compliance: Reflections on Max Weber and Soviet-Type Societies." *British Journal of Political Science* 16, no. 1: 35–56.

Panitch, Leo. 1980. "Recent Theorizations of Corporatism: Reflections on a Growth Industry." *British Journal of Sociology* 31: 159–187.

Parris, Kristin. 1993. "Local Initiative and National Reform: The Wenzhou Model of Development." *China Quarterly* 134 (June): 242–263.

Pearson, Margaret M. 1994. "The Janus Face of Business Associations in China: Socialist Corporatism in Foreign Enterprises." *Australian Journal of Chinese Affairs*, no. 31 (January): 25–46.

———. 1997. *China's New Business Elite: The Political Consequences of Economic Reform*. Berkeley: University of California Press.

———. 1998. "China's Emerging Business Class: Democracy's Harbinger." *Current History* 97, 620 (September): 268–272.

Pei, Minxin. 2006. *China's Trapped Transition: The Limits of Developmental Autocracy*. Cambridge, Mass.: Harvard University Press.

Pempel, T. J. 1999. "The Developmental Regime in a Changing World Economy." In Meredith Woo-Cumings, ed., *The Developmental State*. Ithaca, N.Y.: Cornell University Press.

Perry, Elizabeth J. 2008. "Chinese Conceptions of 'Rights': From Mencius to Mao—and Now." *Perspectives on Politics* 6, no. 1: 41–42.

Pettit, Philip. 2000. "Democracy, Electoral and Contestatory." In Ian Shapiro and Stephen Macedo, eds., *Designing Democratic Institutions*, 105–146. New York: New York University Press.

Przeworski, Adam. 1986. "Some Problems in the Transition to Democracy." In Guillermo O'Donnell, Phillippe C. Schmitter, and Laurence Whitehead, eds., *Transitions from Authoritarian Rule, vol. 3: Comparative Perspectives*. Baltimore: Johns Hopkins University Press.

Przeworski, Adam, Michael E. Alvarez, Jose Antonio Cheibub, and Fernando Limongi. 2000. *Democracy and Development: Political Institutions and Well-Being in the World, 1950–1990*. Cambridge: Cambridge University Press.

Przeworski, Adam, and Fernando Limongi. 1997. "Modernization: Theories and Facts." *World Politics* 49, no. 2 (January): 155–183.

Pye, Lucian W. 1992. *The Spirit of Chinese Politics*. Cambridge, Mass.: Harvard University Press.

Read, Benjamin L. 2003. "Democratizing the Neighborhood? New Private Housing and Home-Owner Self-Organization in Urban China." *China Journal*, no. 49: 31–60.

Rigby, T. H. 1982. "Introduction: Political Legitimacy, Weber and Communist Mono-organizational Systems." In T. H. Rigby and Ferenc Fehér, eds., *Political Legitimation in Communist States*, 1–26. New York: St. Martin's Press.

Roeder, Philip G. 1989. "Modernization and Participation in the Leninist Developmental Strategy." *American Political Science Review* 83, no. 3: 859–884.

Rokkan, Steinl. 1965. "Norway: Numerical Democracy and Corporate Pluralism." In Robert Dahl, ed., *Political Oppositions in Western Democracies*. New Haven, Conn.: Yale University Press.

Rose, Richard, and William Mishler. 2000. *Regime Support in Non-Democratic and Democratic Contexts*. Glasgow: University of Strathclyde.

Rostow, W. Walt. 1991. *Stages of Economic Growth: A Non-Communist Manifesto*. 3rd ed. Cambridge: Cambridge University Press.

Rowen, Henry S. 1996. "The Short March: China's Road to Democracy." *National Interest*, no. 45: 61–70.

———. 2007 "When Will the Chinese People Be Free?" *Journal of Democracy* 18, no. 3 (July): 38–62.

Rueschemeyer, Dietrich, and Peter Evans. 1985. "The State and Economic Transformation: Toward an Analysis of the Conditions Underlying Effective Intervention." In Peter Evans, Dietrich Rueschemeyer, and Theda Skocpol, eds., *Bringing the State Back In*. New York: Cambridge University Press.

Rueschemeyer, Dietrich, Evelyne Huber Stephens, and John D. Stephens. 1992. *Capitalist Development and Democracy*. Chicago: University of Chicago Press.

Saich, Tony. 2000. "Negotiating the State: The Development of Social Organizations in China." *China Quarterly* 161 (March): 124–141.

Scalapino, Robert A. 1998. "Current Trends and Future Prospects." *Journal of Democracy* 9: 35–40.

Schmitter, Philippe C. 1971. *Interest Conflict and Political Change in Brazil*. Stanford, Calif.: Stanford University Press.

———. 1975. *Corporatism and Public Policy in Authoritarian Portugal*. London: Sage.

———. 1979. "Still the Century of Corporatism?" In Philippe C. Schmitter and Gerhard Lehmbruch, eds., *Trends toward Corporatist Intermediation*. Beverly Hills, Calif.: Sage.

Schumpeter, Joseph A. 1947. *Capitalism, Socialism, and Democracy*. New York: Harper.

Scissors, Derek. 2009. "Deng Undone: The Costs of Halting Market Reform in China." *Foreign Affairs* 88, no. 3 (May/June 2009): 24–39.

Seligson, Mitchell A., and Edward N. Muller. 1980. "Democratic Stability and Economic Crisis: Costa Rica, 1978–1983." *International Studies Quarterly* 31: 301–326.

Shapiro, Ian. 1999. *Democratic Justice*. New Haven, Conn.: Yale University Press.

Shi, Tianjian. 1997. *Political Participation in Beijing*. Cambridge, Mass.: Harvard University Press.

———. 1999a. "Village Committee Elections in China: Institutional Tactics for Democracy." *World Politics* 51, no. 3 (April): 385–412.

———. 1999b. "Voting and Nonvoting in China: Voting Behavior in Plebiscitary and Limited-Choice Elections." *Journal of Politics* 61, no. 4: 1115–1139.

———. 2008. "China: Democratic Values Supporting an Authoritarian System." In Yun-han Chu et al., eds., *How East Asians View Democracy*. New York: Columbia University Press.

Shi, Weimin, and Lei Jingxuan. 1999. *Zhijie xuanju: Zhidu yu chengxu* [Direct elections: System and procedure]. Beijing: Chinese Academy of Social Sciences Press.

Shin, Eui Hang. 1999. "Social Change, Political Elections, and the Middle Class in Korea." *East Asia: An International Quarterly* 17, no. 3: 28–60.

Silver, Brian D. 1987. "Political Beliefs of the Soviet Citizen: Source of Support to Regime Norms." In James R. Millar, ed., *Politics, Work, and Daily Life in the USSR: A Survey of Former Soviet Citizens*, 100–142. Cambridge: Cambridge University Press.

Skocpol, Theda. 1985. "Bringing the State Back In: Strategies of Analysis in Current Research." In Peter Evans, Dietrich Rueschemeyer, and Theda Skocpol, eds., *Bringing the State Back In*. New York: Cambridge University Press.

Smith, H. Peter. 2005. *Democracy in Latin America: Political Change in Comparative Perspective*. New York: Oxford University Press.

Smith, Tony. 1987. *Thinking Like a Communist: State and Legitimacy in the Soviet Union, China, and Cuba*. New York: Norton.

Steinfeld, Edward S. 1998. *Forging Reform in China: The Fate of State-Owned Industry*. New York: Cambridge University Press.

Stepan, Alfred C. 1978. *The State and Society: Peru in Comparative Perspective*. Princeton, N.J.: Princeton University Press.

Sun, Yan. 2004. *Corruption and Market in Contemporary China*. Ithaca, N.Y.: Cornell University Press.

Tang, Wenfang. 2005. *Public Opinion and Political Change in China*. Stanford, Calif.: Stanford University Press, 2005.

Tang, Wenfang, and William L. Parish. 2000. *Chinese Urban Life under Reform: The Changing Social Contract*. Cambridge: Cambridge University Press.

Tanner, Murray Scot. 1999. *The Politics of Lawmaking in Post-Mao China: Institutions, Processes, and Democratic Prospects*. New York: Oxford University Press.

Tao, Jianqun, and Wen Zhao. 2003. "Siying qiyezhu zou xiang zhengzhi wutai" [Private entrepreneurs' marching toward political stage]. *Shidai Chao* [Tide of Times] 3, no. 1 (May): 15–19.

Thelen, Kathleen. 2003. "How Institutions Evolve: Insights from Comparative Historical Analysis." In James Mahoney and Dietrich Rueschemeyer, eds., *Comparative Historical Analysis in the Social Sciences.* New York: Cambridge University Press.

Thomassen, Jacques J. A. 1989. "Economic Crisis, Dissatisfaction, and Protest." In M. Kent Jennings, Jan W. van Deth, et al., eds., *Continuities in Political Action: A Longitudinal Study of Political Orientations in Three Western Democracies,* 103–134. New York: Walter de Gruyter.

Tsai, Kellee S. 2002. *Back Alley Banking: Private Entrepreneurs in China.* Ithaca, N.Y.: Cornell University Press.

———. 2005. "Capitalists without a Class: Political Diversity among Private Entrepreneurs in China." *Comparative Political Studies* 38, no. 9: 1130–1158.

———. 2006. "Adaptive Informal Institutions and Endogenous Institutional Change in China." *World Politics* 59: 116–141.

———. 2007. *Capitalism without Democracy: The Private Sector in Contemporary China.* Ithaca, N.Y.: Cornell University Press.

Unger, Jonathan. 1996. "'Bridges': Private Business, the Chinese Government and the Rise of New Associations." *China Quarterly,* no. 147 (September): 795–819.

Unger, Jonathan, and Anita Chan. 1996. "Corporatism in China: A Developmental State in an East Asian Context." In Barrett L. McCormick and Jonathan Unger, eds., *China after Socialism: In the Footsteps of Eastern Europe or East Asia?* Armonk, N.Y.: M. E. Sharpe.

Wade, Robert. 1990. *Governing the Market: Economic Theory and the Role of Government in East Asian Industrialization.* Princeton, N.J.: Princeton University Press.

Walder, Andrew. 1998. "Zouping in Perspective." In Andrew G. Walder, ed., *Zouping in Transition: The Process of Reform in Rural North China.* Cambridge, Mass.: Harvard University Press.

Wang, Xiaoyan. 2007. *Siying qiye jia de zhenzhi canyu* [The political participation of private entrepreneurs]. Beijing: Social Science Academy Press.

Wang, Yuanqi. 2007. "Siying qiyezhu zhengzhi canyu de jiedu" [Understanding of private entrepreneurs' political participation]. *Guangdong Shehui Zhuyi Xeuyuan Xeubao* [Journal of Guangdong Socialist College] (July).

Wang, Zhongtian. 1998. *Xingde bi'an: Zouxiang 21st shiji de zhongguo minzhu* [A new horizon: Marching toward the Chinese democracy in the 21st century]. Beijing: The Party School of the CCP's Central Committee Press.

Wank, David L. 1999. *Commodifying Communism: Business, Trust, and Politics in a Chinese City.* New York: Cambridge University Press.

———. 2002. "The Making of China's Rentier Entrepreneur Elite: State, Clientelism, and Power Conversion." In Françoise Mengin and Jean-Louis Roca, eds., *Politics in China: Moving Frontiers,* 118–139. New York: Palgrave Macmillan.

Wedeman, Andrew H. 2004. "The Intensification of Corruption in China." *China Quarterly*, no. 180 (December): 895–921.

White, Gordon, ed. 1988. *Developmental States in East Asia*. London: Macmillan.

———. 1994a. "Democratization and Economic Reform in China." *Australian Journal of Chinese Affairs*, no. 31: 73–92.

———. 1994b. "Prospects for Civil Society in China: A Case-Study of Xiaoshan City." *Australian Journal of Chinese Affairs* 29: 73–92.

White, Gordon, Jude Howell, and Shang Xiaoyuan. *In Search of Civil Society: Market Reform and Social Change in Contemporary China*. Oxford: Oxford University Press, 1996.

White, Stephen. 1986. "Economic Performance and Communist Legitimacy." *World Politics* 38, no. 3: 462–482.

Whiting, Susan. 2001. *Power and Wealth in Rural China: The Political Economy of Institutional Change*. New York: Cambridge University Press.

Wiarda, Howard J. 1981. *Corporatism and National Development in Latin America*. Boulder, Colo.: Westview Press.

———. 1997. *Corporatism and Comparative Politics: The Other Great "Ism."* Armonk, N.Y.: M. E. Sharpe.

Woo-Cumings, Meredith, ed. 1999. *The Developmental State*. Ithaca, N.Y.: Cornell University Press.

Wu, Jinglian. 2005. *Understanding and Interpreting Chinese Economic Reform*. Singapore: Thomson/South-Western.

Xia, Ming. 2007. *The People's Congresses and Governance in China: Toward a Network Mode of Governance*. London: Routledge.

Xiao, Gongqin. 2003. "The Rise of the Technocrats." *Journal of Democracy* 14, no. 1: 59–65.

Yang, Dali L. 2004. *Remaking the Chinese Leviathan: Market Transition and the Politics of Governance in China*. Stanford, Calif.: Stanford University Press.

Yang, Henan. 2007. "Siying qiyezhu jiecan zhengzhi canyu de tezheng ye duice fenxi" [The characteristics of private entrepreneurs' political participation and its policy implications]. *Tequ Jingji* [Economy of the Special Economic Zone].

Yang, Keming. 2007. *Entrepreneurship in China*. Aldershot, England: Ashgate.

Yusuf, Shahid, Kaoru Nabeshima, and Dwight Perkins. 2006. *Under New Ownership: Privatizing China's State-Owned Enterprises*. Palo Alto, Calif., and Washington, D.C.: Stanford University Press and the World Bank.

Zhang, Chunmin. 2005. "Zhongchan jieceng de zhengzhi canyu" [Political participation of the middle class]. In Zhou Xiaohong, ed., *Zhongguo zhongchan jieceng diaocha* [Survey of the Chinese middle classes]. Beijing: Social Sciences Academic Press.

Zhang, Houyi. 2004. "Jinru xin shiqi de Zhongguo siying qiyezhu jiceng" [Chinese private entrepreneurs enter a new era]. In *2004 nian: Zhongguo shehui xingshi fenxi yu yuce* [Blue book of China's Society 2004: Analysis and forecast of China's social development]. Beijing: Shehui kexue wenxian chubanshe.

———. 2005. "Kuaisu chengzhang de Zhongguo siying qiyezhu jiceng" [The rapid growth of China's private entrepreneurs]. In *2005 Nian: Zhongguo shehui xingshi fenxi yu yuce* [Blue book of China's society 2005: Analysis and forecast of China's social development]. Beijing: Shehui kexue wenxian chubanshe.

Zhang, Houyi, Hou Guangming, Ming Lizhi, and Liang Chuanyun. 2005. *Zhongguo siying jing qiye fazhan baogao* [A report on the development of China's private enterprises]. Beijing: Social Sciences Academic Press.

Zhao, Ziyang. 2009. *Prisoner of the State: The Secret Journal of Premier Zhao Ziyang.* New York: Simon and Schuster.

Zheng, Yongnian. 2004. *Will China Become Democratic? Elite, Class, and Regime Transition.* Singapore: Eastern Universities Press.

Zhong, Yang. 1996. "Legitimacy Crisis and Legitimization in China." *Journal of Contemporary Asia* 26, no. 2: 201–220.

Zhong, Yang, and Jie Chen. 2002. "To Vote or Not to Vote: An Analysis of Peasants' Participation in Chinese Village Elections." *Comparative Political Studies* 35: 686–712.

Zhou, Kate Xiao. 1996. *How the Farmers Changed China: Power of the People.* Boulder, Colo.: Westview.

Zhou, Xueguang. 2004. *The State and Life Chances in Urban China.* Cambridge: Cambridge University Press.

Zysman, John. 1983. *Governments, Markets, and Growth: Financial Systems and the Politics of Industrial Change.* Ithaca, N.Y.: Cornell University Press.

Index